FROM WORK–FAMILY BALANCE TO WORK–FAMILY INTERACTION

Changing the Metaphor

FROM WORK–FAMILY BALANCE TO WORK–FAMILY INTERACTION

Changing the Metaphor

Edited by

Diane F. Halpern
Susan Elaine Murphy
Claremont McKenna College

LEA LAWRENCE ERLBAUM ASSOCIATES, PUBLISHERS
2005 Mahwah, New Jersey   London

Lawrence Erlbaum Associates, Inc., Publishers
10 Industrial Avenue
Mahwah, New Jersey 07430

Cover design by Kathryn Houghtaling Lacey

Library of Congress Cataloging-in-Publication Data

Kravis-deRoulet Leadership Conference (13th : 2002 : Claremont McKenna College)
From work-family balance to work-family interaction : changing the metaphor / edited by
Diane F. Halpern, Susan Elaine Murphy.
    p. cm.
Papers from the 13th annual Kravis-de Roulet Leadership Conference held in
February 22, 2002 at Claremont McKenna College.
Includes bibliographical references and index.
ISBN 0-8058-4886-X (cloth. : alk. paper) — ISBN 0-8058-4887-8 (pbk. : alk. paper)
1. Work and family.   2. Family policy.   3. Dual-career families.   4. Social networks.
I. Halpern, Diane F.   II. Murphy, Susan E.   III. Title.

HD4904.25.K73   2002
306.3'6—dc22   2004056432
                                                                         CIP

Books published by Lawrence Erlbaum Associates are printed on acid-free paper,
and their bindings are chosen for strength and durability.

Printed in the United States of America
10 9 8 7 6 5 4 3 2 1

Contents

Preface

This book is dedicated to working families and the many people who help them make it all work—the neighbors who help each other in countless large and small ways, the employers with family-friendly policies, the physicians, dentists, and other professionals with office hours that allow working families to care for their health without losing time from work, and the policymakers who understand that public policies support societal values. To all of you who help—we offer our thanks and applause.

We thank the many people who worked so hard in making this book a reality. We especially thank Dr. Ron Riggio, Director of the Kravis Institute for this support. We thank Sandra Counts, Beth Donaghey, Lynda Mulhill, Sherylle Tan, and many wonderful students at Claremont McKenna College, and we thank our own husbands for their continued support: Copil Yáñez and Sheldon Halpern.

THE KRAVIS-DE ROULET LEADERSHIP CONFERENCE

The Kravis–de Roulet Leadership Conference, which began in 1990, is an annual leadership conference funded jointly by an endowment from financier Henry R. Kravis and the de Roulet family. This perpetual funding, along with additional support from the Kravis Leadership Institutes and Claremont McKenna College, enables us to attract the finest leadership researchers, scholars, and practitioners as conference presenters and participants. The conference topics alternate between leadership research and more practitioner-oriented topics. The 13th Annual Kravis–de Roulet Conference, Leadership in Work/Family Balance, was held February 22, 2002.

THE BERGER INSTITUTE FOR WORK, FAMILY, AND CHILDREN

The Berger Institute for Work, Family, and Children advances knowledge about the interactions between work and family through education, dissemination, research, and community service. Integrating the fields of psychology, economics, sociology, and public policy to effect change and to study the challenges that face working individuals, families, communities, labor, and business.

THE KRAVIS LEADERSHIP INSTITUTE

The Kravis Leadership Institute plays an active role in the development of young leaders via educational programs, research and scholarship, and the development of technologies for enhancing leadership potential.

About the Authors

Rosalind Chait Barnett is a senior scientist at the Women's Studies Research Center at Brandeis University and Director of its Community, Families & Work Program. Alone and with others, she has published more than 90 articles, 20 chapters, and six books. *She Works/He Works: How Two-Income Families Are Happy, Healthy and Thriving* was published in paperback in 1998 by Harvard University Press. She is the recipient of several national awards, including the American Personnel and Guidance Association's Annual Award for Outstanding Research, the Radcliffe College Graduate Society's Distinguished Achievement Medal and Harvard University, Kennedy School of Government's 1999 Goldsmith Research Award. A 1997 journal article co-authored with Robert Brennan received the "Best paper award for 1997" from the *Journal of Organizational Behavior*. She is currently working on a new book with Caryl Rivers entitled *The Seduction of Difference*.

David Bruce Bell is a senior research psychologist at headquarters of the U.S. Army Research Institute (ARI) in Alexandria, Virginia. Dr. Bell holds a BA and MA in psychology from the University of Texas at Austin and a PhD in Counseling Psychology from Texas Tech University in Lubbock, Texas. He has been studying Army families since 1985. He was the contract monitor for a 6-year, $10-million, worldwide research project that linked family factors to soldier readiness and retention. He has also studied the ability of both Active and Reserve families to cope with the stresses of deployment during the Gulf War, Somalia, Bosnia, peacekeeping in the Sinai, and other military deployments. Dr. Bell's family research is recorded in several widely used book chapters, reports, invited addresses, and Army manuals.

Nigel Boyle is Associate Professor of Political Studies at Pitzer College and Acting Director of the European Union Center of California. His research interests focus on the welfare state and labor market policy in Europe. Recent publications include articles entitled "Varieties of neo-liberalism in the domestic response to global turbulence: Youth labor market policy under Thatcher and Blair" and "Feeding the Celtic Tiger: FAS and the transformation of the Irish labor market 1987–2001" (both to be published in 2005 in edited volumes). He has benefited from paid, semester-long parental leaves while at Pitzer.

Wayne F. Cascio received his PhD in industrial and organizational psychology from the University of Rochester. Currently he is professor of management and international business at the University of Colorado at Denver. In 1988 he received the Distinguished Faculty award from the HR Division of the Academy of Management, in 1994 he received the Bemis award for excellence in HRM from the International Personnel Management Association's Assessment Council, and in 1999 he received the Distinguished Career award from the HR Division of the Academy of Management. Dr. Cascio is past chair of the HR Division of the Academy of Management and past president of the Society for Industrial and Organizational Psychology. He has authored numerous texts, has published more than 80 journal articles and 30 book chapters, and has consulted with more than 150 organizations on six continents. Currently he serves on the Boards of Directors of CPP, Inc. and the Society for Human Resource Management Foundation.

Stephan Desrochers is an applied social psychologist with interests in managerial science and family science. Within these fields of study, he is interested in the attitudes, roles, self-identities, and interpersonal relationships relating to work, family, gender, and other domains of people's lives. He received his PhD in Interdisciplinary Social Psychology at the University of Nevada, Reno. He is an Assistant Professor at the University of Maine, Farmington.

Robert Drago is a professor of labor studies and women's studies at Pennsylvania State University. Before moving to Pennsylvania, Dr. Drago was a professor of economics at the University of Wisconsin–Milwaukee. He holds a PhD in economics from the University of Massachusetts at Amherst and has been a Senior Fulbright Research Scholar. Bob also moderates the work/ family newsgroup on the Internet (http://1sir.la.psu.edu/workfam). The newsgroup is an excellent resource for information including summaries of recent research, conference announcements, legislation, and books and articles summarized by Dr. Drago. As of January 2002, the list had 700 members. Dr. Drago's recent research includes a study of teachers and their time for work and family, and a study of faculty and family issues, both funded by the Alfred P. Sloan Foundation. He is the 2001 recipient of the R. I. Downing Fellowship from the University of Melbourne (Australia), serves on the Boards of the Alliance of Work/Life Professionals and of the College and University Work/Family Association, is an advisory council member for the "Top 100" list compiled annually by *Working Mother* magazine, and is a proud soccer dad.

Ellen Galinsky is President and Co-founder of the Families and Work Institute (FWI), a Manhattan-based nonprofit organization, which conducts research on the changing family, workplace, and community. Prior to co-founding the FWI in 1989, Galinsky served on the research faculty of the Bank Street College of Education. Galinsky earned a BA degree from Vassar College and a MS from Bank Street College. She authored the ground-breaking book, *Ask the Children: The Breakthrough Study That Reveals How to Succeed at Work and Parenting*, which was selected by the *Wall Street Journal* as one of the best work–life books of 1999. In 2002, Galinsky co-authored FWI's major new Ask the Children study: *Youth and Violence: Students Speak Out for a More Civil Society*. Galinsky has co-authored The National Study of the Changing Workforce, a nationally representative study of the U.S. workforce, updated every 5 years. For more information about FWI, visit www.familiesandwork.org.

Adele Eskeles Gottfried is a professor in the Department of Educational Psychology and Counseling at California State University, Northridge. She is a Fellow of the American Psychological Association, recipient of the MENSA Award for Excellence in Research, and was Invited Speaker for the Esther Katz Rosen Annual Lecture at the 2001 Annual Meeting of the American Psychological Association. She has been engaged in longitudinal research on maternal employment and children's development over a long-term period, and is the author and co-editor of numerous books, chapters, and articles including *Maternal Employment and Children's Development, Redefining Families: Implications for Children's Development*, and Maternal and Dual-Earner Employment Status and Parenting in the 1st and 2nd editions of the *Handbook of Parenting*. She serves on the editorial boards of several journals. Her research on maternal employment and children's development has been cited as a foundation for a key ruling in parental custody by the California State Supreme Court.

Diane F. Halpern is Professor of Psychology and Director of the Berger Institute for Work, Family, and Children at Claremont McKenna College. For the last 20 years, she was a professor in the psychology department at California State University, San Bernardino. She has won many awards for her teaching and research, including the 2002 Outstanding Professor Award from the Western Psychological Association, the 1999 American Psychological Foundation Award for Distinguished Teaching, 1996 Distinguished Career Award for Contributions to Education given by the American Psychological Association, the California State University's State-Wide Outstanding Professor Award, the Outstanding Alumna Award from the University of Cincinnati, the Silver Medal Award from the Council for the Advancement and Support of Education, the Wang Family Excellence Award, and the G. Stanley Hall Lecture Award from the American Psychological Association. She is the author of several books: *Thought and Knowledge: An Introduction to Critical Thinking* (4th ed., 2003), *Thinking Critically About Critical Thinking* (with Heidi Riggio, 2003), *Sex Differences in Cognitive Abilities* (3rd ed., 2000), *Enhancing Thinking Skills in the Sciences and Mathematics* (1992), *Changing College Classrooms* (1994), *Student Outcomes Assessment* (1987), and *States of Mind: American and Post-Soviet Perspectives on Contemporary Issues in Psychology* (co-edited with Alexander Voiskounsky, 1997). Diane has served as president of the Western Psychological Association, the Society for the Teaching of Psychology, and the Division of General Psychology of the American Psychological Association. She co-chaired the Education Work Group of the American Psychological Society with Milton Hakel. She recently chaired a conference on "Applying the Science of Learning to the University and Beyond: Cognitive, Social, and Motivational Factors" that was funded by the Spencer Foundation and Marshall–Reynolds Trust. She presented the outcomes from the conference to the White House office of Science and Technology and the Science Committee of the U.S. House of Representatives. Diane is the current President of the American Psychological Association.

Maggie Jackson, author of *What's Happening to Home: Balancing Work Life and Refuge in the Information Age* (Sorin Books) is an award-winning columnist who helped pioneer U.S. coverage of workplace and work–life issues. She has won three Front Page awards from the Newswomen's Club of New York, the 2001 Work–Life Leadership Council's Media Award from The Conference Board, and a 2000-2001 travel and research grant from the Alfred P. Sloan Foundation. The former national workplace columnist of the Associated Press, Jackson now contributes regularly to *The New York Times, The Boston Globe*, and other national publications. A graduate of Yale University and the London School of Economics, she lives in New York City with her family.

Donna Klein guides the strategic formation, planning, development, implementation, and management of corporate-wide diversity and work–life initiatives as Vice President of Diversity & Workplace Effectiveness at Marriott International, Inc. In 1999, she initiated Marriott's Women's Leadership Initiative with a focus on the development and retention of minority and women talent. She is also a nationally known authority on work–life issues and has been the catalyst for many employer-based collaborative projects addressing the complex needs of the lower income worker. Currently, Mrs. Klein is leading breakthrough work to launch Corporate Voices for Working Families, a coalition focused on organizing the voices of the private sector. Corporate Voices for Working Families will convene, communicate, and educate policymakers around policy support needed for working families. At a national level, Mrs. Klein is Chair of The Conference Board's Work–Life Leadership Council, is a member of The Conference Board's Diversity Council, and is a member of Boston College's Work and Family Roundtable. She is also a founder and current co-chair of The Employer Group, a partnership of employers engaged in identifying quality of life solutions for hourly workers. In 1996, Mrs. Klein and Marriott International were recipients of The Business Enterprise Trust Award for creation of Marriott's Associate Resource Line. She is a frequent speaker at local and national business conferences and spoke at the Ten Downing Street Summit on Women in the New Economy during 1999.

Christina Maslach is Vice Provost for Undergraduate Education and Professor of Psychology at the University of California at Berkeley. She received her AB, magna cum laude, in Social Relations from Harvard–Radcliffe College in 1967, and her PhD in Psychology from Stanford University in 1971. She has conducted research in a number of areas within social and health psychology. She is best known, however, as one of the pioneering researchers on job burnout, and the author of the *Maslach Burnout Inventory* (MBI), the most widely used research measure in the burnout field. In addition to numerous articles, her books on this topic include *Burnout: The Cost of Caring*; the co-edited volume, *Professional Burnout: Recent Developments in Theory and Research* (with Wilmar Schaufeli); *The Truth About Burnout* (with Michael Leiter); and *Preventing Burnout and Building Engagement: A Complete Program for Organizational Renewal* (with Michael Leiter).

V. Sue Molina leads the Deloitte & Touche Initiative on the Retention and Advancement of Women. In this capacity, she provides guidance to a variety of programs on career counseling, mentoring, and leadership training, and is a frequent speaker on flexibility and work–life balance. With a focus on women in leadership, the Women's Initiative Vision 2005 has created bold, new goals with an emphasis on succession planning to ensure proportionate representation of women in senior leadership. Ms. Molina is on the

Deloitte & Touche Management Committee and is a Tax Partner with 24 years of experience focusing on public and privately owned real estate development, management, and investment companies. Ms. Molina currently serves on the boards of the Shakespeare Theater in Washington, DC, and the Vital Voices Global Partnership. In 2001, she was named as one of the 100 Most Influential People by Accounting Today. Ms. Molina received a BS in Business Administration and a Master's of Accounting from the University of Arizona. She is married with two children.

Susan Elaine Murphy is Associate Professor of Psychology at Claremont McKenna College and Associate Director of the Kravis Leadership Institute. She earned her PhD, MS, and MBA from the University of Washington. She is an adjunct professor at Claremont Graduate University. She has published articles and presented research investigating the contribution of personality characteristics and early leadership experiences in effective leadership and the role of mentoring in career and leadership development. Her most recent published work is an edited book, *Multiple Intelligences and Leadership* (Lawrence Erlbaum Associates, 2002). Prior to joining Claremont McKenna College, Dr. Murphy worked as a research scientist at Battelle Seattle Research Center, where she designed and delivered leadership development programs for senior-level managers in a wide range of industries.

Paul Orfalea, with a single copying machine, a $5,000 loan, and an unfailing vision, built Kinko's from a one-man operation in a converted food stand into a corporate powerhouse with more than 1,100 branches worldwide and 25,000 "co-workers." His rise through the business world was sparked by a belief in the power of entrepreneurship and a strong commitment to customer relationships and corporate responsibility. Orfalea's story is also testimony to the strength of the American dream. A chronically struggling student, he spent his school years frustrated by severe dyslexia and educational challenges that were not equipped to accommodate or even recognize his needs. After overcoming this giant obstacle, Orfalea now strives to improve resources for the next generation through his family's philanthropic efforts and public speaking on early care and education, intergenerational care, and learning distinctions. At the podium, Orfalea shares his inspiring road to success, provides an indispensable model of corporate leadership and illustrates how, in today's technologically driven economy, putting people first is still the key to winning customer loyalty and maintaining co-worker productivity.

Phyllis Stewart Pires' experience spans 18 years of work in child-care center management and program development and the broader work–life field. In her current position at Cisco Systems as a Senior Benefits Program Manager, Family Services, Phyllis worked with Bright Horizons Family Solutions to bring the Cisco Family Connection child-care center to San Jose. The center is the largest facility in Northern California, providing onsite child care for more than 440 children ranging in age from 6 weeks to 5 years as well as back child-care services, summer holiday programs for school-age children, family focused events, and parent resources. Phyllis also manages the other Family Services provided by Cisco—dependent care resource and referral, adoption assistance, breastfeeding support, baby gift program, discount programs, and parent educational programs. Prior to joining Cisco in June 2000, she was the project manager for Bright Horizons Family Solutions, Inc. In that capacity, she provided her child-care center design expertise and participated in the city planning and approval process while interpreting child-care licensing regulations. Phyllis also participated in policy and procedure decision making, the enrollment process, communication plan development, and overall design. Before joining Bright Horizons, Phyllis directed child-care centers for Apple Computers, Inc., and Pacific Gas & Electric. She received her BA in Early Childhood Education from the University of the Pacific in Stockton, California and her Master's in Developmental Studies from the University of California, Los Angeles. Phyllis is currently the co-chair of One Small Step—an organization promoting the development and expansion of work–life programs among employers in the Northern California area.

Betty Purkey is the Work/Life Program Manager at Texas Instruments. Her responsibilities focus on work/life strategy, dependent care community investment, workplace flexibility and diversity metrics. Betty is a member of the Conference Board Work/Life Leadership Council, Corporate Voices for Working Families and the Executive Board for Work Friendly Dallas, a coalition of Dallas-area employers. She also represents Texas Instruments as a member of the American Business Collaboration for Quality Dependent Care. She is a graduate of Leadership Richardson and Leadership Texas. Betty has been a speaker at many conferences on work–life issues and has appeared in local and national print and broadcast media. Betty received her undergraduate degree in mathematics and her Master's degree in computer science from Southern Methodist University.

Heidi R. Riggio is a social psychologist and currently a visiting assistant professor in the Department of Psychology at Clarement McKenna College, and was also a visiting assistant professor in psychology at Pomona College. Her research interests include adult family relationships, including sibling and parent–adult child relationships, and adulthood relationship consequences of parental marital conflict and divorce. She is also interested in the development of attitudes toward relationships, family, and work, as well as resistance to persuasion and behavioral confirmation of attitudes.

Walter R. Schumm is Professor of Family Studies at Kansas State University in the School of Family Studies and Human Services in the College of Human Ecology. He earned his PhD in family studies from Purdue University in 1979 and has taught at Kansas State since then. He recently retired (July 2002) after more than 30 years reserve component service in the Army Reserve, Army National Guard, and the Active Army, last commanding a brigade in the U.S. Army Reserve. He has published numerous scholarly articles and chapters on military families, among many other topics. His biography was recently featured in the book *Pioneering Paths in the Study of Families*. He resides with his wife and seven children in Manhattan, Kansas.

Gail L. Thompson taught in public junior high and high schools for 14 years. During this time she won a civic award for outstanding teaching, as well as teaching awards from student organizations. Thompson served as a district-selected mentor teacher, and later developed an after-school literacy program for struggling elementary school students. She is an associate professor in the School of Educational Studies at the Claremont Graduate University, and the author of three books: *Through Ebony Eyes: What Teachers Need to Know But Are Afraid to Ask About African American Students*; *African American Teens Discuss Their Schooling Experiences*; and *What African American Parents Want Educators to Know*, as well as numerous journal articles. In 2002, one of her essays, "Teachers' Cultural Ignorance Imperils Student Success," was published in *USA Today*. In addition to serving as a guest editor for *Educational Horizons, The Urban Review*, and *The High School Journal*, Thompson has appeared on National Public Radio, KPCC, and KXAM radio in Scottsdale, Arizona, and has been quoted in several newspapers. She serves as a reviewer for *The Reading Teacher, The California Reader, The High School Journal*, and *The Journal of Adolescent and Adult Literacy*. In addition to serving as a keynote speaker for many organizations, she has presented papers at numerous national, regional, and state conferences, and done consultant work in many K–12 schools. Thompson is married to Rufus, an educator, and they have three children, Nafissa, NaChe', and Stephen.

Faith A. Wohl is President of Child Care Action Campaign. She is a former political appointee in the Clinton Administration, where she was on staff at the National Performance Review (NPR). Her assignment there was to accelerate the use of "family-friendly" policies in the Federal workplace. She also worked on more affordable child-care for low income workers, as part of the President's welfare-to-work initiative. Previously, she was Director of the Office of Workplace Initiatives at the U.S. General Services Administration, where she oversaw policy and development of worksite child-care centers and telecommuting centers for Federal employees. Before joining the Federal government, Ms. Wohl was with The DuPont Company for more than 20 years, serving in successive management roles as Director of Corporate Communications, Corporate Affairs, Community Affairs, and Work-force Partnering. As one of the company's first women in senior manage-ment, she was its spokesperson on women and family issues to the community and the national media, and an advocate and resource to women at all levels in the corporation.

Clifford E. Young is Professor and Director of the Undergraduate Business program at The Business School, University of Colorado at Denver. He re-ceived his PhD in business from the University of Utah. Dr. Young's primary trust is in the area of marketing research methodology, survey develop-ment, and research analysis. He also has experience in selling and sales de-ployment analysis. Dr. Young has published articles in *Journal of Marketing, Journal of Retailing, Journal of Public Policy and Marketing, Journal of Personal Selling and Sales Management, The Journal of the Academy of Marketing Science, The Academy of Management Journal,* and others.

David Zagorski completed his doctoral studies at Claremont Graduate Uni-versity's School of Behavioral and Organizational Sciences in 2004. His ar-eas of interest are the changing nature of work–life balance and organiza-tional justice. Dave also holds an MBA in management and an MA in research psychology, both from California State University, Los Angeles. He currently handles recruiting, outreach, and employee relations for WesCorp, a multibillion-dollar financial services company based in San Dimas, California.

Part I

INTEGRATING THE DEMANDS OF WORK AND FAMILY

From Balance to Interaction: Why the Metaphor Is Important

Diane F. Halpern
Susan Elaine Murphy
Claremont McKenna College

We have all seen the images of the modern and harried adult, racing from work to home. If there is ever a still moment, the androgynous pant-suited (or overall-covered) adult is at the fulcrum of a large balance beam seemingly burdened with children and a spouse on one side and work-related paraphernalia, usually a briefcase and computer, on the other. The balance is delicate and any false movement to one side will start the items on the other side in a downward slide. The message in this balance metaphor is clear—spend too much time at work and your family will suffer and vice versa. There are similar other metaphors that offer similar dire outcomes. There is the juggler—similarly dressed, usually androgynous in appearance, but now with a baby, computer, spouse, client, and other work and family "balls" in the air. If this harried worker/family juggler holds on to any one of these objects too long the others will crash. It is like juggling a bowling ball, chain saw, and penknife at the same time. The juggler had better pay close attention or she or he will be crushed/slashed/stabbed. These metaphors are not only anxiety provoking; the message that they send is wrong. Work and family are not a zero-sum game. Although there are reasonable limits to all activities, there are many benefits that accrue to people who both work and have families and other out-of-work life activities. It is time to change the metaphor.

Work–Family Interaction: From Zero-Sum Game
to Win–Win Interactions

The idea of an interaction comes from statistical models where two effects combine to provide something that is greater than would have been predicted from either one alone. In the example of positive work–family interactions, think about a household task—like shopping for a new lawn rake (not very exciting for most people) and spending a rainy afternoon indoors with a preschool child. When they are combined in a way that makes the most of both, the excitement of a child's trip to a hardware or lawn store can make the mundane task much more enjoyable and the afternoon with the preschool child can be fun and productive as you both explore lawn tools and share a glass of milk at the lunch counter while discussing other topics. This is an example of a "win–win" situation. Numerous other examples are provided in a study of business school graduates who managed to make work and family either allies or enemies, depending on how they arranged work schedules, priorities, employment-related resources, and had access to behavioral and emotional support from others (Friedman & Greenhaus, 2000).

It may seem that stay-at-home moms have it best because they have the least stress, but the research does not support this supposition. It is interesting to note that, in general, women who work outside the home are both happier and healthier than those who do not. In Barnett and Rivers' (1996) review of the literature, they conclude that working women are less depressed and report better physical health than women who are not employed. In their review of the Framingham heart study (a large study of precipitating factors for cardiac-related illness), they conclude that the only group of working women that shows an employment-related increase in heart disease is women in low-paid jobs, with high work demands and little control over their work, with several children at home, and little support to help with the children. The entry of large numbers of mothers into the workforce has not reduced life expectancies for women as some had predicted. The gap in life expectancy between women and men is narrowing, but the narrowing is more likely caused by increases in male life expectancy, and the narrowing between life expectancies for women and men has not been found for African-Americans in the United States, so it is not related to work status per se.

The Good Old Days

There are many people who express nostalgia for the "Good Old Days," when there were stay-at-home moms who greeted children with warm cookies and milk after school, but the nostalgia is for a time that existed only in

the black-and-white world of television land, or for the precious few real
children who had two parents with sufficient incomes to live a middle-class
life, insurance to protect against financial disaster, and none of the other
tragedies such as illness, crime, alcoholism, and array of family problems
that are far more common than any sitcom television viewer would believe.
The idyllic life where tragedies were touched with humor and neatly solved
by a wise father who "always knew best" within their televised time slot was,
we are sorry to say, as much a fiction as the cookie monster.

Poor women always worked and rich women always had nannies and
other child care and household help. Prior to the development of our industrialized society, both men and women worked long and hard, often in
close proximity—on the farm, tending stores or other businesses in or near
their homes, and watching children die at young ages to an assortment of
diseases we rarely think about today. Poor children worked long hours in
coal mines, on farms, on ships, hauling heavy bundles, and as hired help
in homes and small businesses. During World War II, women went to work
in large numbers as the popular press touted the benefits to children who
were sent to preschools and to women who worked outside the home. Pe-
rusal of "women's magazines" from World War II shows strong women who
reap the benefits of working outside the home and happy children who
advanced because of early education and socialization. It is only during
that short "blip" in modern history after World War II when middle-class
women stayed at home to raise families and their men, returning from war,
took back their jobs from the women. Yet, this period is often idealized as
the norm.

Time Is an Important Variable

The idea that time is finite and working families are starved for time has an
intuitive appeal, so it is not surprising that a default notion is that working
parents are depriving their children of the time they need with their parents. Unfortunately, like many intuitively appealing notions, and despite
the fact that many people report that they wish they had more time, the underlying concept can rarely be reduced to black-or-white. Working parents
are, indeed, stressed, and often tired, but so are stay-at-home parents and
working adults without children or other care responsibilities. We all want
more time, but does this mean that children with two working parents are
not getting enough time with their parents for healthy development?

For most working families (and most everyone else)—it's about *time*. On
average, men are spending more time than women at work (an average of
48 hours a week for men—includes some commuting time and 46 hours a
week for women—although estimates vary among surveys). Men are also
spending more time on child care and household chores than their own fa-

thers did, but still less than their wives—a condition that virtually defines conflict. These data are described in more detail in the chapters by Galinsky and Barnett in this volume. On average, working mothers spend an additional 25 hours a week on child care and household tasks while working fathers are spending an average of 15 hours a week on child care and household tasks. Mothers and fathers are tired, but this seems to be universal and not restricted to parental status. There is a need for quality part-time jobs, especially at the professional level where there is a stigma associated with part-time employment and remuneration is not proportional to the full-time rate. There is still much that needs to be done to make work and family more compatible and to close the motherhood wage gap for part-time work.

Gender Is Also an Important Variable

Because most job categories are segregated by gender, it is difficult to consider any work and family interaction without also discussing the roles of males and females in society. There is a large increase in the proportion of managerial jobs going to women in the last decade and women are now receiving the majority of undergraduate degrees and master's degrees, although they still tend to be overrepresented in the helping professions such as teaching, nursing, and social work. By contrast, men are still in the majority in physics, engineering, and chemistry, with other job categories such as medicine, law, and journalism approaching equality.

Similarly, household chores and childcare tasks tend to be gender-segregated, but in ways that differ from a generation ago. Fathers are spending more time with their children, especially when their spouse is employed outside the home. One in every five single-parent households is headed by a father, and noncustodial fathers pay child support when they understand their importance in children's lives. Children with involved fathers have better outcomes—they become more compassionate adults (according to a 26-year longitudinal study), have higher IQ scores (controlling for other variables), and fewer behavioral problems.

PAID EMPLOYMENT IS RARELY OPTIONAL

Few families can afford "luxuries" like health insurance, mortgage payments, and grocery bills on one salary (Warren & Tyagi, 2003). The two-parent, single wage-earner family is going the way of the dodo bird. In a careful study of bankruptcy in America, Warren and Tyagi found that few families with children can afford to own a home with only one wage earner, and even with two incomes, most families are living so close to the edge of financial collapse that an extended illness or loss of a job begins a rapid financial free-fall that ends with bankruptcy. Far from the fiction of affluent families who are spending frivolously on fancy clothing and food, most two-income families with children are barely making it. The second income is being used to pay for a home in a neighborhood with "good schools"—the classic dream of good education for one's children—not logos on overpriced clothes.

Going It Alone

If it is difficult to make it financially with children in dual-income households, it is even harder for those who are supporting children alone. Children in single-parent homes are more likely to live in poverty and suffer negative outcomes associated with poverty, but these risks can be reduced when parents are provided with supportive services, such as parenting classes, job training, psychological services, and assistance with child care. Yet, U.S. labor law permits workers to be fired if they refuse to work overtime, but many parents cannot work overtime because they cannot find or cannot afford child care for long hours when they have to work extra shifts. Child care and, increasingly, elder care, is *the central issue* for working families. Low-wage workers cannot afford quality child care unless it is subsidized.

The minimum wage in the United States is $5.15 an hour, and many families rely on workers at or near minimum wage! Numerous groups including the NOW Legal Defense Fund (2003, June) have calculated the savings to society for programs, such as wraparound school where the school hours actually coincide with the hours most adults work, the school year matches the work year, and child and elder care is available for working families. The savings to society occur in several ways: Caregivers are absent from work less frequently and suffer less illness of their own, sick children and adults are not sent to school and the workplace to spread illness, illnesses are treated sooner so fewer hospitalizations are required and treatments for chronic illnesses are shorter, fewer people lose their jobs because of absences and then need to go on public assistance, reduced use of health benefits should reduce health insurance, and more. We know of no study that has incorporated all of these potential savings into the "costs" of paid family medical leave or other leave programs.

IT'S EVERYONE'S BUSINESS

Work, family, and children are primary concerns to every policymaker, employer, and family member. Everyone has parents, and workers without nuclear families have friends and neighbors who function as family and will, at some time, need others to care for them. Sound policies can be consistent with our values and our bottom line, and these are the reasons for this book—the reasons why we brought together a superb panel of experts from different disciplines to look at work and family issues and the way they interact. The book is divided into five sections. Part I is an overview, with a brief discussion by a psychologist, an economist, and a political scientist, each of whom provide their own interpretation of how their discipline views this hybrid field that none exclusively "owns."

In Part II, we consider the business case or the question of why employers should invest in family-friendly work policies. This is probably the question that is asked most frequently. How can employers afford to offer family-friendly policies and remain competitive? Given the competition for talent, the changing nature of the workforce, and the savings to employers who meet worker needs, a better question might be how they can afford not to. In chapter 3, Susan Murphy and David Zagorski offer a management view of work–family interaction. In chapter 4, Wayne Cascio and Clifford Young analyze the financial outcomes of the top family-friendly companies in America and answer the important question of whether it pays dividends to be good to employees.

The employer response to work–family interactions is the focus of Part III. Paul Orfalea, whose red curly hair inspired the name "Kinko's," the large chain of stores that have become home and haven for college students and businesses of all sizes, sums it up well. Do you want to bite the hand that opens the cash register? In his own short but to-the-point style, Orfalea shows the wisdom of being good to one's employees. In chapter 6, four corporate insiders tell what it is like to be sitting at the corporate table when the decisions are made and how they help to influence work–family policies in good and bad financial times. Bruce Bell and Walter Schumm (chap. 7) write about the special needs of being the employer that just won't take "no" for an answer—the military. They tell about the support services for families that help the military succeed at its unique work. The final chapter in this section describes "burnout," the psychological phenomenon that hurts workers and their work. Christina Maslach, who is best known for her work in this area, provides insights into the variables that create burnout and what employers can do to prevent it.

Families are the focus of Part IV. Gail Thompson (chap. 9) shows how African Americans face many barriers starting with poor education that make later transitions to higher education and good jobs even more difficult to achieve. On the other end of the family spectrum is Maggie Jackson's chapter 10, where she shows how technology has brought work and family together in ways that can be both beneficial and harmful, depending on the choices we make for how we work and live. Families are more in touch, but so are our bosses and coworkers. Even with the added time constraints of dual-earner families, children are spending as much time with parents or more as children did in single-earner families a generation ago, as Barnett explains in chapter 11, showing that dual-earner families are caring well for their children.

In many ways, the children are at the heart of work and family interaction—the topic of Part V. How does having working parents affect adolescent and young adult expectations for their own ability to handle work and family? Heidi Riggio and Stephan Desrochers answer these and other questions about the expectations of young adults. The effects of childcare on the children are overall positive, according to an extensive review by Adele Gottfried who shares some of the results of multiyear longitudinal studies. And the children themselves, they also believe that they are doing well, according to data reported by Ellen Galinsky, who asked the children about their own well-being.

There are many lessons to be learned about work–family interaction from these experts. It is clear that some people have learned how to combine work and family in ways that are mutually supporting, at least much of the time, and some employers have created work environments and policies that make positive interdependence of these two spheres more likely to occur. What is obvious is that work and family are not two independent spheres of life, especially as technology is increasingly blurring the lines between them, the theme of Jackson's chapter in this volume. The purpose of this book is to consider a broad range of topics that pertain to work and family with the goal of helping employers and working families understand the work-life options that are available so they can make choices that offer returns-on-investments to employers, families, and society at large that are consistent with personal and societal values—a lofty, but an achievable goal. We have only to look around to realize that many wonderful people are building a richer and fuller life by integrating work and family in positive and healthy ways.

REFERENCES

Barnett, R. C., & Rivers, C. (1996). *She works/he works: How two income families are happier, healthier, and better off.* San Francisco: Harper.

Friedman, S. D., & Greenhaus, J. H. (2000). *Work and family—Allies or enemies?* New York: Oxford University Press.

NOW Legal Defense and Education Fund. (2003, June). *Family initiative: Better child care, preschool and afterschool.* Washington, DC: Author.

Warren, E., & Tyagi, A. W. (2003). *The two-income trap.* New York: Basic Books.

Chapter 2

How We Study Work–Family Interactions

In this chapter, a psychologist, an economist, and a political scientist discuss their disciplinary perspectives on the many questions that pertain to work and family life.

METHODS, MODELS, AND MEASURES: PSYCHOLOGICAL APPROACHES TO WORK–LIFE ISSUES

Diane F. Halpern

Psychologists view work–life issues through a psychology-colored lens. Although it is a fuzzy boundary that distinguishes the psychological approach to work–life issues from those used by our sister disciplines of sociology, anthropology, economics, history, political science, and human relations, I believe there are some systematic differences in how we study questions about the intersection of work and life and, perhaps more importantly, how we decide what to study when we are looking at the ways that the part of our lives we call "work" and the parts we call "nonwork" overlap and interweave. In fact, there are even differences in where we draw boundaries between work and life, and these boundaries are becoming increasingly blurred, a point that is convincingly made by Jackson in chapter 10 of this volume. It will not surprise anyone who knows academic life close up—by which I mean the soft underbelly of academic life—that we each believe our own discipline to have the clearest views.

We certainly respect work done by those in other disciplines and we support the language of multidisciplinary research, but in fact, sometimes we might secretly believe the other disciplines would surely benefit from the application of our corrective lenses to their somewhat myopic views. My own doctorate was in experimental psychology. What is interesting about this area of specialization is that it specifies a research method rather than a substantive content area, like personality or psychopathology. This means that my graduate education was more concerned with the tools that we use to ask and answer questions in the social sciences than in knowing the answers that define a particular area of interest.

The study of work–life interactions really poses special research problems, especially for someone like me whose academic mantras include: "The only good experimental method is the one that permits you to make causal explanations," and "The only legitimate way that you can make causal explanations is to decide if one variable actually causes changes in the other variable." We look with envy at the causal designs that psychologists can use in the laboratory. As a research psychologist, I understand that I cannot conclude that X caused Y to occur, or, for example, whether having an employed mother causes children to engage in criminal behavior, unless I can randomly assign people to different conditions. The only way I could design an experiment that could show that having an employed mother caused children to become criminals is to randomly assign mothers to different categories, with some not working outside of the home, some working part-time, and some working full-time, and then, depending on which group their mothers were in, see, on average, how the children fared at some point later in life.

Of course, such experimental designs are not possible for the various ethical reasons that are immediately apparent; yet, the questions we want to answer beg causal explanations. What are the effects of growing up without a father? Will working adults have more stress-related illnesses if they cannot take time off to care for their own sick parents? Would workplaces be friendlier or yield more profits if women had a majority of high-level executive positions? These are just a small sample of the types of questions we address while being handicapped by the strict inability to infer cause because we cannot assign people at random to having sick parents or to high-level positions in corporations.

Psychological study of work–family issues often uses a variety of less preferred research strategies, usually pretending they are just as good as experimental designs that would permit causal conclusions. Psychologists may use natural experiments, where some event mimics random assignment to treatment conditions. For example, there are studies of the work–life consequences of being drafted into the army at different ages and at different life stages. We also use samples that are matched on variables that we believe are important in determining an outcome. An example of a matched sample design is comparisons of men and women who are at the CEO (chief executive officer) or COO (chief operating officer) level in a large corporation, matched on educational background, age, and years of employment. How do these two groups differ in their management style or salary level? There are many problems with "matched group designs," but often that is the best we can do.

I have presented research papers at various conferences and psychology departments and sometimes I am told (politely or not) that the study of work–life interactions is not a scientific field, that psychologists should not sully their reputations by working in this area until we can find ways to utilize true experimental designs. In other words, it is a "soft" field. In response to the denigrating term *soft*, some of the best models of work–life (or work–family) interaction require a high level of sophistication for their statistical tests—the sort of sophistication that requires multiple years of doctoral and postdoctoral training and access to the sorts of data sets that few people are likely to have. Unfortunately, the results are often stated in terms of abstractions that seem far removed from practitioner recommendations. I assume that translators will continue to build bridges between the world of research consumers and high level researchers, so that the newest research findings can be made accessible to a broader range of practitioners.

Any broad generalization about psychological research, especially of work–life issues, will fall far short of reality because of the wide range of methods of inquiry that are used by the many hundreds of thousands of psychologists—some of whom are doing work that is more closely aligned with other specializations than they are with psychology. Yet, on the whole, psychological research is usually identified along a handful of dimensions at the core of which is the singular fact that psychologists measure everything. Sometimes this disturbs people, mostly people who are outside of psychology, but also some of us inside as well. Still, psychologists do measure everything.

There is an old saying that has been attributed to many different people: "If it exists, then it exists in some quantity. If it exists in some quantity, then we can measure it." I would add that when we care about something, we measure it, and that one way of generating interest in a topic, in fact, is to measure it. For better or for worse, psychologists measure variables like marriage satisfaction, intelligence, personality, fear, and motivation, to name a few. Perhaps psychology's greatest contribution as a science lies in the psychometric methods that are used to measure fuzzy variables such as work–family life conflict, role satisfaction, parenting quality, and virtually any construct that might pertain to work and family life. The questions we address are also broad. Recent work has focused on the way and the extent to which multiple roles can be beneficial to mental and physical well-being. Psychologists also work in the area of program assessment where we have found that family-friendly work policies are both good for the health of the employees and for the employer's "bottom-line." Results from these studies can be used to inform business practices, as they support the business case for pro-family benefits.

Sometimes our successes are also our downfalls. I must have at least 15 to 20 different scales of work–life conflict or some variation on that theme. Of course, some scales of measurement are better than others. Among the general public there is very little understanding of the fact that the scales we come up with need to have multiple known validities and reliabilities. We often are too accepting of any group of questions that are formatted in ways that make them look like they measure just what they claim. And that is certainly a real danger because the public is too willing to accept poorly executed and sometimes even worthless studies as science.

Another problem with measurements is that they tend to take on a life of their own. People tend to use IQ scores as if they were synonymous with intelligence, instead of seeing these scores as a number that someone gets on a test and recognizing the multidimensional nature of intelligence. Similarly, if you have 15 to 20 different scales measuring work–life conflict, it becomes very difficult to think about work and family in any way that does not include conflict. So when can we break that sort of mental set, and instead think about work–life enhancement or think about the way that work and life add to each other and create something positive? If we focus on the measurement scales on hand (conflict scales), this kind of thinking becomes much more difficult.

Although it is always dangerous to attempt to summarize a field of inquiry in a few sentences because of the variability in research methods and topics, psychologists, as compared to researchers in other disciplines, often prefer models of interacting variables. By modeling data, we can see a "larger picture" with multiple variables exerting mutual influences on each other and on the outcome of any study. These multivariable models may resemble the "real-world" situation more than the experimental manipulation of one variable while holding all others steady, but they can become unwieldy and difficult to interpret, just like the real world. I believe that psychological research tends to be more model-oriented than most of the other social sciences, and thus rely heavily on structural equation modeling, which has grown in popularity over the last decade. If I were giving advice to people entering the arena, I would tell them that modeling is something they need to know.

It is a little known secret that psychologists measure more often than carpenters but with nowhere near the same sort of precision. Perhaps we would be better off if we adopted that old carpenters' creed and measured twice, at least before we interpreted our data. I have little doubt that psychologists see different research questions than social scientists educated in our sister disciplines, and that some of these differences come from the tools we use. Perhaps we are like the surgeon who sees every illness as a need for surgery. I would expect that the economists see the finances as the heart of work–life issues and political scientists see the core importance of political belief systems. It is only when we use multidisciplinary approaches that we get the whole picture and can even begin to explore the way work and life may conflict or cooperate given a particular political belief system and financial incentives.

THE ANALYSIS OF WORK–FAMILY ISSUES THROUGH ECONOMICS[1]

Robert Drago

For most economists, their domain of study is defined by markets for goods and services, and behavior is assumed responsive to monetary and other material incentives. Behind the idea of incentives lie the further notions that individuals rationally choose courses of action based on preferences for goods and services in tandem with constraints on possible courses of action. This general framing of the field helps to explain why economists are often accused of limiting the scope of human motivation to greed.

Most economic research relevant to work and family can be traced to the ideas of the Nobel prize–winning labor economist, Gary S. Becker (1976). Whether one believes the model is fundamentally "true" or not, Becker's research on human capital, dating to the late 1950s, facilitated the now widespread belief that education, productivity, and pay should be intimately connected, and established the terrain over which women would fight for equality at the highest levels of professional careers. His research on the allocation of time across the home and the workplace, dating to the mid-1960s, addressed gender, women's entry into the labor force, and issues around the division of child care that would become so central to research on work and family once dual-earner families became pervasive. As if this were not enough, economic theories of discrimination can also be traced to Becker's research.

To be sure, there were flaws in Becker's work. His theory of discrimination was based on the notion that some people do not like being around others. This theory helps explain workplace, occupational, and residential

[1]Thanks to the Alfred P. Sloan Foundation for financial support, and to Jennifer Fazioli for research assistance.

segregation, but does not translate well into home settings where men oppress women, and where White families employ women of color to perform tasks ranging from cleaning to child care in close physical proximity.

Of greatest importance, Becker took economics outside the realm of markets. The bad news was that once this boundary was breached, the validity of the models became increasingly dubious. Some family sociologists may be accepting of the "marriage market" metaphor for analyzing marriage, but most individuals still flinch at the comparison between purchasing an apple and finding a mate. Similarly, and for related reasons, parents do not typically view negotiations around caring for children as akin to those surrounding the purchase of a car.

This downside to Becker's research should not be minimized or ignored. But the upside was equally important: Economics would have very little to say about work and family conflicts without his research because such conflicts involve nonmarket behavior (Anderson, 1988; Waring, 1988). Three topics emerged where economists have made substantial contributions, in large part due to Becker's work. These concerned unpaid work and the national accounts, the division of labor in the home, and the motherhood wage gap.

Unpaid Work

The unpaid work debate started in the developed nations when constructing national accounting systems in the 1930s and 1940s (Eisner, 1989). The central question was whether unpaid labor should be counted as work. My favorite answer was provided by Margaret Reid in 1934. Reid viewed work as any "*activity . . . that . . . might be delegated to a paid [employee]*" (p. 11; the italics are mine, and the word "employee" has been substituted for the word "worker" in the quotation to preclude the use of the term being defined within the definition). The logical deficiencies of ignoring unpaid labor lay in the treatment of housework and housewives as productive if paid but unproductive if unpaid. Therefore, for example, if two househusbands hired each other to perform the same "work" in each other's houses, they suddenly switched from being nonproductive to productive.

The problem of how to account for unpaid labor and its worth to a nation was sufficiently obvious that a steady stream of well-known economists, starting in the 1940s, argued for an extension of the national income accounting system to include unpaid work (Eisner, 1989). Such extended accounts now exist, but are far from replacing Gross Domestic Product (GDP) as the primary yardstick for measuring economic well-being and devising economic policies.

The ominous implications of using GDP to gauge the health of the economy include, for example, a tendency to permit environmental degradation, to push women, men, and children into paid work, and to reduce fertility rates. Anything that is unpaid, whether it is work in the home or maintaining clean air, is necessarily excluded and devalued. Thus, one result of excluding unpaid work from the way we tabulate the wealth of nations is that household work, which is usually the women's work, has also been devalued, even though we acknowledge that it assumes value when we pay others to perform the same tasks.

For purposes of this chapter, the key implication of repeating the GDP mantra—unpaid work does not count toward national wealth—at policy levels is that the government ends up weighing in on work–family conflicts in a lopsided fashion: in favor of the "work" side. As Folbre (2001) and Schor (1991) argued, family supports and time with families, whether facilitated by corporate or government policies, are antithetical to GDP growth. They both conclude that the exclusion of unpaid work is improper measurement of GDP and that should be changed.

Division of Labor in the Home

Becker (1976) first turned to issues of direct concern to work and family research in the 1965 article, *A Theory of the Allocation of Time*. Prior research on working time viewed time allocation as a labor–leisure tradeoff. Supposing the goal of employment is to make money in order to purchase and ultimately consume products, individuals select an amount of working time in order to balance the amount of consumption goods they can purchase and the leisure time available to enjoy those goods. (For more on the labor–leisure tradeoff, see Drago & Wooden [1992]. This discussion ignores complications around time spent on investment in human capital, and around the money spent on investment goods.)

Becker introduced a third potential use of time, for household production, or housework and child care. The basic notion was that consumption can be generated by purchases of consumption goods and the allocation of time to leisure, *or* by spending unpaid time in the home on the production of consumption goods. For examples, a meal can be purchased at a restaurant or instead cooked at home, or laundry can be sent out or instead cleaned in the home.

In retrospect, the key insights from the model concerned the forces driving women into the labor force. Consider the following statement: "[A]n increase in the value of a mother's time may induce her to enter the labor force and spend less time cooking by using pre-cooked foods and less time on child-care by using nurseries, camps or baby-sitters" (Becker, 1976, p.

110). Becker provides two sound reasons for women's entry into employment: Wages were rising, drawing women in, and new technologies were reducing the amount of time required for household tasks, pushing women into paid work. The latter hinged on the development and distribution of automatic washers and dryers for clothing and dishes, vacuum cleaners, and of refrigerators and electric and gas stoves.

It took Becker another 20 years to get around to the questions of whether child care should be classified as "work," and to a direct confrontation with the division of labor in the home. In the 1965 paper, the term *work* applied only to paid employment. By 1985, in a piece in the *Journal of Labor Economics*, the distinction has become far muddier, and the division of labor around children is of central concern.

In the later paper, Becker argued that differences in wages between men and women are partly attributable to differences in hours of work and human capital investments, but also due to the fact that women devote substantially more time and effort to children and the household. In short, Becker had discovered that raising children is work, and that jobs are structured to advantage those who perform no child care, an argument that fits the newer motherhood wage gap literature discussed next.

For many of us in the field of work and family research, the central issue here is whether it is possible for couples to equally share child care and labor market participation (e.g., Risman, 1998, or Deutsch, 1999). Becker responds that equality is possible, but not desirable in any given household. The root argument here concerns the advantages of specialization. For example, a woman qualified as an airline mechanic would either be a poorly qualified parent or we would waste valuable resources training her to be a good parent. Similarly, her househusband would have become so qualified as a parent that if he also sought to, for example, become a pastry chef, he would be poorly equipped for that venture and his parenting skills would be wasted on the endeavor. This does not mean that gender equity is a hopeless goal, but rather that we are unlikely to do away with the division of labor in a particular home. If we take the division of labor as given, then other routes to gender equity need to be pursued. As Becker (1985) concluded regarding the possibilities for a more equal division of labor between men and women in the future: "[Because of the advantages to unencumbered workers,] husbands would be more specialized to housework and wives to market activities in about half the marriages, and the reverse would occur in the other half" (p. S56).

This dismal conclusion is probably wrong. Many employed parents may believe they should spend more time with their children, but none that I am aware of consider their parenting skills inadequate, nor do they fear the loss of job skills due to the performance of parenting tasks. This argument is consistent with all of the findings reported by Galinsky (chap. 14, this volume).

Motherhood Wage Gap

Becker's later research suggested that there might be a wage penalty associated with parenting. Because most parenting work was and continues to be performed by mothers, his research implied that there might be a wage gap specifically associated with motherhood: Among women, mothers may systematically earn less than nonmothers. Other economists skirted similar arguments by around the mid-1980s (e.g., Bergmann, 1986). These works suggested the existence of a motherhood wage gap. But, in retrospect, the gap was still emerging at that time. Only later was the new pattern clearly identified and documented, a task performed by Jane Waldfogel in 1998. Waldfogel compared wage figures from the 1980 and 1990 respondents at age 30, and found the gender wage gap had shrunk substantially over the period. The overall wage gap between women and men, corrected for differences in education and the like, was $4.73 per hour in 1980, a figure that fell to $1.86 per hour by 1990. In both years, men experienced higher wages. This decline in the gender gap reflected dramatic gains for women in the labor market.

However, Waldfogel found a new wage gap affecting women who are employed and responsible for dependent children. Among women in the sample, the motherhood gap rose from $.42 in 1980 to $2.07 in 1990. The difference in hourly wages between women who are and are not mothers became larger than the overall difference between men and women. The main question this research raises is whether in fact the work of mothering leaves employees with less energy, time, and commitment for their jobs. I suspect that the trade-off here afflicting most adults committed to parenting involves a choice between being highly productive for a limited number of hours on the job or being relatively unproductive over a longer span of hours. If this trade-off exists, and it has yet to be documented, then long-hours parents are probably in fact less productive than nonparents, while short-hours parents may experience wage discrimination even though their hourly productivity is high. (This argument is implicit in the work of Williams [1999].) Only further research could document whether and where such a trade-off exists. (To be fair to noneconomists, it is worth noting that Becker, Waldfogel, Budig, and England are all employed in sociology and not economics departments.)

Additional Considerations

Becker's research helps us to understand all three of the issues outlined above: the importance of including unpaid work in the national accounts, the division of labor in the home, and the motherhood wage gap. What his approach cannot help to explain are changes in attitudes. To understand those shifts, we need analyses of norms and ideology, such as those found in the works of Joan Williams (1999). Relevant efforts to combine economic and noneconomic models, or to at least think through the issues with these various facets of social reality in mind, are indeed appearing of late. Works by Frank (1995), Schor (1998), Appelbaum, Bailey, Berg, and Kalleberg (2000), and Folbre (2001) all provide wonderful templates for combining the best of economic thinking with the messier issues of belief systems, norms, and customs.

In addition, the empirical tools of economists remain very useful for analyzing a variety of economic and less economic phenomena. For example, research currently being conducted by Yi-Ping Tseng and Mark Wooden at the University of Melbourne is using such tools to analyze Australian data regarding the division of labor in the home, in the hope of ascertaining the constraints stopping some couples but not others from achieving an egalitarian split. Other researchers are, for example, using economic tools to analyze the factors leading parents to leave their children in "latch-key" arrangements (Brandon, 1999). The value of large-sample survey data, and of economic tools for analyzing those data, cannot be doubted.

The most substantial and difficult challenge for economists interested in understanding conflicts between work and family is, however, incorporating the information gathered by ethnographic research into their theories or thinking. Ethnographers gather samples of rich, detailed qualitative data from a handful of research participants, and strive to let the resulting interpretation of reality come from the participants themselves. Excellent examples of this approach in the work–family field can be found in the works of Hochschild (1997), Risman (1998), Deutsch (1999), or Garey (1999). These works rely upon the inductive rather than deductive method common to economic theorizing, and what generalizations are found are based on samples that are sufficiently small that they would never see the light of day in the pages of any reputable economics journal.

Economists could continue to ignore ethnographers. But I believe that would be a mistake. What I have instead tried to do in my own research is to take hypotheses generated by ethnographic research and test these in larger data sets, using economic methods to do so. For example, in Drago (2001), I take the notion of "time transfer" as developed in Rogers' (2001) ethnographic study, to understand and test in a relatively large survey data set for transfers of work tasks from parents to nonparents in the workplace. Research of this type is promising, but also leads us down a very daunting path, because an acceptance of the value of ethnographic research among economists would have us generating theoretical predictions from a mixture of empirical work and deductive thinking. Such an approach is likely to prove somewhat confusing, to say the least.

Nonetheless, for ascertaining where the crux of work–family conflicts will be found, and for identifying viable solutions, the combining of traditional economic methods with ethnographic research offers us a great source of hope. Whether others will follow that path remains to be seen.

A POLITICAL SCIENTIST PERSPECTIVE: UNDERSTANDING RECONCILIATION OF WORK AND FAMILY IN THE EUROPEAN UNION

Nigel Boyle

The primary focus of this section is to investigate the lessons that people working in various areas of work and family might draw from the application of different approaches. To this extent, I am supposed to represent the field of political science, and to give a perspective on the European model. I won't be able to do this, mainly, because there is no such thing as the European model. There are actually three different models in Europe, and, in fact, they are not really European at all but span across all of the OECD countries, the cluster of first-world capitalist democracies. There are three very different groupings of countries regarding child care and family issues, which are, in turn, nested in a larger array of social institutions.

Although as a political scientist everything seems to break down into politics in the end, I remain greatly impressed by the work of sociologists and economists, and of demographers in particular. In fact, I think this field, the relationship between work and family, is uncovering factors that are immensely important for social scientists, ranging from developing economies to shifts in politics as well as dramatic changes in demographics. Birth rates, death rates, morbidity, and even physiological changes in human population can all be traced back to these issues of what is going on between work and family.

There are some rather quirky data that point strongly to the differing attitudes between the advanced capitalist countries. The French government is presently undertaking a national survey on the physical size and measurements of French people, both men and women. It is being produced, in part, for the fashion and apparel industries as the old measurements of people's dimensions no longer apply. This issue of how (and why) people physiologically are changing is an international one, and one whose effects vary by country. The British are shaped differently than the French who are shaped differently than the Americans. You might expect that Americans are getting kind of pear shaped. The French people are changing, but interestingly, men are not changing in the gut, but in the shoulders; in just the last few years French men have been getting a lot bigger around the shoulders. They are becoming more "buff," as it were. How is this explained? Well, participation in sports clubs, health clubs, and fitness centers has skyrocketed in France, particularly in the last 5 years. One of the reasons for this is the introduction of the 35-hour workweek. The French already have very extensive holidays and leave policies, but now they have shorter workweeks, and a lot of French people are spending time at the club getting fit. There is also evidence that a lot of French men are spending more time with their children, more time with their families, and, over the past 5 years, the relationship between work and family in France has been changing dramatically.

A related matter is the dramatic rise over the past 5 years in the French birth rate. Recall that the advanced capitalist democracies in Europe right now have the lowest birth rates in the world. The birth rates in Italy and Spain are below 1.3, way below the replacement rate of 2.1 children per woman. In comparison, the Swedes are breeding like crazy, and only the French have begun to catch up. What is going on is in large measure a function of the different ways in which work and family relations are being treated in different European countries. There are, as I said, three different models.

The model that most people are familiar with, as it applies to the United States, the United Kingdom, Australia, New Zealand, and Canada, is the liberal model. This model holds the work ethic as its core value and institutions are designed to provide minimum interference in the free market function of the economy. We see the consequences of this orientation in the political debates over welfare reform and other social issues.

The second model is the social–democratic model, most familiar in the case of Scandinavia. There, government policies try to insulate people from the market. This model provides extensive public provision of day care and child care, with care-giving being a relatively high-status occupation. There are also very extensive leave policies: 15-month leaves available to parents of newborns and strong encouragement for men to participate in parental leave as part of a national campaign to de-gender parenting. Now about 15% of Swedish men are actually taking time off for child leave when they have a newborn.

The third, and most often overlooked, model is called variously the continental, the conservative, or the Christian–Democratic model. The last of these terms is my preference, although, as the grouping also includes Japan, it is occasionally a rather unfortunate name. In these societies, there is a great emphasis on a social system based on the male breadwinner and the female homemaker. Fiscal systems, tax laws, and benefits programs all are designed in just a way to facilitate and encourage the continuation and propagation of this model.

These are the three worlds that are out there. Again, this is not just interesting as an outcome of other factors but it has immense consequences on the economic development of each country as well. The Scandinavian participation rate of women working outside the home is enormous: More than 85% of women work outside the home. In the countries based on the conservative model, the female participation rate is lower than 60%. In places like Italy, only 40% of women work outside the home. The liberal cases are usually somewhere in between these extremes.

These fundamental social orientations also ultimately explain some of the demographic features of various countries. Italian and Spanish women are not having babies because it is immensely costly for a woman to have a child. Becoming a mother means leaving the labor market for about 15 years. The costs of doing such without public provision are enormous, particularly for women who also want careers. On the other hand, in Scandinavia, and now in France as well, the incentives have changed significantly, particularly where the state is attempting to de-gender parenting. As a result, women are perhaps more willing to have more children, producing a more demographically stable society.

This is just a taste of the value of comparative analysis. There are really different ways of organizing this relationship between work and family, although I would not go so far as to say one country can borrow easily from other models. You cannot create a Swedish system in the United States overnight. These policies and programs are nested in a whole array of labor market institutions, social institutions, cultural practices, and cultural norms. It is not easy to just graft from one to the other. Different countries are in different courses of national development; there are differences in national trajectories. Still, there is much to gain in comparative analysis, particularly in the way it aids the understanding of one's own country and its policies. It should be interesting to see how a work–life professional with expertise in the business end of these models sees the research landscape.

REFERENCES

Anderson, M. (1988). *The American census: A social history.* New Haven, CT: Yale University Press.

Appelbaum, E., Bailey, T., Berg, P., & Kalleberg, A. L. (2000). *Manufacturing advantage: Why high-performance work systems pay off.* Ithaca, NY: Cornell University Press.

Becker, G. S. (1976). *The economic approach to human behavior.* Chicago: University of Chicago.

Becker, G. S. (1985). Human capital, effort, and the sexual division of labor. *Journal of Labor Economics,* special supplement, January, S33–S58.

Bergmann, B. (1986). *The economic emergence of women.* New York: Basic Books.

Brandon, P. D. (1999). Determinants of self-care arrangements among school-aged children. *Children and Youth Services Review, 21*, 497–520.

Deutsch, F. (1999). *Halving it all: How equally shared parenting works.* Cambridge, MA: Harvard University Press.

Drago, R. (2001). Time on the job and time with their kids: Cultures of teaching and parenthood in the U.S. *Feminist Economics, 7*(3), 1–31.

Drago, R., & Wooden, M. (1992). The determinants of labor absence: Economic factors and workgroup norms across countries. *Industrial and Labor Relations Review, 45*(4), 764–778.

Eisner, R. (1989). *The total incomes system of accounts.* Chicago: University of Chicago Press.

Folbre, N. (2001). *The invisible heart: Economics and family values.* New York: New Press.

Frank, R. H. (1995). *The winner-take-all society: Why the few at the top get so much more than the rest of us.* New York: Penguin.

Garey, A. I. (1999). *Weaving work and motherhood.* Philadelphia, PA: Temple University Press.

Hochschild, A. (1997). *The time bind: When work becomes home & home becomes work.* New York: Metropolitan Books.

Reid, M. (1934). *Economics of household production.* New York: Wiley.

Risman, B. (1998). *Gender vertigo: American families in transition.* New Haven, CT: Yale University Press.

Rogers, J. K. (2001). There's no substitute: The politics of time transfer in the teaching profession. *Work and Occupations, 28*, 64–90.

Schor, J. B. (1991). *The overworked American: The unexpected decline of leisure.* New York: Basic Books.

Schor, J. B. (1998). *The overspent American: Why we want what we don't need.* New York: Basic Books.

Waldfogel, J. (1998). Understanding the 'Family Gap' in pay for women with children. *Journal of Economic Perspectives, 12*(1), 137–156.

Waring, M. (1988). *If women counted: A new feminist economics.* San Francisco: Harper & Row.

Williams, J. (1999). *Unbending gender: Why work and family conflict and what to do about it.* New York: Oxford University Press.

Part II

THE BUSINESS CASE OR "WHY SHOULD MY FIRM INVEST IN FAMILY-FRIENDLY WORK POLICIES?"

Organizations first introduced Family Friendly work policies in the late 1980s to compete for talent in a shrinking labor pool. Many of the Fortune 500 companies found that these policies such as flexible working hours accommodated the increasing numbers of working mothers and dual-career couples. Giving employees flexible work hours let them attend to family needs while minimizing work disruption.

Today organizations face additional challenges in managing work–family initiatives. Top management often demands that human resource directors provide evidence of the return on investment for these initiatives. This process of making a "business case," which refers to demonstrating the costs and benefits of a particular organizational decision, is an important step to ensuring organizational-wide support for work–family initiatives. Organizations must also work to ensure that families can in fact utilize many of the policies set out to accommodate working families. Studies find that although many organizations have family-friendly policies on the books, their implicit norms discourage employees from using these policies. Thus, official policies and actual usage of policies can be disparate—and employees learn that what they see in benefits manuals is not always what they get, at least not if they want to get ahead in their careers.

In this section, we showcase two chapters that focus on how and why businesses should adopt policies to help employees integrate work and family. The first, by Murphy and Zagorski, traces some of the causes and consequences of work–family conflict, as well as the ways in which these programs reduce work–family conflict. They also consider how an organization's culture and management can work to make sure employees utilize the policies they have in place. The second chapter by Cascio and Young focuses on the impact of family-friendly policies on an important business outcome: shareholder return. Using *Working Mothers 100 Best Companies,* the chapter analyzes shareholder rates of return for this group of companies versus standard stock indexes over a number of years.

These two chapters make the case for why organizations should assist employees in raising their families. In this section, we also focus on what organizations can do to help.

Chapter 3

Enhancing Work–Family
and Work–Life Interaction:
The Role of Management

Susan Elaine Murphy
Claremont McKenna College

David A. Zagorski
Claremont Graduate University

Today's organizations have more than a passing interest in retaining their productive employees. Company estimates put turnover costs, including recruiting and selecting, at about $10,000. An additional 2% of an employee's salary goes to training (Van Buren & King, 2000). Especially in lean times, organizations cannot afford to lose those employees on whom they rely most. To compete for qualified employees, many organizations have continued to offer nonjob benefits that help them attract and retain these top performers. These benefits include both work–family and/or work–life employee accommodations. Although many organizations offer these programs, the promised benefits do not always materialize. Many researchers and organizations speculate as to the reasons for the shortcomings of the programs, although some evidence suggests that the strongest predictor of the efficacy of these programs is how they are implemented and supported throughout all levels of organizational management (Nord, Fox, Phoenix, & Viano, 2002).

Efforts to address work–family conflict began as a set of initiatives to give employees more control over their home life, and included the widespread use of flexible working hours, or flex time. Currently, about 29% of full-time and salary workers have flexible work schedules, which is nearly double the proportion of 10 years earlier (Bureau of Labor Statistics, 2001). Interestingly, for about 11% of employees a flexible schedule was part of a formal program, while for other employees it was discretionary. The proportions of employees utilizing these programs vary greatly by occupation.

The data showed that while 45.5% of executive, administrative, and sales personnel vary their work hours, the figure is much lower for hourly employees.

Another major method for improving work–family balance was the introduction of cafeteria-style benefit programs that allowed employees to craft their benefits package to meet their specific needs and family status. In 1997, 13% of medium and large organizations offered these types of flexible benefits as compared to only 5% 10 years earlier (Bureau of Labor Statistics, 2001). Job sharing, time off for caring for sick children, and on-site day care facilities are a few more of the ways in which corporations tout their "family friendly" status to prospective employees. In 2000, 12.8% of all civilian workers (employees of state and local government and private industry) had access to child care resources and referral service, with only 4% of these same workers having access to on-site or employer-sponsored day care centers.

The need for work–family benefits occurs at a time when many statistics suggest that U.S. employees are working harder than ever. U.S. employees work more hours than any other industrialized country. In the past decade alone, U.S. workers have added 58 hours per year to their work schedules (Brady, 2002). Compared to European countries, the average U.S. worker takes 14 days of vacation versus about 33 days (Engle, 2003). The impact of this additional workload is reflected in current attitudes toward work. A survey by TrueCareers reports that 70% of workers feel they have no balance between their work life and home life (Armour, 2002; see also Cascio & Young, chap. 4, this volume). Combine these statistics with the major changing demographic shift in the increasing number of working mothers, increases in dual-earner families, and single-parent households (Barnett, chap. 11, this volume), and you have an increasingly pressure-filled situation. Moreover, these changing statistics and increased feelings of overwork do not just affect women. Relatively equal percentages of women and men are concerned with work–family issues (Galinsky & Bond, 1998). In fact, when surveyed, equal numbers of men and women said they would turn down promotions to accommodate family responsibilities (Milkie & Peltola, 1999). In addition, men are increasing the amount of time they devote to child care and other home responsibilities, and work–family issues will become an even more critical issue for organizations as they work to keep their valuable human assets (Bond, Thompson, Galinsky, & Prottas, 2002). (See Riggio & Desrochers, chap. 12, this volume, for a discussion of the changing attitudes of men toward work and family issues.)

In light of these various factors affecting work, employers face a number of challenges in understanding and remedying work–life issues. One of the challenges in addressing work–life conflict is getting past the misconception of what Friedman, Christensen, and Degroot (1998) call the "zero sum game" of employee benefits. Rather than focusing exclusively on the costs to the organization, organizations should instead focus on how benefits can not only help the organization attract and retain employees, but can impact the bottom line. In fact, work–life balance was among the three most important factors considered by job applicants in accepting a new position (Galinsky, Bond, & Friedman, 1993). Greenblatt (2002) noted that in McKinsey & Company's book, *The War for Talent,* work–life balance factors account for more than two thirds of those work characteristics rated absolutely essential to attracting and recruiting talent. Other authors have gone so far as to suggest that corporations have a social responsibility to foster work–life balance (Drucker, 2002; Jones, 2003).

Another employer challenge in the work–life area is the shift in focus from work–family balance to work–life balance. This shift is reflected in organizational policies that now look to address balance issues for employees without families (Grover & Crooker, 1995; Hall, 1990) and attempt to meet the needs of increasing numbers of unmarried employees. *Business Week* (Conlin & Hempel, 2003) reported that according to the U.S. Census Bureau, "married-couple households—the dominant cohort since the country's founding—have slipped from nearly 80% in the 1950s to just 50.7% today." Furthermore, the latest census data shows that married couples with kids make up only 25% of all households, and 42% of the workforce is unmarried. These changes are sure to affect the way in which employers decide on the how and why of benefit options.

A third challenge for employers is defining what constitutes an effective work–life outcome for an individual. Most of the current thinking implies that employees are attempting to achieve a life in which each realm of their lives is in balance or at least not in conflict. As the title of this volume suggests, balance may not be an appropriate goal. The term *balance* might suggest that employees are giving less effort to their work and nonwork domains in some sort of a compromise. In the research literature on conflict resolution between parties, the optimal solution for resolving conflict is one of collaboration because compromise results in each party giving up something. Collaboration occurs when a win–win solution is achieved (i.e., a solution that allows both sides to get more and give up nothing). As noted by Greenhaus, Collins, and Shaw (2003), a number of researchers have used other terms such as accommodation, compensation, resource drain, segmentation, spillover, work–family conflict, work–family enrichment, and work–family integration to explain the nature of the relationship between these two spheres of employee life. (See Greenhaus et al., 2003, for an extensive discussion of different conceptualizations of balance.) In this edited volume, we are using the term *interaction* to suggest that a collaborative solution occurs where work and nonwork life integrate in such a way that both sides are enhanced (see Halpern & Murphy, chap. 1, this volume).

Reducing work–life conflict and increasing work–life interaction is currently a priority for many companies, whereas for others it will become increasingly important for establishing competitive advantage and for ensuring a productive workforce. Many of the challenges surrounding work–family and work–life interaction imply that organizations will need to define more broad-reaching methods for accommodating individual needs for employees to achieve effectiveness in both their work and personal lives. The purpose of this chapter is to provide an overview of the organizational support structures to ensure intended utilization of work–life benefits. In addition, the chapter demonstrates how managers and leaders can assist employees in increasing the effectiveness of the interaction of their work and home life. We first outline some of the important findings regarding work–life conflict and work performance, followed by a brief summary of some steps organizations are currently taking, and concluding by offering the next steps organizations can take.

BACKGROUND ON CAUSES AND CONSEQUENCES OF WORK–LIFE AND FAMILY CONFLICT

The study of work–family conflict was initially based on the assumption that work and family were two separate, incompatible, and therefore, competing roles individuals attempted to fulfill (Edwards & Rothbard, 2000). More recent research has considered the multiple ways in which an individual's work and nonwork life interact. Some of these theories now take into consideration possible benefits that can transfer between one domain to the other. Even though the transfer can be positive, overwhelmingly the view is that many factors in the workplace do in fact cause work and nonwork to be in conflict with one another, and therefore, results in many negative consequences. In this next section we briefly overview some of the causes of work/nonwork life conflict, its consequences, and research on the efforts by organizations to reduce the conflict.

Causes

Greenhaus and Beutell (1985) defined work–family conflict as "a form of interrole conflict in which the role pressures from the work and family domains are mutually incompatible in some respect" (p. 77). Work–life and work–family conflict becomes an issue for organizations as employees attempt to fulfill roles in the workplace and roles at home that may be in conflict. Researchers have identified three different types of conflict. Time-based conflict occurs when time demanded by family competes with work activities. Individuals who have inflexible work schedules and working women experience the greatest time-based conflict. Strain-based conflict occurs when stress from one domain spills over into another. In other words, when the stress of household duties, relationship problems, and the needs of children interfere with work, or when work stress spills over into home life. The bidirectional nature of work–family conflict has been investigated in a number of studies. For example, Frone, Yardley, and Markel (1997) distinguished the conflict that arises from work interfering with family life (work-to-family; WTF conflict) from the type of conflict that occurs when family life interferes with work (family-to-work; FTW conflict). The third type of conflict, role behavior conflict, occurs when the way a person has to behave at work conflicts with the way they need to behave at home. For example, a caring compassionate mother may have to be strict and bottom-line oriented in the workplace.

In addition to different conflict causes, such as time-based, strain-based, and incompatible roles, certain job features are more likely to cause strain, stress reactions, or burnout. For example, stress-inducing job characteristics include jobs that are challenging and require long hours, give no employee control over work time or work processes, consist of a heavy workload, or jobs in which employers have unlimited access to their employees. For example, Families and Work Institute (Bond et al., 2002) revealed that 32% of employees surveyed say they are contacted outside work hours about work matters regularly; 28% are contacted occasionally, and 40% report this never happens. Most companies recognize technology as one of the drivers of increased work–life conflict. Cellular phones, pagers, and e-mail make employees accessible around the clock every day of the year (see Jackson, chap. 10, this volume).

Another issue driving incompatibility between work and home is the paradox that in these times of job instability, people seem to be turning to their families for security and work is becoming less important. For example, as reported by Cascio and Young (chap. 4, this volume), according to the Society for Human Resource Management in 2002, 70% report they would rather spend time with their families than at work; in 2000, the proportion was only 54%. Some attribute this renewed emphasis on family and personal life and reordering of priorities such that family is seen as more important than work to the terrorist attacks of September 11th, 2001 (Armour, 2002). Many articles and books conclude that people seem to be calling a kind of a time-out and asking, "What is really important to me? And why I am here?" (Shellenbarger, 2002).

In addition to the need to care for families or other life demands, many workers must provide care for their elderly parents or other elderly relatives. Most likely, the increased numbers are directly related to the fact that the largest group of employees come from the baby boom generation and are facing the stress of elder care. Some individuals in the baby boomer group, those who waited to have children until they were older, are actually sandwiched between concerns for child care in addition to elder care, adding even more stress to their lives. Care for children and elderly dependents causes high levels of family domain stress. Employers are becoming increasingly aware of this employee need. A survey by Hewitt Associates in 1999 showed 47% of large companies offered elder-care benefits compared to 20% in 1993 (Mendels, 2001).

In understanding the causes of work–life conflict, it is important to consider individual differences. As much research suggests, one person's stress is another person's motivation. Individual differences in personality, coping styles, or other resources will determine how two individuals react to the same stressor or the same occurrences of work to family or family to work conflict.

Consequences

According to the American Stress Institute, stress is estimated to cost U.S. businesses approximately $300 billion per year because of lower productivity, higher absenteeism, turnover, alcoholism, and medical costs (McShane & Von Glinow, 2003). Work–family conflict has been shown to be positively associated with overall life stress (Parasuraman, Greenhaus, & Granrose, 1992) and increased turnover intention (Greenhaus, Parasuraman, & Collins, 2001). In another study, Frone (2000) showed that both work-to-family and family-to-work conflict produced mood, anxiety, and substance dependence disorders. In one study, working mothers were found to have significantly higher levels of stress hormones after work than fathers or women who were not mothers (Lundberg & Frankenhaeuser, 1999). Kossek and Ozeki's (1998) meta-analytic review found that both WTF and FTW conflict were negatively related to job and life satisfaction. The FTW conflict can be even more devastating to families. For example, a recent study of adolescents showed that parents' work-related stress led to problem behaviors in adolescents, through more conflict at home and less positive adjustments (Crouter & Bumpus, 2001). These children tended to withdraw from the family.

Some employees hold specific expectations for balancing work and family. In their eyes, not meeting these expectations may violate the psychological contract. Psychological contracts in organizations consist of an individual's beliefs about the nature of the exchange relationship between employers and employees (Rousseau & Parks, 1993). The two types of contracts, transactional and relational, vary in the degree of commitment between the employer and employee. The transactional type is short term and primarily an exchange of pay for work, whereas the relational psychological contract is reflected in a longer term relationship characterized by mutual obligations between employer and employee. Research suggests that employees in the latter type of psychological contract exhibit job behaviors that go above and beyond the call of duty, otherwise known as organizational citizenship behaviors (Organ, 1990; Podsakoff, Ahearne, & MacKenzie, 1997). Robinson and Morrison (1995) found that if the psychological contract is violated and trust is broken, the individual is less likely to engage in organizational citizenship behaviors. Psychological contract violations have two implications for work–life conflict. First, the rapid increase in work–life benefits may lead many employees to take them for granted, and to perceive a violation of the implicit contract when they are not offered. Consequently, these employees may engage in fewer organizational citizenship behaviors. Second, employees may perceive psychological contact violation if the organization has a work–life policy in place, but the organizational culture or management discourages employees from using such benefits.

Employers may need to accommodate various strategies for combining work and family life effectively. What are the options? In a qualitative study of women executives in television, Ensher, Murphy, and Sullivan (2002) found that women used three types of tactics in dealing with work and family and only one resembled balance as traditionally described. Some women chose to be exclusively career-focused, eschewing any kind of a family or personal life. The strategy of putting career first is similar to the one described in a controversial book by Hewlett (2002). Alternatively, others used a sequential focus in which early in their career they showed exclusive dedication to a career, and then after 10 to 15 years focused on personal and family life by cutting back on assignments or switching to part time. Some planned to re-enter the workforce eventually at their previous pace, whereas others were not sure. Cardozo back in 1986 called this "sequencing." The third group was composed of women who were simultaneously career- and family-focused (what many people envision when working toward balance), and reported that they were taking more of a compromise-based approach to work–family balance. Each of these three strategies came with its own advantages and disadvantages.

Less research has described the attempts of men to reconcile the competing demands of family and work, but as Kimmel (1993) noted, the corporate man of today is much less likely to have a stay-at-home wife than was his corporate boss, but is simultaneously more likely to be interested in being an involved father. This new organizational man also finds that organizations are not set up to meet the seemingly contradictory needs for both a challenging career and involved fatherhood. A number of popular books have addressed these issues for men. Some research has looked at differences between men and women in how they cope with these issues, but have not found many differences. For example, Anderson, Coffey, and

Byerly (2002) found no difference between men and women with respect to work-to-family and family-to-work outcomes. Hall (1990) mentioned the "invisible mommy and daddy tracks" that arise when men and women keep their fast track jobs by using informal strategies to attend to nonwork duties. Behson (2002a) found that some of the informal employee work accommodations to family included arranging for a coworker to switch duties, working through lunch, and leaving work early but completing tasks that night.

EFFECTIVENESS OF EFFORTS
TO REDUCE WORK–FAMILY CONFLICT

In offering these various benefits to reduce work–family or work–life conflict, companies want to know if they are actually effective. A number of studies in the 1990s looked at the bottom line effectiveness with mixed results. CCH, Inc., recently found that "programs such as a compressed workweek that increase work time flexibility are among the most effective strategies to combat unscheduled absences—a problem that costs some large companies as much as $1 million a year in lost productivity" (Weber, 2003, p. 26). The study also found that job sharing, alternative work arrangements, and telecommuting were also effective.

Other research has focused on the relationship of different work arrangements to affective outcomes such as organizational commitment and job satisfaction (Scandura & Lankau, 1997). For example, Families and Work Institute data from the 2002 National Study of the Changing Workforce (Bond et al., 2002) indicate that companies that offer greater work–life supports have employees who report higher job satisfaction, higher levels of commitment to the organization, and a greater likelihood of remaining in their jobs. In addition, employees with supervisors who were supportive of their employees' family and personal lives were highly satisfied with their jobs. Moreover, the study revealed that employees with more access to flexible work arrangements were more loyal and willing to work harder than required to help their employers succeed.

Beyond tangible accommodations such as paid parental leave and telecommuting, there are both formal and informal practices in every workplace regarding the acceptable use of family friendly options (Anderson et al., 2002). Case in point: Autodesk, a software development firm, has relatively few formal policies related to work–life balance, but its employees consistently rate it among the most family-supportive companies in America because the company's managers are willing to work with employees individually to determine customized solutions to their work–life balance challenges (*Business Week*, 1997). Whether accommodations are formal or informal, however, the availability of benefits alone is not enough to guarantee an effective work–life program.

ROLE OF MANAGEMENT IN ASSISTING EMPLOYEES IN ADDRESSING THE COMPETING DEMANDS OF WORK AND NONWORK LIFE

Organizational leaders and managers at all levels play three critical roles with regard to implementation and success of work–life policies: agenda-setters, gatekeepers, and role models. An organization's top management, in conjunction with the Human Resource department, is responsible for introducing and administering benefit policies, or in other words, setting the agenda. They may also act as gatekeepers by putting up roadblocks for employee utilization of benefits, for example, by requiring employees to obtain multiple levels of approval to use a benefit. Or they may serve as role models when they engage in efforts to improve their own personal situations (Milliken, Martins, & Morgan, 1998). First-line supervisors and managers have a large effect on whether individuals actually feel comfortable using the policies set out by top management, and may have input into what policies are adopted. Also, the more first-line supervisors refuse to support a policy, the more that value will be manifested in the overall organizational culture. Although efforts at the top management or first-line supervisor/manager level are somewhat overlapping, the distinction is important for addressing problems in fully implementing work/family/life benefits. In the following two sections, we delineate the way in which organizational management and manager/first-line supervisors can improve the use and effectiveness of the policies.

Organizational/Top Management Level: Agenda Setting

At the top level of organizational functioning, executives make decisions to help the organization adapt to competitive pressures (Zaccaro & Klimoski, 2001). In addition, top leaders and managers also have a direct influence on developing and sustaining the organization's culture, which consists of the shared values and norms that distinguish one organization from another (Schein, 1996). Starrels (1992) noted that "corporate culture may either advance or thwart the development and effectiveness of work–family programs" (p. 261).

With respect to organizational culture, the challenge for leaders then is to create a "family-friendly" or "balance-supportive" environment. Thompson, Beauvais, and Lyness (1999) found that supportive work–family culture was related to higher levels of benefits utilization, higher affective commitment, reduced employee turnover, and lowered self-reported levels of work–life conflict. A number of additional studies have identified the importance of organizational context—including climate and culture—in the employee's ability to balance work and family (Bailyn, 1997; Bond, Galinsky, & Swanberg, 1998). Over and over, culture emerges as a key element—*Business Week* (1997) noted in their annual survey of corporate work–life balance programs: "Lacking visible support from the top, work–family efforts can quickly be crippled."

Schein (1996) offered one framework for understanding how top management, as well as first-line supervisors or managers, affect organizational culture, which in turn affects the success of work–life programs. Top management and leaders can use five primary mechanisms for "embedding and reinforcing" an organization's culture. Foremost among these is attention, which refers to communication about priorities and values by what a leader asks about, measures, comments on, praises, and criticizes. Additional mechanisms include reactions to crises, role modeling, allocation of rewards, and criteria for selection and dismissal. Employees look to these signals regularly to affirm their understanding of the organization's culture of unwritten rules and norms. For work–family or work–life benefits, it is readily apparent which aspects are supported by the organization through these very mechanisms.

Terms like *overtime culture* (Fried, 1998) and *work devotion* (Blair-Loy & Wharton, 2002) have been coined to describe the unspoken corporate norm that regardless of an organization's official policies regarding work–life integration, long hours and impression management are often seen as the true keys to advancement (Bankert & Googins, 1996; Lizotte, 2001). Hill, Miller, Weiner, and Colihan (1998) suggested that for leaders to truly embrace work–life balance, the workplace must shift from a "face-time culture" to a "results-oriented culture." Bailyn (1997) believes that the way in which managers define "control" has an effect on work–family balance (i.e., whether managers choose to focus on recording attendance as opposed to productivity).

What types of organizations have come the farthest in offering the types of management initiatives and support needed for employees to experience work–life balance? In companies where turnover costs are high, such as many types of professional organizations, there are more initiatives to balance work and home life. Some research suggests that companies adopt family-friendly policies to signal their own adaptation to societal norms and pressures (Goodstein, 1994). Therefore, it is expected that large organizations, or those with professional reputations, might be first to offer these programs. Overall, the finance, insurance, and real estate industries lead the way. Service industries for the most part fall behind other types of organizations, with a few exceptions such as Marriott Corporation (see chap.

6, this volume). Those with more hourly workers are less likely to provide work–life policies (Bond et al., 2002) despite research that indicates that work–family policies, like flexible work arrangements, are positively associated with lowered turnover (Bond, 2003a, 2003b) and increased job satisfaction, which both impact an organization's bottom line. There is also a trend that larger companies offer more benefits, although, so do some of the very small organizations.

One interesting statistic shows that the proportion of top executive positions filled by women will predict whether or not a company offers these types of benefits. Specifically, 82% provide traditional flex time if half or more of top positions are filled by women, versus 56% of firms with no women in top positions (Bond et al., 2002). Disney Channel President Anne Sweeny is in the position to make decisions about family issues and encourages parents to take time off from work to accompany their children to the first day of school (Ensher et al., 2002). She is an agenda-setter in her position to influence the culture of her organization, and as a working mother has a better understanding of the family needs as opposed to traditional male executives. A study conducted in 1994 showed that in a sample of executives, predominantly males, 53% had wives that did not work outside of the home, and that on the whole, the executives spent very little time with their families and a disproportionate amount of time at work (Judge, Boudreau, & Bretz, 1994). As this trend changes we may see more support for other home arrangements from the top levels of management as the agenda-setters have experiences trying to reconcile different domains of their lives, we expect to see changes in organizational culture.

Finally, work–family support may not be enough for employees, however. Behson (2002b) found that more general organizational context was more strongly related to job satisfaction and affective commitment than were the actual work–family policies. He studied the effects of general perceived organizational support, perceived fair interpersonal treatment, and overall trust in management on the typical outcomes researchers investigate for work–family culture and family-supportive organization perceptions. His findings, however, did corroborate that specific work–family policies make a difference for employees with families and especially for those who chose to use the policies. The implications of his findings suggest that the type of organizational values such as concern for employees, etc., may be needed in conjunction with family-friendly policies to bring about effectiveness in work and home life domains.

Managerial and Supervisory Support

Leaders throughout the organization can also consciously or unconsciously influence the effectiveness of corporate work–life policies by displaying what Thompson et al. (1999) term "support sensitivity." This trait manifests itself whenever managers and other opinion leaders throughout the company encourage or discourage employee participation in benefits such as flextime or telecommuting, or by reinforcing cultural norms that favor "face time" or "overtime culture" above bottom-line results (Perlow, 1997; Starrels, 1992; Thompson, Thomas, & Maier, 1992). Employees who take advantage of family-related leave policies, for example, are often seen as uncommitted (Greenhaus et al., 2003), and are subject to negative career consequences such as lower performance ratings, proportionally smaller salary increases, and decreased promotional opportunities (Lobel & Kossek, 1996; Perlow, 1997). If benefit usage is punished, no matter how subtly, employees are unlikely to use them (Allen, 2001).

In further analyses of the Thompson et al. study, they examined three aspects of work–family culture: organizational support, career consequences, and managerial support. They found that beyond the influence of demographic variables, only one of the three elements—managerial support—contributed significantly to the variance in benefit usage. They suggest that day-to-day managerial support may be the most critical cultural variable in employees' decisions to use family-based workplace benefits, and more recent findings by Zagorski (2004) found that this is true of all forms of work–life accommodations, not only those related to dependent care.

As noted by one researcher (Behson, 2002b), it is important to distinguish between the generic term *management*, which might entail multiple levels of management, or managers a number of levels above the employee, and the employee's direct supervisor or manager. Although one might hope that a supervisor would be supporting the policies of the larger organization, this may not always be the case. Therefore, while many supervisors will follow policy in an organization, and even go so far as to be supportive of employees in utilizing a benefit, it takes effective leadership to balance the needs of their employees with the needs of the organization.

What does a supportive supervisor look like? According to Pitt-Catsouphes (2002), workplace relationships that are "respectful of employees' . . . work–life responsibilities are an essential component of balance-friendly workplaces." Similarly, a nationwide study commissioned by Canada's Department of Labour (2003) found that 70% of employees surveyed attributed problems with their respective companies' work–life balance programs to treatment by their immediate supervisors. Their primary complaints concerned managers who did not treat employees respectfully, failed to see people as a priority, or barred employees from using work–life accommodations. Conversely, successful programs were associated with managers who were supportive and approachable, understanding of the importance of balance—often from first-hand experience, and willing to give workers the option of flexibility.

To corroborate these nonempirical findings, a wealth of recent research has emphasized the role of first-line supervisors, whose supportiveness has been directly linked to reduced stress and interrole conflict and improved physical health (Burke, 1988; Thomas & Ganster, 1995), decreased turnover (Allen, 2001), and increased employee productivity, citizenship, job satisfaction, and family functioning (Clark, 2001; Galinsky & Stein, 1990; Repetti, 1987). Supportive supervisory attitudes and behaviors have also been linked to increased use of work–life benefits (Thomas & Ganster, 1995), higher perceptions of organizational fairness, and greater satisfaction with the company's overall efforts to help employees balance work and personal matters (Zagorski, 2004). Thomas and Ganster (1995) suggested two mechanisms by which leader support contributes to positive outcomes for employees. The first proposes that supervisory supportiveness engenders a sense of control over limited resources; the second posits that supportive attitudes increase perceived social support and thereby decrease employees' experience of work–life conflict (Greenhaus & Parasuraman, 1987).

In recent research by Zagorski (2004), a list of 26 items related to work–family culture was presented to survey participants. He found that 7 of the 9 items that were most strongly related to the success of work–life balance programs were related to supervisory attitudes and behaviors. The strength of the relationship between employees' ratings of supervisory supportiveness and their overall satisfaction with employee-sponsored work–life programs was nearly twice as strong as that between actual benefits and satisfaction. Similarly, 5 of the 7 items most strongly related to the perceived fairness of work–life programs had to do with treatment by supervisors, not overall organizational factors. In addition, Hartwell (2003) found that physicians with high psychological contract fulfillment believe that their organizations have fulfilled their supervisory relationship obligations to them to a much greater extent than those with low psychological contract fulfillment.

Can all leaders be helpful in this additional task of management? Current theories of leadership may help demonstrate what types of leaders may be effective in assisting employees in reducing work and family conflict. For example, Leader Member Exchange (LMX) is a well-researched theory of leadership that views leadership as a dyadic relationship between a leader and each of his or her direct reports (Graen & Scandura, 1987). The quality of these relationships can range from high to relatively low. Individuals in high-quality relationships find a supervisor who treats them with loyalty and trust, rather than merely as part of a transactional exchange of work for money. In fact, these higher quality relationships are somewhat more like a mentoring relationship. Research evidence from a recent study showed that employees involved in mentoring relationships had reduced work–family conflict (Nielson, Carlson, & Lankau, 2001). One would expect that individuals involved in higher quality relationships would have supervisors who helped them reconcile the competing demands of home and work. This type of supervision requires a wealth of relational skills that help not only in managing people day-to-day, but also in situations in which work and nonwork life collide (Uhl-Bien, 2003).

Transformational leadership theory is another type of leadership that describes leaders who possess the skills to help understand and to respond to the specific needs of an employee. According to Bass and his colleagues (Bass & Avolio, 1994), a leader who is considered transformational is engaged in a number of behaviors that would facilitate encouraging employees to have balance. The theory utilizes four dimensions: individualized consideration, intellectual stimulation, inspirational motivation, and idealized influence. Leaders who use individualized consideration would be more likely to recognize the unique work–life needs of each employee.

Hartwell and Torbert (2004) described leadership practices that can help to create work environments that support professionals hoping to reduce work–family conflict. Specifically, they suggest that leaders must be able to meet employees at the psychological level and correct incongruities between employees' and managements' beliefs. Based on adult developmental theory, they describe the Strategist type of leader (Fisher, Rooke, & Torbert, 2003) as one who intuitively appreciates the value of communicating openly with employees so that they can be sure there is an alignment in their understanding of each other's goals and terms.

Regardless of the theoretical lens, enhancing a supervisor's leadership skills is important. Future research should consider LMX, transformational leadership, and strategist-type leadership as three possible theories to determine what types of leaders are more likely to support their subordinates. Understanding what types of managers or supervisors can assist employees is the first step. The second step is making it clear to all managers that it is an organizational priority by including some measure of commitment to their employees' work–life balance in their performance reviews.

PUTTING LESSONS INTO PRACTICE

Given the crucial role of leaders at all levels of the organization in creating and sustaining a workplace culture that is conducive to work demands and life–family demands, what are the take-home lessons?

1. The foremost task for organizations is to understand the importance of personal and organizational benefits (see Cascio & Young, chap. 4, and Maslach, chap. 8, this volume) and to make work–life programs a strategic

priority. The next step is to create a menu of benefits that is based on employee focus groups, competitive benchmarking, and an eye toward fairness.

2. Once those benefits are in place, the biggest challenge is to fulfill the commitment to the policies by examining the way in which work is completed. This means challenging leaders to shift the organization's focus from time-oriented to task-oriented (Bailyn, 1997), to reexamine long-standing priorities about how, when, and where jobs must be performed, and to guarantee that employees who choose flexible options will not be punished.

3. Another important method for ensuring balance or integration is to establish clear communication that gatekeepers at all levels must follow. At the most basic level, this means being explicit about the company's expectations and accommodations. As one respondent in the Canadian Department of Labour's survey (2003) wrote, "I would like to get something in writing from the company to describe the policy for flextime, personal days, sick days. Employees would be much happier if they were clear on the company's standpoint because they could take needed time off without guilt." Even more important is a willingness to engage in constructive dialogue with employees about the importance of work–life balance, helping them to establish reasonable boundaries between work and nonwork domains, and making sure that employees are aware of their options—both formal programs and informal solutions (Behson, 2002a). As mentioned previously, effective leaders should have these communication skills in their behavioral repertoire.

4. Because first-line supervisors appear to be the linchpin in an effective balance program, the selection and development of managers must be handled with care (Thomas & Ganster, 1995). Supervisors must be trained to manage and motivate workers in nontraditional arrangements, to be more accommodating during family crises (Galinsky & Hughes, 1987), to deal effectively with employees' balance concerns, and to administer policies appropriately and fairly (Allen, 2001). The Canadian workforce survey (2003) concluded that "When work–family programs are applied unevenly and denied to many, they only serve to further demoralize an already beleaguered workforce." Conversely, leaders who are proficient in dealing with balance issues reap the reward of loyalty.

Some organizations are taking the lead by recognizing the role that supervisors play and setting up policies to ensure that they do not become a roadblock in the process. One study by the Families and Work Institute in Boston (Bond et al., 2002) found that 55% of the participants surveyed said that their organizations encouraged supervisors to be supportive of employees with family problems; 66% reported equal support from both the supervisor and the organization; 43% reported that their organizations in fact trains supervisors to provide support; and 56% reported that their organizations consider how well supervisors manage the work–family issues of employees within the formal performance appraisal system. These numbers are quite encouraging. Moreover, according to *Business Week's* (1996) corporate work–life survey, supervisors at First Tennessee National Corporation who were rated by their subordinates as supportive of work–family balance retained their employees twice as long as those were seen as less supportive.

5. Just as any working adult, leaders have limited resources, and they often benefit when the responsibility for managing schedules shifts to the workgroup rather than to supervisors (Bailyn, 1997). The critical message for leaders? Walk the talk. Most people see their managers as role models. When managers take advantage of benefits, they are telling employees that it is okay to use benefits. This also means that leaders must be careful to avoid playing the martyr and sending out mixed messages, such as sending employees home early on Fridays and then complaining about the long weekend they had to spend in the office.

6. Perhaps the most important lesson for leaders is that they must understand their workforce and be sensitive that each employee has unique balance needs. For example, although men and women report similar levels of work–life conflict (Burden & Googins, 1987), they may choose to resolve their respective role strains by choosing to adopt one of a variety of coping strategies, ranging from avoidance to problem solving to seeking social support. In dealing with workplace stress, men tend to favor a problem-solving approach, whereas women use social support in concert with other solutions. Rosario, Shinn, Morch, and Huckabee (1988), however, noted that under identical types of stress, gender differences in coping strategies often vanish. Generational differences are equally important to consider. A recent book by Warren Bennis and Robert Thomas (2002) provides an interesting narrative of the different values and corresponding needs of three generations: Generation Y (those born between 1979–1994); Gen X (those born between 1965–1978); and Boomers (those born between 1946–1964); distinctions that are important for organizations to consider in designing work life policies. Beyond gender roles and generational differences, workplace demographics also affect how organizations should consider benefits. Organizations also need to use a "life cycle" approach based on employee demographics to anticipate when employee family concerns such as children or elder care would occur.

Cultural factors can also influence employees' perceptions of supportiveness. Zagorski (2004) found that non-White employees felt less safe than their White counterparts in discussing nonwork issues in the workplace, and reported that their immediate supervisors were more critical of their efforts to balance work and nonwork concerns. Although work–family supports were designed originally to help ease the competing demands of working parents, it may be employees without children who are most susceptible to the influence of management support. Zagorski (2004) also found that after factoring out all other demographic and job-related variables, the willingness of childless employees to request access to work–life benefits was heavily dependent on the level of supportiveness of their immediate supervisor. Working parents, on the other hand, were comparatively immune to supervisory attitudes, suggesting that employees without children may be receiving cultural messages that their nonwork needs are viewed as less legitimate than those of working parents. As the number of childless employees increases, this disparity becomes increasingly relevant.

THE NEXT STEPS

Even if we can identify all of the elements of supportive cultures, from sensitive leaders to relevant programs, can we find ways to ensure that they are optimized? If we can find the magic formula to create a workplace climate that allows employees to find the optimal integration of work and life roles, can we design longitudinal studies to measure the effects—both on employees and on the organization—over time? How do we identify and train supervisors who will encourage their employees to integrate their work and nonwork roles while still helping the company remain competitive? And finally, can change be both top-down and bottom-up, as Thompson, Beauvais, and Lyness (1999) suggested? Can leadership in work–life interaction truly come from all levels? (See Purkey, Molina, Klein, & Pires, chap. 6, this volume for a discussion of organizations that tried different approaches emanating from different levels.) As *Business Week* (1997) noted, "Programs . . . are relatively easy to slap into place. Cultural change is far more compelling, but far tougher, too."

In this chapter, we focused on the causes and consequences of work and nonwork conflict, and outlined the role of management in helping employees achieve effectiveness in both the work and nonwork realm of their lives. We did not focus on the many pressures, which even in the presence of a supportive supervisor, that nevertheless make it very difficult to "do it all" or "have it all." Today's world of working is increasingly becoming more rapid-paced and more complex. As Robert Reich (2000), former U.S. Secretary of Labor, noted, work is changing in ways we cannot even anticipate. To benefit organizations, and ultimately society in the end, it is important that employers anticipate employee needs and help them determine realistic methods for bringing together their work and nonwork lives successfully.

REFERENCES

Allen, T. D. (2001). Family-supportive work environments: The role of organizational perceptions. *Journal of Vocational Behavior, 58,* 414–435.

Anderson, S., Coffey, B. S., & Byerly, R. T. (2002). Formal organizational initiatives and informal workplace practices: Links to work–family conflict and job-related outcomes. *Journal of Management, 28*(6), 787–810.

Armour, S. (2002). More Americans put families ahead of work. *USA Today,* December 5. Retrieved using Lexis Nexis.

Bailyn, L. (1997). The impact of corporate culture on work–family integration. In S. Parasuraman & J. H. Greenhaus (Eds.), *Integrating work and family: Challenges and choices for a changing world* (pp. 209–219). Westport, CT: Quorum Books.

Bankert, E. C., & Googins, B. K. (1996). Family-friendly—says who? *Across the Board, 33*(7), 45.

Bass, B. M., & Avolio, B. J. (1994). *Improving organizational effectiveness through transformational leadership.* Thousand Oaks, CA: Sage.

Behson, S. J. (2002a). Coping with family-to-work conflict: The role of informal work accommodations to family. *Journal of Occupational Health Psychology, 7*(4), 324–341.

Behson, S. J. (2002b). Which dominates? The relative importance of work–family organizational support and general organizational context on employee outcomes. *Journal of Vocational Behavior, 61,* 53–72.

Bennis, W. G., & Thomas, R. J. (2002). *Geeks and geezers.* Boston, MA: Harvard Business School Press.

Blair-Loy, M., & Wharton, A. S. (2002). Employees' use of work–family policies and the workplace social context. *Social Forces, 80*(3), 813–845.

Bond, J. T. (2003a). *The impact of job and workplace condition on low-wage and -income employees and their employers.* New York: Families and Work Institute.

Bond, J. T. (2003b). *Information for employers about low-wage employees from low-income families.* New York: Families and Work Institute.

Bond, J. T., Galinsky, E., & Swanberg, J. E. (1998). *The 1997 national study of the changing workplace.* New York: Families and Work Institute.

Bond, J. T., Thompson, C., Galinsky, E., & Prottas, D. (2002). *Highlights of the national study of the changing workplace.* New York: Families and Work Institute.

Brady, D. (2002). Rethinking the rat race. *Business Week,* August 26. Retrieved November 30, 2003, from http://www.businessweek.com/magazine/content/02_34/b3796646.htm

Burden, D. S., & Googins, B. (1987). Balancing job and homelife study. *Managing work and family stress in corporations.* Boston, MA: Boston University School of Social Work.

Bureau of Labor Statistics. (2001). Retrieved November 5, 2003, from http://data.bls.gov/cgi-bin/surveymost

Burke, R. J. (1988). Some antecedents and consequences of work–family conflict. *Journal of Social Behavior and Personality, 3,* 282–302.

Business Week. (1996). Special report: Balancing work and family. Retrieved October 11, 2003 from http://www.businessweek.com

Business Week. (1997). Special report: Work and family. Retrieved October 11, 2003, from http://www.businessweek.com

Canadian Department of Labour. (2003). Voices of Canadians: Seeking work–life balance. Retrieved October 11, 2003, from http://labour.hrdc-drhc.gc.ca/worklife/vcswlb-tcrctvp/p010105.cfm

Cardozo, A. R. (1986). *Sequencing.* Philadelphia: Athenaeum.

Clark, S. C. (2001). Work cultures and work–family balance. *Journal of Vocational Behavior, 58,* 348–365.

Conlin, M., & Hempel, J. (2003). Unmarried America: Say good-bye to the traditional family. Here's how the new demographics will change business and society. *Business Week*, October 20. Retrieved November 27, 2003, from http://www.businessweek.com/magazine/content/03_42/b3854001_mz001.htm

Crouter, A. C., & Bumpus, M. F. (2001). Linking parents' work stress to children's and adolescents' psychological adjustment. *Current Directions in Psychological Science, 10*, 156–159.

Drucker, P. (2002, February). They're not employees, they're people. *Harvard Business Review*, 70–77.

Edwards, J. R., & Rothbard, N. P. (2000). Mechanisms linking work and family: Clarifying the relationship between work and family constructs. *Academy of Management Review, 25*, 178–199.

Engle, J. (2003, July 13). The American vacation does a disappearing act. *Los Angeles Times*. Retrieved November 30, 2003, from http://www.latimes.com

Ensher, E. A., Murphy, S. E., & Sullivan, S. (2002). Reel women: Lessons from female TV executives on managing work and real life. *Academy of Management Executive, 16*(2), 1–14.

Fisher, D. D., Rooke, D., & Torbert, W. (2003). *Personal and organizational transformations: Through action inquiry*. Boston: Edge\Work Press.

Fried, M. (1998). *Taking time: Parental leave policy and corporate culture*. Philadelphia: Temple University Press.

Friedman, S. D., Christensen, P., & Degroot, J. (1998, November–December). Work and life: The end of the zero-sum game. *Harvard Business Review*, 119–129.

Frone, M. R. (2000). Work–family conflict and employee psychiatric disorders: The national comorbidity survey. *Journal of Applied Psychology, 85*, 888–895.

Frone, M. R., Yardley, J. K., & Markel, K. S. (1997). Developing and testing an integrative model of the work–family interface. *Journal of Vocational Behavior, 50*, 145–167.

Galinsky, E., & Bond, J. T. (1998). *The 1998 Business Work–Life Study: A sourcebook*. New York: Families and Work Institute.

Galinsky, E., Bond, J. T., & Friedman, D. E. (1993). *The changing workforce: Highlights of a national study*. New York: Families and Work Institute.

Galinsky, E., & Hughes, D. (1987, August). *The Fortune magazine child care study*. Paper presented at the meeting of the American Psychological Association, New York.

Galinsky, E., & Stein, P. J. (1990). The impact of human resource policies on employees: Balancing work/family life. *Journal of Family Issues, 11*(4), 368–383.

Goodstein, J. D. (1994). Institutional pressures and strategic responsiveness: Employer involvement in work–family issues. *Academy of Management Journal, 37*, 350–382.

Graen, G. B., & Scandura, T. A. (1987). Toward a psychology of dyadic organizing. *Research in Organizational Behavior, 9*, 175–208.

Greenblatt, E. (2002). Work–life balance: Wisdom or whining? *Organizational Dynamics, 31*(2), 177–193.

Greenhaus, J. H., & Beutell, N. J. (1985). Sources of conflict between work and family roles. *Academy of Management Journal, 10*, 76–88.

Greenhaus, J. H., Collins, K. M., & Shaw, J. D. (2003). The relation between work–family balance and quality of life. *Journal of Vocational Behavior, 63*, 510–531.

Greenhaus, J. H., & Parasuraman, S. (1987). A work-nonwork interactive perspective of stress and its consequences. *Journal of Organizational Behavior Management, 8*, 37–60.

Greenhaus, J. H., Parasuraman, S., & Collins, K. M. (2001). Career involvement and family involvement as moderators of relationships between work–family conflict and withdrawal from a profession. *Journal of Occupational Health Psychology, 6*, 91–100.

Grover, S. J., & Crooker, K. J. (1995). Who appreciates family-responsive human resource policies: The impact of family-friendly policies on the organizational attachment of parents and non-parents. *Personnel Psychology, 48*, 271–288.

Hall, D. T., (1990). Promoting work/family balance: An organization change approach. *Organizational Dynamics, 18,* 5–18.

Hartwell, J. K. (2003). *Making reduced hours work: The role of psychological contract fulfillment on reduced-hour physicians' intent to leave their positions.* Unpublished doctoral dissertation, Boston College.

Hartwell, J. K., & Torbert, W. R. (2004). Leadership for Retaining Reduced-Hour Professionals. Kravis Leadership Institute *Leadership Review,* Winter (http://leadershipreview. org).

Hewlett, S. A. (2002). *Creating a life.* New York: Hyperion.

Hill, J. E., Miller, B. C., Weiner, S. P., & Colihan, J. (1998). Influences of the virtual office on aspects of work and work/life balance. *Personnel Psychology, 41,* 667–683.

Jones, A. M. (2003). Managing the gap: Evolutionary science, work/life integration, and corporate responsibility. *Organizational Dynamics, 32*(1), 17–31.

Judge, T. A., Boudreau, J. W., & Bretz, R. D. (1994). Job and life attitudes of male executives. *Journal of Applied Psychology, 79*(5), 767–782.

Kimmel, M. S. (1993, November–December). What do men want? *Harvard Business Review, 71*(6), 50.

Kossek, E. E., & Ozeki, C. (1998). Work–family conflict, policies, and the job–life satisfaction relationship: A review and directions for organizational behavior–human resources research. *Journal of Applied Psychology, 83,* 139–149.

Lizotte, K. (2001). Are balance benefits for real? *Journal of Business Strategy, 22*(2), 32–34.

Lobel, S. A., & Kossek, E. E. (1996). Human resources strategies to support diversity in work and personal lifestyles: Beyond the "family friendly" organization. In E. E. Kossek & S. A. Lobel (Eds.), *Managing diversity: Human resource strategies for transforming the workplace* (pp. 221–244). Cambridge, MA: Blackwell.

Lundberg, U., & Frankenhaeuser, M. (1999). Stress and workload of men and women in high-ranking positions. *Journal of Occupational Health Psychology, 4,* 142–151.

McShane, S. L., & Von Glinow, M. A. (2003). *Organizational behavior.* New York: McGraw-Hill.

Mendels, P. (2001). Elder care: A growing concern. *Business Week,* January 16. Retrieved January 13, 2004, from http://www.businessweek.com/careers/content/jan2001/ca20010116_110.htm

Milkie, M. A., & Peltola, P. (1999). Playing all the roles: Gender and the work–family balancing act. *Journal of Marriage and the Family, 61,* 476–490.

Milliken, F. J., Martins, L. L., & Morgan, H. (1998). Explaining organizational responsiveness to work–family issues: The role of human resource executives as issue interpreters. *Academy of Management Journal, 41,* 580–592.

Nielson, T. R., Carlson, D. S., & Lankau, M. J. (2001). The supportive mentor as a means for reducing work–family conflict. *Journal of Vocational Behavior, 59,* 364–381.

Nord, W. R., Fox, S., Phoenix, A., & Viano, K. (2002). Real-world reactions to work–life balance programs: Lessons for effective implementation. *Organizational Dynamics, 30*(3), 223–238.

Organ, D. W. (1990). The motivational basis of organizational citizenship behavior. *Research in Organizational Behavior, 12,* 43–72.

Parasuraman, S., Greenhaus, J. H., & Granrose, C. S. (1992). Role stressors, social support, and well-being among two-career couples. *Journal of Organizational Behavior, 13,* 339–356.

Perlow, L. A. (1997). *Finding time: How corporations, individuals and families can benefit from new work practices.* Ithaca, NY: ILR Press.

Pitt-Catsouphes, M. (2002). Family-friendly workplace (A Sloan Work and Family Encyclopedia Entry). Retrieved February 10, 2003, from http://www.bc.edu/bc org/avp/wfnetwork/rft/wfpedia/wfpFFWent.html

Podsakoff, P. M., Ahearne, M., & MacKenzie, S. B. (1997). Organizational citizenship behavior and the quantity and quality of work group performance. *Journal of Applied Psychology, 82,* 262–270.

Reich, R. (2000). *The future of success.* New York: Alfred A. Knopf.

Repetti, R. L. (1987). Individual and common components of the social environment. *Journal of Personality and Social Psychology, 52,* 710–720.

Robinson, S. L., & Morrison, E. W. (1995). Psychological contracts and OCB: The effect of unfulfilled obligations on civic virtue behavior. *Journal of Organizational Behavior, 16,* 289–298.

Rosario, M., Shinn, M., Morch, H., & Huckabee, C. B. (1988). Gender differences in coping and social supports: Testing socialization and role constraint theories. *Journal of Community Psychology, 16,* 55–69.

Rousseau, D., & Parks, X. (1993). The contracts of individuals and organizations. *Research in Organizational Behavior, 15,* 1–43.

Scandura, T. A., & Lankau, M. J. (1997). Relationships of gender, family responsibility and flexible work hours to organizational commitment and job satisfaction. *Journal of Organizational Behavior, 18,* 377–391.

Schein, E. H. (1996). *Organizational culture and leadership* (2nd ed.). San Francisco: Jossey-Bass.

Shellenbarger, S. (2002). Trends point to future of more-focused work, parenting, and learning. *Wall Street Journal.* January 9, p. B1.

Starrels, M. E. (1992). The evolution of workplace family policy research. *Journal of Family Issues, 13,* 259–278.

Thomas, L. T., & Ganster, D. C. (1995). Impact of family-supportive work variables on work-family conflict and strain: A control perspective. *Journal of Applied Psychology, 80*(1), 6–15.

Thompson, C. A., Beauvais, L. L., & Lyness, K. S. (1999). When work–family benefits are not enough: The influence of work–family culture on benefit utilization, organizational attachment, and work–family conflict. *Journal of Vocational Behavior, 54,* 392–415.

Thompson, C. A., Thomas, C. C., & Maier, M. (1992). Work-family conflict and the bottom line: Reassessing corporate policies and initiatives. In U. Sekaran & F. T. Leong (Eds.), *Woman-power: Managing in times of demographic turbulence* (pp. 59–84). Englewood Cliffs, NJ: Prentice Hall.

Uhl-Bien, M. (2003). Relationship development as a key ingredient for leadership development. In S. Murphy & R. Riggio (Eds.), *The future of leadership development* (pp. 129–147). Mahwah, NJ: Lawrence Erlbaum Associates.

Van Buren, M., & King, S. (2000). *The 2000 ASTD international comparisons report.* Alexandria, VA: American Society for Training and Development.

Weber, G. (2003). Flexible jobs mean fewer absences. *Workforce Management, 82*(12), 26.

Zaccaro, S. J., & Klimoski, R. J. (Eds.). (2001). *The nature of organizational leadership: Understanding performance imperatives confronting today's leaders.* San Francisco, CA: Jossey-Bass.

Zagorski, D. A. (2004). *Balancing the scales: The role of justice and organizational culture in employees' search for work–life equilibrium.* Unpublished doctoral dissertation, Claremont Graduate University.

Work–Family Balance: Does the Market Reward Firms That Respect It?

Wayne F. Cascio
Clifford E. Young
University of Colorado at Denver

Although many countries in the developed world have cut back the annual number of hours worked per person since the mid 1990s, Americans have headed in the opposite direction, *adding* an average of 58 hours to their annual total. The Japanese, by contrast, have cut an average of 191 hours. Unionized workers in France and Germany now work an average of 35 hours per week, and, according to data from the World Tourism Association, enjoy approximately 35 annual vacation days on average. By contrast, U.S. workers enjoy an average of 13 annual vacation days. To make matters worse, U.S. workers do not even take what few holidays they get, giving back to their employers an average of 1.8 days, or almost $19.5 billion in unused vacation time each year, according to a survey commissioned by online travel agent Expedia.com.

In the aftermath of the terrorist attacks of September 11, 2001, however, Americans are rethinking the meaning of work in their lives, and their priorities among work and nonwork activities. According to a survey by American Demographics/TeleNation, Market Facts, Inc. (2002), almost 3 in 4 people (73%), say helping others means more to them now than before September 11, 2001. More specifically, these percentages of respondents endorsed the following items:

- Spending time with family—77%
- Helping others—73%

- Serving the country—67%
- Doing things I enjoy—63%
- Getting ahead—30%
- Retiring young—27%
- Making lots of money—19%

To be sure, workers are demanding more flexibility in their work schedules (Conlin, Merritt, & Himelstein, 2002; Shellenbarger, 2001, 2003a; Strope, 2003). As job time has encroached on leisure time, however, so too has leisure crept into the job. As Brady (2002) noted:

> Workers increasingly are Internet shopping, exercising, chatting with friends, or otherwise building breaks into their day. They may work at midnight, but they also feel free to take off at 3 p.m. to see a child's school play. The aging of the workforce, and the need for constant education, are creating a less rigid view of careers—one that lets people dip in and out of the job market, work into their 70s, or take time off in their 30s to study, travel, or raise children. (p. 142)

Citing a variety of survey results, the Society for Human Resource Management (2002) reported that the following comprise what employees want most:

- 70% say that family is their most important priority, compared to 54% in 2000.
- 70% do not think there is a healthy balance between work and personal life.
- 46% either feel overworked, overwhelmed by the quantity of their work, or lack the time to step back and reflect on their work.
- 61% say they would give up some of their pay for more time with their families.
- Finding time for family is a more pressing concern than layoffs (32% vs. 22%).
- 36% say they would be willing to take a pay cut of 10% or more for a shorter commute to work.

These are important trends that employers ignore at their peril. Many, but certainly not all, employers would rather dole out stock options or bonuses than time off. In extreme cases, employees have been fired for taking Family and Medical Leave Act benefits (Shellenbarger, 2003b). Not surprisingly, therefore, the U.S. Department of Labor found that the number of complaints by employees fired in family-leave fights in 2002 was up more than 34% over the number in 2001.

Despite the reluctance of some organizations to address work and family conflicts, others have responded in an exemplary manner. Consider General Mills Chairman and CEO, Steve Sanger, who has headed the Minneapolis-based food company since 1995. "You know what's really expensive? Turnover. If we've invested in recruiting and developing good people, then we want them to stay" (quoted in Rubin, 2002, p. 1). General Mills offers flexible work arrangements, on-site childcare and health care, timesaving employee perquisites, and back-up child care programs. The CEO's commitment to advancing women's careers also won General Mills a 2001 award from Catalyst, which honors companies for strategies that encourage women to achieve their maximum potential.

Given current economic conditions, it might seem surprising for a CEO to dedicate company resources to employee wellbeing. Sanger sees it another way. He cites the company's family perks as initiatives that will benefit General Mills for years to come. Take those family-leave policies. "It's a far better outcome for someone to take a leave than it is to lose someone who could make a contribution not just next month but fifteen or twenty years from now," he says (quoted in Rubin, 2002, p. 2).

General Mills is by no means the only company that "gets it." As is well known, every year *Working Mother* magazine compiles a list of the best 100 firms for working mothers. Companies must apply in order to be considered for inclusion on the list. When a company does apply, its human resources executives are asked to complete a 67-page questionnaire that includes detailed information about the company's benefits policies and practices. Companies are rated on a 1 to 5 scale (with 5 being the highest) in the following categories: child care, flexibility, leave for new parents, work–life benefits, and advancement of women. A subsequent profile of each company that makes the 100-Best list appears in *Working Mother* magazine. The profile describes the company's accomplishments, flaws, and plans for improvement. The magazine also lists the five companies that scored highest in each of its five categories, along with the 10 best companies for working mothers.

It is understandable that employees who are parents, and working mothers in particular, would want to work for firms that respect the demands that families impose, and that try to accommodate those demands. The firms, in turn, have the luxury of choosing from larger pools of applicants, and they enjoy reduced employee absenteeism, turnover, and tardiness. Many such firms also report positive returns on investment from their work–life programs (Cascio, 2000).

Not included, however, is the relative economic performance of firms that comprise the *Working Mother* 100-Best list. Are companies that are good to their employees also good to their investors? To address this question we compiled a database of companies that comprised the *Working Mother* 100-Best lists from 1995 to 2001. We then observed the performance of the companies, relative to their industries and to established equity-performance benchmarks, in terms of three key outcome variables: profitability, productivity, and total return on common stock. The following section describes our methodology in greater detail.

RESEARCH METHOD

We began by compiling lists of the 100-Best companies for Working Mothers, as published each year in *Working Mother* magazine, from 1995–2002. Our objective was to use the Standard & Poor's Compustat database to examine financial and stock-return results for the companies. Compustat includes comprehensive financial and employment information on all companies that are traded publicly. We used Compustat data from 1995 through the end of 2002.

Two factors limited our ability to include data from all 100 companies each year. First, not all of the companies on the *Working Mother* magazine 100-Best list are publicly traded. Hence, their financial data are not included in the Compustat database. Second, mergers and acquisitions sometimes lead to changes in the names of the companies. Table 4.1 shows the number of publicly traded companies from the *Working Mother* 100-Best list in each year from 1995 through 2002.

To confirm that a company on the 100-Best list was not publicly traded, we accessed that company's Web site. We also used search engines to learn the name of a newly merged company. Following these procedures, we compiled a list of the remaining "Best Companies for Working Mothers" in each year from 1995 through 2002. For each remaining company on the

TABLE 4.1
Number of Publicly Traded Companies
From *Working Mother* "100-Best"

Year	Companies
1995	51
1996	58
1997	54
1998	58
1999	68
2000	68
2001	76
2002	70

100-Best list in each year, we computed three variables: profitability, productivity, and total return on common stock. To measure profitability, we computed each company's return on assets. Return on assets is a standard measure of the financial performance of a firm. We measured it as Operating Income Before Depreciation, Interest, and Taxes (OIBDP, or pretax operating income) divided by Total Assets (AT). For example, others who have examined the financial performance of firms in response to managerial actions (Healy, Palepu, & Ruback, 1992; Kaplan, 1989; Ofek, 1994), focused on OIBDP/AT as a measure of the cash-flow return on assets before and after the event they were studying. In the present study, the event of interest was listing of a company in a given year of *Working Mother* magazine as one of the 100-Best companies for working mothers.

We measured employee productivity for each company in our sample for each year by expressing it as Total Sales divided by Total Employees, or sales per employee. An explanation of our procedures for analyzing companies that might have a disproportionate impact on overall averages can be found in note 1 at the end of the chapter.

In addition to financial performance, as reflected in our measures of profitability and productivity, management also is interested in stock performance. This is the ultimate performance measure from the shareholders' point of view. Consequently, for each company in our sample, we used the total return on common stock (dividends plus capital appreciation) as a measure of performance for evaluating the benefits of being named as one of the 100-Best companies for working mothers.

Some of the earliest explorations of stock market efficiency (Ball & Brown, 1968; Watts, 1978) showed that news regarding a firm's earnings is reflected quickly in stock prices. If publication in *Working Mother* magazine as one of the 100-Best companies for working mothers might cause investors to expect higher future earnings, that event should lead to increases in stock prices.

For each company, we collected measures of profitability, productivity, and stock return, along with industry-aggregate measures of each of the variables. Measures of industry-aggregate variables are defined in the COMPUSTAT User's Guide (2000). The specific variables that we used are listed below with the same acronyms as used in the COMPUSTAT CD-ROM database.

- Operating income before, depreciation, interest, and taxes (OIBDP)
- Total assets (AT)
- Dividends on common stock (DVPSX)
- Price of Common Stock, end-of-year close (PRCC)

We used industry-aggregate variables to generate industry-adjusted measures for the financial performance measures (profitability and productivity ratios) by subtracting from them the corresponding industry ratios. For financial-performance measures relative to the industry, the empirical question is, *"Are companies doing any better or worse relative to their industries?"* With respect to the stock return, by subtracting the industry-average stock return, we are implicitly factoring out the return on stocks with the same level of systematic market risk (beta), because firms in the same industry typically have about the same level of market risk.

To provide a broader perspective, and comparisons to benchmark-equity performances, we also computed average annual and aggregated returns from the Standard & Poor's 500 and the Russell 3000 indexes. The S&P 500 is one of the most widely used benchmarks of the performance of U.S. equities. It represents leading companies in leading industries, and consists of 500 stocks chosen for their market size, liquidity, and industry-group representation. Each stock's weight in the index is proportionate to its market value (stock price times number of shares outstanding). However, the stocks that comprise the index do not remain constant over time. In fact, from its inception in 1926 through September 15, 2000, 1,001 companies exited the S&P 500, the overwhelming majority as a result of mergers and acquisitions (Bos & Ruotolo, 2000).

The Russell 3000 is an index of the 3,000 largest U.S. companies weighted by market-capitalization. It includes only common stocks incorporated in the United States and its territories, and represents approximately 98% of the investable U.S. equity market. As of mid-2002, the market-capitalization of member companies of the Russell 3000 ranged from $128 million to $309 billion (Russell Indexes, 2003).

RESULTS OF DATA ANALYSIS

Total Returns on Common Stock

In terms of indexed, annualized returns from 1995–2002 on the common stock of *Working Mother* 100-Best companies, relative to the Standard & Poor's 500 and the Russell 3000, results were clear and consistent (see Fig. 4.1). The first strategy, "buy and hold," assumes that an investor assembled a portfolio of the publicly traded 100-Best companies in 1995, and held those stocks through the end of 2002. Both the equity-index benchmarks and the 100-Best companies began at an index of about 145 in 1995. *The 100-Best companies consistently outperformed the equity indexes in each of the 8 years of the study.* By the end of 2002, while the S&P and Russell indexes had risen to an index of 225, the 100-Best companies had risen to an index of approximately 345. The difference in percentage return by the end of 2002 was *120%.*

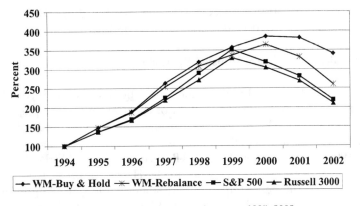

FIG. 4.1. Indexed 1-year stock return: 1995–2002.

The results for a portfolio of 100-Best companies, rebalanced each year, were similar, although not quite as highly elevated relative to the equity-index benchmarks. By the end of 2002, while the S&P and Russell indexes had risen to an index of 225, the 100-Best companies had risen to an index of approximately 260. The difference in percentage return by the end of 2002 was 35%.

Figure 4.2 shows average annual returns for the "buy and hold" and rebalancing strategies among *Working Mother* 100-Best companies, relative to the average (capitalization-weighted) annual returns of the Standard & Poor's 500 and the Russell 3000. While the average annual return of the S&P 500 from 1995–2002 was 12.55%, that of the Russell 3000 was 11.85%. In contrast, for the *Working Mother* 100-Best companies, the average annual

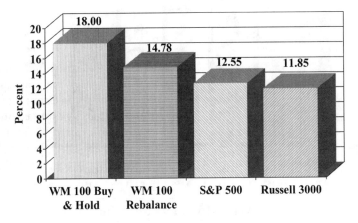

FIG. 4.2. *Working Mother* "100 best" versus stock market annualized return, 1995–2002.

returns were 18% and 14.78%, respectively, for the "buy and hold" and rebalancing strategies over the same time period.

Profitability and Industry-Adjusted Profitability

Our analyses of financial performance span the 8-year period from 1995–2002. Figure 4.3 shows the profitability of the firms in our sample, relative to that of the S&P 500, for each year of the analysis. The results shown in Fig. 4.3 exclude outliers in the sample for each year, as described in note 1. From 1995–1998, *Working Mother* 100-Best companies and S&P-500 companies were approximately equally profitable. However, from 1999–2002 the *Working Mother* 100-Best companies were somewhat less profitable than the S&P-500 companies. Over that time period, the range of incremental profitability of the S&P 500 over the *Working Mother* 100-Best companies varied from 1.8% (in 1999) to 3.6% (in 2001).

These results, however, are unadjusted for industry-average profitability. Thus, it is possible that a disproportionate number of the 100-Best companies were in highly profitable industries, relative to the broad range of industries represented in the S&P 500. To account for that possibility, and to compare the profitability of each of the *Working Mother* 100-Best companies to competitors in the same industry, we computed the average profitability on an industry-adjusted basis for each year of the analysis. Industry-average adjustment is an important control, because all firms in an industry face the same set of economic conditions in a given time period.

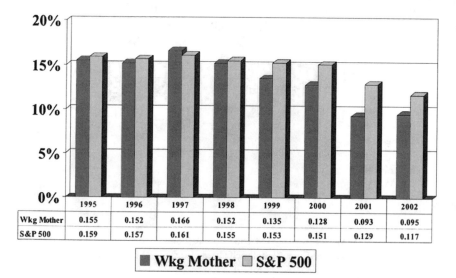

	1995	1996	1997	1998	1999	2000	2001	2002
Wkg Mother	0.155	0.152	0.166	0.152	0.135	0.128	0.093	0.095
S&P 500	0.159	0.157	0.161	0.155	0.153	0.151	0.129	0.117

■ Wkg Mother □ S&P 500

FIG. 4.3. Profitability.

As Fig. 4.4 demonstrates, the industry-adjusted profitability of the *Working Mother* 100-Best companies was uniformly higher for the first 3 years of our analysis (1995–1997), and it was uniformly lower for the remaining 5 years of our analysis (1998–2002). Incremental differences ranged from 1.9% in favor of the *Working Mother* 100-Best companies in 1995, to 2% in favor of the S&P 500 in 2001. As a general conclusion, however, it is not possible to state with confidence that *Working Mother* 100-Best companies are more or less profitable than S&P-500 companies.

Productivity and Industry-Adjusted Productivity

Like the analyses for profitability, all of the analyses of employee productivity exclude outlier cases that fell more than five standard deviations from the mean. In terms of productivity (in thousands of dollars per employee), employees in the *Working Mother* 100-Best companies were slightly more productive in 7 out of the 8 years of our analysis, relative to the average productivity of employees in firms comprising the S&P 500 (see Fig. 4.5). Year 2000 was the lone exception. Differences in productivity ranged from $78,000 more per employee in *Working Mother* 100-Best companies in 2002, to $21,700 more per employee in S&P-500 companies in 2000.

On an industry-adjusted basis, however, a slightly different picture emerges with respect to productivity per employee. Industry-adjusted employee productivity is higher in *Working Mother* 100-Best companies in 5 out

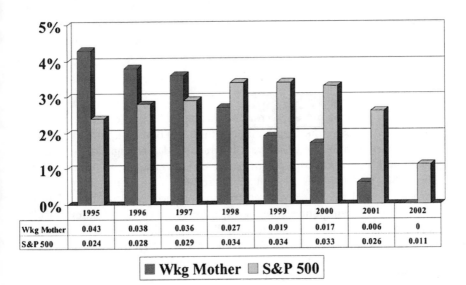

	1995	1996	1997	1998	1999	2000	2001	2002
Wkg Mother	0.043	0.038	0.036	0.027	0.019	0.017	0.006	0
S&P 500	0.024	0.028	0.029	0.034	0.034	0.033	0.026	0.011

■ Wkg Mother ▢ S&P 500

FIG. 4.4. Profitability (industry-adjusted).

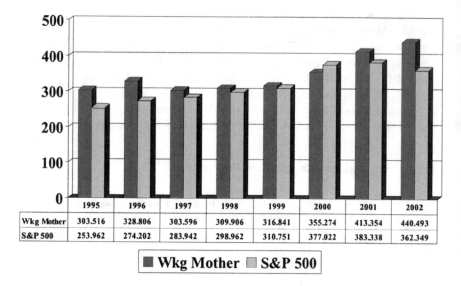

	1995	1996	1997	1998	1999	2000	2001	2002
Wkg Mother	303.516	328.806	303.596	309.906	316.841	355.274	413.354	440.493
S&P 500	253.962	274.202	283.942	298.962	310.751	377.022	383.338	362.349

■ Wkg Mother □ S&P 500

FIG. 4.5.   Productivity ($000 per employee).

of the 8 years of the analysis (see Fig. 4.6). However, industry-adjusted employee productivity in S&P-500 companies was higher in 1998, 1999, and in 2000. Differences ranged from $20,005 more per employee in *Working Mother* 100-Best companies in 1996, to $50,416 more per employee in S&P-500 companies in 2000. As a general conclusion, therefore, it is not possible to state with confidence that *Working Mother* 100-Best companies are consistently more or less profitable than S&P-500 companies.

Discussion of Results

Using data from each year from 1995 through 2002, we compared the financial and stock-market performance of the 100-Best companies for working mothers, as published each year by *Working Mother* magazine, to that of benchmark indexes of the performance of U.S. equities, the Standard & Poor's 500 and the Russell 3000. With respect to stock-market performance, we found that the total returns on common stock among *Working Mother* Best-100 companies consistently outperformed the broader market benchmarks. Consider a "buy and hold" strategy, based on a portfolio of the Best-100 companies in 1995. By the end of 2002, the publicly traded companies in that list had achieved total returns on common stock that were 120% higher than the S&P 500 and the Russell 3000. If instead an investor had rebalanced the portfolio each year that a new Best-100 list was

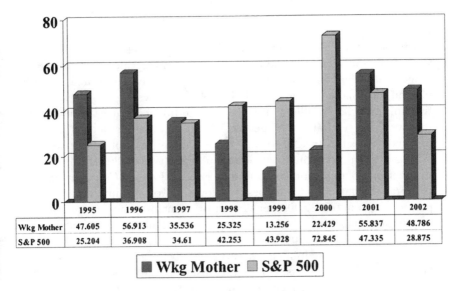

FIG. 4.6.   Productivity (industry-adjusted).

published, he or she still would have achieved returns that were 35% higher than the average of the S&P 500 and the Russell 3000.

In terms of profitability (operating income before depreciation and taxes divided by total assets), the *Working Mother* best companies were not consistently more profitable than the S&P-500 companies. On an industry-adjusted basis, the profitability of the *Working Mother* Best-100 companies was slightly higher than that of the S&P-500 companies from 1995 to 1997, and it was slightly lower from 1998–2002.

Finally, in terms of employee productivity (total sales divided by the total number of employees), the productivity of the *Working Mother* Best-100 companies exceeded that of the S&P 500 average in 7 of the 8 years of our analysis. Industry-adjusted employee productivity was higher in *Working Mother* 100-Best companies in 5 out of the 8 years of the analysis. Differences ranged from $20,005 more per employee in *Working Mother* 100-Best companies in 1996, to $50,416 more per employee in S&P-500 companies in 2000. In general, therefore, employees of *Working Mother* 100-Best companies are not consistently more or less productive than their counterparts in S&P-500 companies.

Perhaps the most significant conclusion from this study is that the total returns from the common stock of the *Working Mother* 100-Best companies that are publicly traded, on average, are consistently higher than those of S&P-500 companies. At the same time, however, *Working Mother* 100-Best companies are not consistently more profitable, nor are their employees consistently more productive, than their counterparts in S&P-500 companies.

Although there are numerous possible causes of higher stock prices, one study of financial analysts and portfolio managers revealed that, for the average analyst, 35% of his or her investment decision is determined by nonfinancial information (Low & Siesfield, 1998). Interestingly, one of the top five nonfinancial variables considered by the financial analysts was "ability to attract and retain talented people." As far as attracting talent, "Best employers to work for" typically receive twice as many job applications per position as firms not designated as best employers (Cascio, 2000). In fact, the number of job applications received by Edward Jones & Company, named by *Fortune* magazine as the #1 best employer to work for in 2002 and 2003, jumped from about 40,000 per year prior to making the "Best employer" list, to more than 400,000 after making the list (Holmes, personal communication, January 16, 2003).

With respect to retaining talent, work–family programs show positive relationships with constructs such as job satisfaction (Kossek & Ozeki, 1998), affective and continuance commitment (Grover & Crooker, 1995; Mellor, Mathieu, Barnes-Farrell, & Rogelberg, 2001; Roehling, Roehling, & Moen, 2001), and negative relationships with role conflict, role stress, burnout, and intentions to quit (Christensen & Staines, 1990; Dalton & Mesch, 1990; Grandey & Cropanzano, 1999). In short, "Best employers" are more likely to be able to attract and retain top talent, and financial analysts consider that information in making investment decisions.

It is important to note that firms offering a wide range of work–family policies are also likely to employ broader bundles of progressive management practices, such as empowered teams and democratic decision making. To the extent that this is true, then recognition for exceptional work–family practices may be viewed as a proxy for a broader platform of sound HR management practices. Such management practices should lead to recognition of the same organizations by other publications, using somewhat different criteria, as "best places to work." Partial support for this hypothesis comes from the fact that in 2002, 30% of the *Working Mother* 100-Best companies were also named by *Fortune* magazine as "Best Employers" or "Best Employers for Minorities."

What factors might explain the fact that *Working Mother* 100-Best companies are not consistently more profitable, nor are their employees consistently more productive than their counterparts in S&P-500 companies? Although it is purely speculative, generous leave policies may contribute to these outcomes. This is so because if employees are not working, either at an office or plant, or by means of virtual work arrangements, then the firm receives no productive benefit, and no contribution toward profitability, from their labor. Of necessity, this affects aggregate-level productivity and profitability as well. On the other hand, even if *Working Mother* 100-Best companies are not consistently more profitable, and even if their employees are not consistently more productive, we found no evidence to indicate that such companies are handicapped in the marketplace by offering family-friendly policies.

Indeed, employers have an opportunity to take advantage of an important social trend that emphasizes how important flexibility and family-related concerns are to employees. Our results indicate that there is a positive payoff in terms of stock return for doing so. In addition, employees who work for companies that address concerns that are most important to them, such as child care and back-up child care, tend to be more productive than they otherwise would be if such programs were not available to them. They are less likely to be distracted during the workday, worrying about family-related matters. If the programs were not available, then absenteeism rates would most likely rise, and that would hurt overall productivity and profitability. Finally, investors should take comfort in knowing that what might appear to be frivolous expenses on noncore activities really do have positive payoffs in terms of improved stock performance.

Our results are likely to be underestimates of the true relationships between family-friendly benefits and financial and stock market outcomes in the population of companies. Several reasons bolster this argument. First, companies selected to appear on *Working Mother* magazine's list of best companies for working mothers must affirmatively apply for inclusion by completing a 67-page questionnaire. It is highly likely there are companies that have progressive work–family benefits that do not apply. At least some of those firms may well be included in the S&P 500 and the Russell 3000 indexes. To the extent that is true, then any subsequent comparison of the *Working Mother* 100-Best companies to the equity indexes and to the financial performance of their member companies will, of necessity, underestimate the true difference in financial and stock-market performance among family-friendly firms and those that do not offer such benefits.

Additional support for this argument comes from a study by Bardoel, Tharenou, and Moss (1998). Their study sought to identify characteristics of organizations that are associated with the adoption of work–life programs. Five such characteristics were investigated: organizational size (measured on a 10-point scale from 1, *fewer than 25 employees*, to 10, *more than 8,000 employees*), the percentage of women in the organization, the percentage of employees under age 35 in the organization, public- versus private-sector ownership, and the organization's track record in HR management (good vs. poor).

Only two of the five characteristics were associated with the adoption of work–life programs. Larger organizations were better able to provide a broad base of work–life benefits than smaller organizations. Larger organizations tended to adopt more policies related to individual support (e.g., personal counseling, relocation assistance), leave, life-career strategies, and child- and dependent-care benefits than were smaller organizations. Similarly, organizations rated as having good track records in HR management tended to implement more flexible work options, individual growth, and life-career policies. However, the percentage of women in the organization, the percentage of employees under age 35, and public- versus private-sector ownership were unrelated to the adoption of work–life programs.

Finally, it is important to emphasize an important limitation in our results. We have demonstrated *associations* between firms that adopt family-friendly work practices, and financial and stock-market outcomes. We cannot say that family-friendly work practices *cause* changes in financial and stock-market performance. It may well be that firms with superior financial and stock-market performance have the luxury of offering such programs. It is the task of future research to determine the direction of the causal arrow.

NOTE

1. A preliminary analysis of the profitability and productivity measures revealed that certain companies accounted for a disproportionate impact on overall averages, particularly with respect to the productivity measures. This was due to large values of sales divided by very small values of employees. In one case, the productivity measure was so large as to double the average value of productivity for the S&P 500 in that year.

To minimize the impact of these outlier cases, we eliminated values for profitability and productivity that were five standard deviations or more from the mean. Assuming the distribution of the measures was normal, one would expect to eliminate less than one case in a million. In our sample of companies, however, we removed as many as 10 values of productivity and/or profitability in each year from the S&P data. We performed a similar elimination of outliers for the *Working Mother* Best-100 samples, again using five standard deviations as the benchmark for eliminating outliers. We eliminated only three cases over the 8-year period of our study from those samples.

REFERENCES

American Demographics/TeleNation, Market Facts, Inc. (2002). Survey results cited in *Workplace visions: Exploring the future of work* (Vol. 4, p. 7). Alexandria, VA: Society for Human Resource Management.

Ball, R., & Brown, P. (1968). An empirical evaluation of accounting income numbers. *Journal of Accounting Research*, Autumn, 159–178.

Bardoel, E. A., Tharenou, P., & Moss, S. A. (1998). Organizational predictors of work–family practices. *Asia Pacific Journal of Human Resources*, *36*(3), 31–49.

Bos, R. J., & Ruotolo, M. (2000, Sept.). *General criteria for S&P U.S. Index membership*. Retrieved from the World Wide Web at www.standandpoors.com on February 9, 2002.

Brady, D. (2002, Aug. 26). Rethinking the rat race. *Business Week*, pp. 142–143.

Cascio, W. F. (2000). *Costing human resources: The financial impact of behavior in organizations* (4th ed.). Cincinnati, OH: South-Western College Publishing.

Christensen, K. E., & Staines, G. L. (1990). Flextime: A viable solution to work–family conflict? *Journal of Family Issues, 11*(4), 455–476.

Conlin, M., Merritt, J., & Himelstein, L. (2002, Nov. 25). Mommy is really home from work. *Business Week*, pp. 101–104.

Dalton, D. J., & Mesch, D. J. (1990). The impact of flexible scheduling on employee attendance and turnover. *Administrative Science Quarterly, 35*, 370–387.

Grandey, A. A., & Cropanzano, R. (1999). The conservation of resources model applied to work–family conflict and strain. *Journal of Vocational Behavior, 54*, 350–370.

Grover, S., & Crooker, K. (1995). Who appreciates family-responsive human resource policies: The impact of family-friendly policies on the organizational attachment of parents and non-parents. *Personnel Psychology, 48*, 271–287.

Healy, P., Palepu, K., & Ruback, R. (1992). Does corporate performance improve after mergers? *Journal of Financial Economics, 31*(2), 135–175.

Kaplan, S. (1989). The effects of management buyouts on operating performance and value. *Journal of Financial Economics, 24*(2), 217–254.

Kossek, E. E., & Ozeki, C. (1998). Work-family conflict, policies, and the job–life satisfaction relationship: A review and directions for organizational behavior–human resources research. *Journal of Applied Psychology, 83*, 139–149.

Low, J., & Siesfield, T. (1998). *Measures that matter*. Boston: Ernst & Young.

Mellor, S., Mathieu, J. E., Barnes-Farrell, J. L., & Rogelberg, S. G. (2001). Employees' non-work obligations and organizational commitments: A new way to look at the relationships. *Human Resource Management, 40*, 171–184.

Ofek, E. (1994). Efficiency gains in unsuccessful management buyouts. *Journal of Finance, 46*(2), 637–654.

Roehling, P. V., Roehling, M. V., & Moen, P. (2001). The relationship between work–life policies and practices and employee loyalty: A life-course perspective. *Journal of Family and Economic Issues, 22*, 141–170.

Rubin, B. M. (2002). Think outside the (cereal) box. Accessed October 18, 2002, at http://www.workingwoman.com/thinkoutside.shtml

Russell Indexes. (2003). Retrieved from the World Wide Web on February 17, 2003 at www.russell.com/US/Indexes/US/default.asp

Shellenbarger, S. (2001). Employees are seeking fewer hours; Maybe bosses should listen. *The Wall Street Journal*, February 21, p. B1.

Shellenbarger, S. (2003a). If you'd rather work in pajamas, here are ways to talk the boss into flex-time. *The Wall Street Journal*, February 13, p. D1.

Shellenbarger, S. (2003b). A downside of taking family leave: Getting fired while you're gone. *The Wall Street Journal*, January 23, p. D1.

Society for Human Resource Management. (2002, Dec.). *Workplace visions: Exploring the future of work* (Vol. 4). Alexandria, VA: Author.

Strope, L. (2003). Some seek standards for popular 'flextime.' *The Denver Post*, January 6, p. 2A.

Watts, R. (1978). Systematic "abnormal" returns after quarterly earnings announcements. *Journal of Financial Economics*, June–September, 127–150.

Part III

HOW EMPLOYERS RESPOND TO THE CHALLENGE OF WORK–FAMILY DEMANDS

Research shows that organizations that provide work and family programs do so mostly to retain their best employees, but in addition they also use these programs as a recruitment incentive to attract the best employees, and to increase employee morale and productivity. Business magazines are replete with stories describing the efforts of many organizations that offer these programs to working families. Specific articles such as *Fortune's 100 Best Companies to Work For* as well as *Working Mothers: The 100 Best Companies for Working Mothers* provide details on great companies that understand the importance of providing accommodations for working families. These unique descriptions provide wonderful insight into many of the challenges organizations face as they introduce new programs, as well as the goals, implementation steps, and different types of evaluation metrics they use. From the stories, however, there does not appear to be a "one size fits all" strategy for organizations. For some organizations, top management initiates the programs as either a response to an internal need or to what their competitors are doing, while for others the impetus comes from employees.

In this section, we provide insight into the steps different organizations are taking to accommodate work–family issues. We begin with a presentation from the founder of Kinko's,

Paul Orfalea, a true rags-to-riches businessperson, who shares his philosophy of work. He feels that two key ingredients to employee motivation are trust and working to remove obstacles to employees accomplishing their work. These are in fact also key elements of cultures that support working families. Employees who are allowed to manage their own time through flexible hours or other family-accommodating benefits, are less likely to experience the stress that comes from work–family conflict.

Building on the themes of trust and removing obstacles, the next chapter provides highlights of a panel discussion with managers of various work–family and work–life programs in consulting, technology, and service industries. These organizations have led the way in their respective industries by introducing cutting-edge programs. Each manager in the panel shares how she helped make the business case for the importance of her company's program and how each company works continuously to modify the programs to meet the changing needs of the workforce. The panel also discusses the challenges they faced in implementing the programs and the ongoing metrics they use to assess program effectiveness.

In chapter 7, Bell and Schumm examine the ways in which the Army has attempted to reduce the disruption that military life causes families. Although most work organizations do not find themselves sending employees overseas for extended periods of time, the extensive work the Army has done to alleviate stress is commendable and sets an enviable goal for civilian organizations. The lessons from much of their research are applicable in both its results and its methodology.

In the final chapter in this section, Maslach looks at the phenomenon of burnout and how organizations that do not attend to work–family issues run the risk of having a workforce that shows the classic symptoms of burnout. The chapter ends with some recommendations to ensure that the potential for burnout is lessened.

Chapter 5

Corporate Responsibilities

Paul Orfalea
Chairperson and Founder, Kinko's, Inc.

The title of this chapter is "Corporate Responsibilities," but a more accurate title would really be "Corporate Opportunities." I think there is a big opportunity to inspire workers. At Kinko's, I always used to say that the only competitive advantage we have is the sparkle in our workers' eyes. There is a tremendous business opportunity in taking advantage of motivating workers.

When I was a boy, my father had a factory with about 500 workers. I remember he would never bring work home with him no matter how business was going. But the one problem, the one concern that he would always carry with him, was the difficulty of firing a worker. Be it a janitor or a showroom person, I remember him agonizing over these decisions. He was always empathetic toward his workers, and it left a huge impression on me.

My mother used to say, "How do people do it? I just can't figure it out. We pay these people a hundred dollars a month. They have four children. How do these people make ends meet?" She said, "I know how much the shoes cost. How do they have any peace of mind?"

To be a good businessperson you have to be empathetic. Most importantly, your bread is buttered by your workers. If you are not empathetic toward them, you have lost a big opportunity. This is why what is often called *corporate responsibility* is really a corporate opportunity. One of the greatest problems in the business world right now revolves around this confusion. If we viewed relationships with workers as opportunities, corporate policy would be a lot more beneficial and businesses would be better off.

I firmly believe that workers rise to the level of trust that you give them. I may be the boss, but there is a register in the store even when I'm not. It is my name on the deposit slip. Happy fingers ring happy registers. Do you think you ought to build the workers up or burden them to break down?

A common business misconception is that, in the store, the owner is the boss, that the owner has control. Baloney. How many ways can workers rip off the owner? They can steal, contaminate all the other workers' morale, give bad customer service, and lie about their hours. And owners think they're the boss!

The true role of management is not to control workers, but to remove obstacles. The only reason to have bosses and managers is to make life easier, not harder. As a boss, if you realize the value you get out of a worker's smile, you will know it's priceless.

Corporate bureaucracies often forget just how easy it is to make a worker's life easier, to build a rapport with a worker. At Kinko's everybody used to think we were great—the greatest thing since sliced bread—because of one little thing: We would pay for everybody's lunch on Friday. It cost us $2 per person. Now, if we were to pay somebody $2 to buy their own lunch, we'd have to write a check for $2.80 because of withholdings. If I buy the lunch, factoring in taxes, I'm only spending about $1.10 per person, while it would cost each worker $2.80. I get a 60% discount. How could I pass up such a bargain?

Worker benefits provide companies with many great advantages. We had a program at Kinko's where we would lend people money for their first down payment on a home. We had another program where we put money, tax deductible going in, toward the education of the children of the employees. I have found that these efforts have come back in spades. Not only do you feel good, but it also comes back to you financially.

Doing the right thing for your workers costs you next to nothing; compared with the marginal return you get on it—in motivation, loyalty, workers' morale, everything—is unbelievable. Many modern businesses are afflicted with the debilitating disorder of corporate dyslexia, failing to think of human resources as human opportunities.

This corporate dyslexia shows up in all aspects of a business. It was beginning at Kinko's as well. We used to do passport photos. It costs us 75 cents. We sold it for a dollar. We had almost no customers coming in for passport photos until we bought an ad in the Yellow Pages. Business on the passport photos alone shot up, not including the regular photocopying business these new customers brought with them. Yet when we had a re-budgeting process at Kinko's, one of the first things to go was the Yellow Page ad. The passport photo business followed suit. Now, that's corporate dyslexia!

A lot of times middle management in organizations manage their career and fail to manage the business. They take the path of least resistance and try to placate their bosses. That is the plague on American businesses today: certain middle management and leaders who are interested only in not rocking the boat. Look what happened to Kodak, Xerox, and Polaroid.

A good leader is in the future. Managers are in the present. Accountants are in the past. Companies need a leader constantly fighting the bureaucracy of the organization, taking it places it doesn't want to go, saying, "I want that day-care center come hell or high water."

Companies should look at the human resource programs—the human opportunity programs—offered by the competition. Always remember, the mere fact that a competitor exists means that someone is doing something right. The fact that the competitor has one customer means that they are satisfying somebody. The fact that corporations have offered early-care centers; have done the right thing for elderly employees, have provided orthodontics for their workers' children; and they now can see those smiles in their workers' eyes, means that all organizations can find ways to provide similar services and to take a real interest in their workers.

There are explosions of success throughout corporate America where corporations are doing the right thing. Let's emulate them. The cost to a business is so minute, and the benefits are so enormous.

If your organization does not encourage people to tell them what they don't want to hear, don't work there. That business won't be around much longer. Tell your organization: "I'm a single mother. The amount of money you're paying me is next to nothing. I can't afford to buy shoes for my child. I have no sanity here. Why can't we have an on-site early care center?" Go back and tell them that. You're doing them a favor.

Chapter 6

Sitting at the Corporate Table: How Work–Family Policies Are Really Made

The impressive slate of panelists consisted of Betty Purkey from Texas Instruments; V. Sue Molina, Deloitte & Touche, LLP; Donna Klein, Marriott International, Inc.; and Phyllis Stewart Pires, Cisco Systems, Inc. Each of the panelists was asked to discuss how she became a work–family advocate, how work–family policy decisions are made in corporations, how to make a business case for work–family programs, how to keep work–family initiatives going in an economic downturn, and some of their success stories. In this chapter, their individual contributions to the panel discussion are presented separately and are organized around the above themes.

BETTY PURKEY
Texas Instruments, Work–Life Strategies Manager

On Becoming a Work–Family Advocate. I was on the original team of about 15 or 20 men and women that got this all started back in the early 1990s. I joined that team because I was dealing with elder care issues at the time. My mother was in a nursing home. My father was not well. And I wanted the team to have the perspective of elder care because everybody else in the team was dealing with child care issues. And that's how I got involved. The team convinced HR that we needed to do a needs assessment. We did the needs assessment. They created the job. I bid for it. I got it. It was supposed to last a year.

71

On How Work–Family Policy Decisions Are Made in Corporations. One of the things that is interesting about our corporate culture [at Texas Instruments] is that sometimes we might prefer to ask for forgiveness rather than permission because we can get a lot done from the bottom up. And we have had a lot of success in the work–life arena from having very committed employees and groups of employees who had a real concern, who wanted to see some changes and who were able, through their own energy and commitment, to get things to start happening, and who had the political savvy to also work with the management to get management support, so that we had a management component to our activities.

I always tell people, if you think you can't change something in a company, you're wrong. Our whole work–life program was started by that group of about 15 or 20 men and women back in 1994. Our work–life program resulted from that effort and it has affected the entire company of about 45,000 employees. So you can make a difference, and that's a part of our culture about how things happen.

On Making a Business Case for Work–Family Programs. I think in the work–life field we have a responsibility to our companies, and to the folks that work there as well, to do things that are financially responsible for the company. It really doesn't do us any good if we do something that is not fiscally responsible or that is not sustainable in the kind of environment we're in now. It doesn't do us any good, it doesn't do the company any good, and it doesn't do the employees any good. So I think that part of our thinking all the time has to be: Is this something that is fiscally responsible for this company? And it's different for each company, so we also must ask: Is it something that's sustainable even in bad business times?

Quantifying the impact of work–life programs is an interesting challenge. I think the variables that we want to quantify, such as turnover, absenteeism, and productivity, those kinds of things are so complex that you can't get that nice linear relationship—the sort that one often finds in research. You can say, yeah, our turnover has gone down during this period, but can you say for sure it's because of our work–family programs, or our diversity programs, or something else in our corporate culture or whether it is just the fact that people are glad to have a job now? There are so many different factors that impact work-related variables. You can ask people anecdotally, Are you more productive because of some new policy? Or when people leave you can do postexit interviews and find out why they left. But trying to make a clear, statistically valid connection is very, very difficult. And I don't think it's been very well done. And I don't know that it could be very well done, frankly.

Interestingly enough, sometimes I have found that in addition to giving the ROI—the return on investment—data as best you can, using turnover and self-reports of people about how something influences them or doesn't or what they feel like they need or doing surveys over periods of time, that sometimes anecdotal data can be valuable. Where somebody hears the stories from the people who are affected, especially when managers hear the stories of their employees, they are able to understand work–life issues from the people in their organization. The stories take on a reality that shows that perceived changes are not something made up by HR departments. Stories about the effectiveness of change do not come from another company—they represent one's own people, not some large faceless group that is described in a research report. This is a real story of people in my company, in my organization—that sometimes will get the conversation going in a way that data cannot. We're engineers at TI and one thing engineers do is find fault with any data that you bring before them. That sort of criticism is just a way of life for us. We live in that kind of culture. So sometimes to get beyond that, going into the real stories of people actually can be a lever to get a positive response to your work–life program.

On How to Maintain Work–Family Programs in an Economic Downturn. I think for Texas Instruments we've always been a cyclical industry. Semiconductor is one of those industries that has always had economic downturns—and we're in a terrible cycle now. It's the worst it's ever been. But we have always had these ups and downs—and I've worked at TI 36 years, so I know something about the company. And so from the first, my knowledge of the ups and downs of the economy led me to believe that if I wanted to do something that was sustainable, it had to be done in a way that was responsible in the kind of business climate that we live in—something that would work in the semiconductor industry. It is important to understand one's own business so you are prepared and protected for those times when you're on the down cycle. Work–life professionals understand that the down cycle is coming, whether they wish it to or not. It's going to happen. So, trying to make changes that are sustainable in the down cycles of the economy as well as in times that are good is just a part of being responsible.

V. SUE MOLINA
Deloitte & Touche, LLP, Partner & National Director of the Initiative for the Retention and Advancement of Women

On Becoming a Work–Family Advocate. I did not take the normal career route to a position in HR. I began my role as the national director of our women's initiative 2½ years ago after spending 22 years as a client service tax partner. I have a very narrow tax specialty in partnership and real estate. And I have no HR experience or background.

I've only been with Deloitte & Touche 5½ years. I have 20 years of experience with another one of the big four accounting firms. So it actually says a lot for Deloitte to take a relatively new partner—I was a direct admit partner with only 3 years with Deloitte at the time, when they asked me to assume a national role, especially surprising since I did not have the strong internal network with our leaders and partners.

As I stepped into this national role, one of my biggest challenges was to develop this internal network with the right people in order to influence the key decision makers. I describe my job as one where I have no authority over anyone, but I have to influence everybody. It takes time to build an internal network, to get to know people, to get them to know and trust me so I have influence and access to the leaders of the firm. It's been a great opportunity and has made me develop a whole different skill set. My plan is to stay in this role for another year, and then bring somebody else from client service to be the next national director.

On How Work–Family Policy Decisions Are Made in Corporations. At Deloitte & Touche the corporate strategies are ultimately made in our boardroom. However, before board decisions are made, there is tremendous input and recommendations from partners and national leaders, such as myself, to our managing partner of human resources, our CEO, and our managing partner, who is basically our chief operating officer.

Our women's initiative is a good example of a strategic policy decision made by the board but only after studying the situation and receiving input from many partners. The Women's Initiative became the cornerstone for many HR initiatives to follow. With the policy and vision for the women's initiative set by the board, actual programs, including work–family and flexibility, were developed and implemented by the HR professionals. We like to call the women's initiative an HR revolution. Ten years ago we realized the importance of retaining and advancing all our people, both men and women. So the women's initiative was the catalyst for our work–family policies.

On Making a Business Case for Work–Family Programs. Since we are an accounting firm, we always want to quantify everything that we do. We have built a business case around reduced turnover and client satisfaction. We try to quantify the turnover reduction to the extent that we can. We have tracked our turnover rate since the beginning of our women's initiative in 1993, and the rate has gone down from 28% to 18%. The annual turnover reduction can be quantified with an approximate dollar savings that goes directly to the bottom line.

We also survey our clients every year about their satisfaction with our services. To the extent that we have reduced our turnover, the same people are available to serve our clients, and we're seeing a correlation of high client satisfaction. So we do try to find measurements that support the business case for our work–family issues or programs. We also survey our people at Deloitte every year in order to measure their commitment and satisfaction of working at Deloitte. But it is almost impossible to quantify the commitment level to the bottom line in terms of savings or cost reductions. However, if we move the employee commitment arrow up, we think our employees are more productive and we think our clients are more satisfied, but it's almost impossible to quantify that to the bottom line.

On How to Maintain Work–Family Programs in an Economic Downturn.   The economic downturn hit us the hardest after 9/11. During the last quarter of 2001, we took a hard look at our out-of-pocket expenses and cut budgets across the firm including HR programs. There was a concern that our diversity and our women's initiative programs would be negatively impacted. However, they weren't impacted at all. What happened was we turned from using outside consultants to using our internal resources. And it was amazing, quite frankly, to see some of our people really step up and take leadership roles and additional responsibilities. We began doing some fabulous things by just using our internal resources rather than turning to external sources.

One important initiative that we are exploring is our desire to create a culture of flexibility. Maggie Jackson, I thought, was right on when she talked about all the technology that we use in our lives today and how we are constantly connected 24/7. We are so connected all the time! Now we're looking to turn that 24/7 connectivity into a positive rather than a negative by creating this informal flexibility where people have more control over how they work, when they work, and where they get their job done.

Another important issue for women is lack of role models. There aren't enough female role models at the higher leadership levels. In order to highlight and provide access to role models, we've created an internal database where we ask all our women to fill out a profile template that we post on our database. Then if anyone wants to find a role model, they can search the database. They can search for specific characteristics to try to find someone who looks like them. For example, someone who is at, let's say, a manager level with children, maybe on a reduced work arrangement in the tax practice. With this information, they can reach out and develop internal networks or a mentoring relationship with women who are in similar situations or somebody who is at a higher level.

Success Stories.   It is really, really helpful if your top executive, the CEO, is visibly supportive. We all can build business cases and we can try and quantify it to the bottom line, but in Deloitte & Touche's situation, it was our CEO 10 years ago who decided that we needed to change our culture in order to stop the brain drain of our women.

Somebody else mentioned culture. I agree that the culture of an organization is extremely important. If the organization really wants to have a culture that supports their employees, then work–life issues and child care are going to be important to them. As a professional service organization, we're in the service business with no significant hard assets. The only assets that we have are our people and our clients. And up until the early 1990s, we were totally focused on our clients. We wanted to be the best client service accounting firm in the United States and the world. Our goal was to be number one in meeting our clients' needs.

With the launch of the Women's Initiative in 1993, we realized we had a second asset that is just as important as our clients, and that was our people. It was the Women's Initiative that really changed our focus and put the emphasis on our people and work–family programs. Because the Women's Initiative was a top-down strategy led by our CEO, our work–family programs evolved very differently than Texas Instruments with a bottom-down strategy. I think our Women's Initiative is a great success story, not only because we are retaining and advancing more women every year, but because it has positively affected all our people, both men and women, by helping them manage their work–family commitments and by providing a culture that promotes personal success.

DONNA KLEIN
Marriott International, Vice President, Workforce Effectiveness

On Becoming a Work–Family Advocate. My background, in my pre-Marriott career, was in organization development (OD). When I went to Marriott, the work–life job was created as a 2-year assignment. There was a desire on the company's part to do something around work and family. With my OD background and other experience with start-ups, I walked into the job. But it's been 15 years now, and my 2-year assignment is still not over, which I think speaks to the complexity of the issue and the difficulty of the organizational change. As the years have gone by the scope of the job has become bigger and bigger. The definition and scope of the issue has continued to evolve. And, after 15 years, it is still regarded as a cutting-edge issue.

On How Work–Family Policy Decisions Are Made in Corporations. At Marriott, like what Betty Purkey said about Texas Instruments, we certainly follow the model of "take action and worry about apologizing later." It is a very entrepreneurial spirit. In terms of the working family agenda—and we've been active in it about 14 years—we had issues that existed in the properties—in the hotels actually—that prompted us to create a philosophy statement or policy statement on working families. That's a broad-brush statement that still exists today. A policy statement is something we take to the Board for approval, much like the Deloitte & Touche model. The Board approves the philosophy of the company regarding any issue. Our policy for working families was a very simple statement. We believe in working families. We employ working families; therefore, we will support working families. So there are no budgetary constraints or other restrictions for the policy. I have found that, as a first step, to be more advantageous for developing and designing programs. Because there are no dollars attached to the statement of philosophy, it eliminates the financial barriers involved in getting your foot in the door. Once the Board gave their approval 14 years ago, and approved Marriott's Statement of Philosophy on Working Families, the process began in a bottom-up way. We wanted to do it well and to do it wisely. We researched our employees, both hourly workers and management. The needs were identified and we tried to operationalize programs and policies that could provide some relief for the issues.

On Making a Business Case for Work–Family Programs. I think with their business "hat on," CEOs have expected and we have delivered a business case in the best way that we possibly could. We justified the cost of programs, at a minimum, on a cost-neutral basis. Within Marriott, we certainly have implemented programs on which we have lost money. But the case to sell a set of programs had to be least a cost-neutral or better program. So I think CEOs are conflicted. If you want to isolate a CEO as being the ultimate decision maker as to what goes on in the company, I would have to say that a cost-neutral program is a conflict for them because they have a responsibility to shareholders as well as to their employees to leverage cost to increase revenue. And sometimes these two responsibilities can be oppositional.

On How to Maintain Work–Family Programs in an Economic Downturn. I was trying to think if I could identify a company that during down times— and we all have them—had disbanded work–life programs singularly, in other words, apart from and in a focused way, at a time when many other services and supports were not also dismantled. And I can't think of anyone that has simply eliminated all work–life programs, and only work–life programs, during bad economic times. There are companies who were very prominent in the field in the past, but have now lost a lot of prominence, but that is really due, I think, to major dislocations in those particular industries and not a targeted attempt to get rid of work–life programs.

One thing that certainly I am very biased about: I think we have been in this business of trying to fix work–life problems for our own workforces for a long, long time. The field is stuck. And I think many of us have come to a conclusion that as individual companies there is more we could do. There is always more a work–life professional could do in terms of a programmatic response. But is any particular program going to be "system changing"? Is it going to create the kind of universe of change that Faith Wohl and others have described? I think we all have come to the agreement that that's not going to happen.

So we've done a lot. We continue to do a lot. And I don't see our work trying to help our employees manage the simultaneous demands of work and life ever stopping. But, I think there is a different, and additional role for corporations. Many of us have come to the conclusion that there is a role for public policy. And many of the larger companies, the big brand companies, have coalesced into a coalition to try to influence policy at the federal and state level.

Policy advocacy efforts are only 1½ years old, but they appear to be getting a lot of traction. It's not any single issue—social issues in general are not issues that corporations have traditionally become involved in from a lobbying perspective. Corporations usually save their lobbying resources for really nuts and bolts issues, like tax issues or real estate issues or things like that. But I think we're getting some traction with work–family policies now. I think the time has come as the role of corporations vis-à-vis other sectors of the economy continues to blur. And, hopefully, advocacy for work–family problems can provide another platform to move the field forward.

Success Stories.   I don't think we want to paint a picture that a positive return on the expenditure is necessarily a must-have in all cases. I think that for-profit organizations have a responsibility to be fiscally prudent. So that's the first thing we're going to go for in any kind of solution, no matter what the issue is.

But, our behavior is also motivated in many ways that are not financially based. Marriott is probably a good example of that. We employ a very, very large hourly workforce. Eighty-five percent of our 150,000 employees are hourly workers. And those hourly workers have tremendous challenges in terms of trying to provide care for their families, for their children as well as for the elderly family members they have. So we have invested millions in trying to figure out really what the best solution is for this unique workforce.

And it's a very different model than a Texas Instruments or a Deloitte & Touche because to develop ROI, you can't use the retention costs and training costs to justify the cost of a program because, unfortunately, the retention and training cost associated with hourly workers is very low. The nature of hourly labor makes it a very unique challenge.

We are in the business of selling service; Marriott does not sell luxury or price. Because service is such a major part of our brand, we have been able to justify programs because most service is delivered by that hourly person. It is not delivered by me at headquarters. It is not delivered by anyone on the staff side. It is delivered by the housekeeper or the bellmen or the food servers. They are compelling reasons to make an investment in this work–life intersection. It may not pencil out on the bottom line, but nonetheless the work–family issues of our hourly employees are an important part of our business—they touch our customer on a daily basis.

Work–life within organizations is really an organization development intervention. It is a very long-term intervention. But you can enter into the organization at any time or begin the intervention at various points. Betty Purkey described the work–life program at Texas Instruments as largely bottom-up. Sue Molina described Deloitte & Touche as top-down. The direction for work–life programs in most organizations just depends on what is happening in the organization, what the driving need is at that particular point in time. But then you just go through, you use that entry wedge and then go through your data collection and your assessment and your problem solving, your implementation, and your measurement and go back around and collect data again. It's a closed systems model of organizational development, so it really doesn't matter if they are championed from the hourly worker or management level.

PHYLLIS STEWART PIRES
Cisco Systems, Inc., HR Manager, WW Diversity/Ethics

On Becoming a Work–Family Advocate.   I am a mother, and I also have a background in human development education and training. I had been in the employer-supported child care field for a long time—directing child care centers for companies, designing and developing child care centers, etc. Then, as a work–life consultant, I helped companies examine if a child care center and other dependent care programs would enable them to meet various business goals such as employee recruitment, retention, differentiation as an employer of choice, etc. I worked with the HR team from various companies to form the business case that they delivered back to their leaderships.

The position of launching and managing the various Family Services programs at Cisco was really an opportunity to look at the issue of employer-supported, dependent care programs from an entirely new angle. I was part of the consulting team to Cisco when the company embarked on launching their child care center and other dependent care programs. As a result of getting to know the team at Cisco and a recognition on both sides of my fit to the job of launching and supporting these programs, I was asked to join the Cisco staff. It was a great opportunity because it gave me a chance to be behind the closed door we talked about and to sit at those tables and get a sense of the way that the business cases data get used and talked about, set aside, redefined, etc. It's been a hugely educational experience for me to be in this position for the last 3½ years.

On How Work–Family Policy Decisions Are Made in Corporations. The child care center at Cisco came about as a result of an observation made by our CEO, John Chambers, who hosts monthly forums with our employees. He tells the story of how he was continually being asked the same question: What was Cisco going to do to support families at Cisco? Employees were having a very difficult time finding child care that met their particular needs. As he tells the story, he says he realized if he'd been sitting across a table from a customer and they had been continually asking the same kind of question, he would have acted more quickly. He said that was a lesson for him.

We performed a very traditional needs assessment, ROI analysis, and budget modeling exercise, all of which culminated in a recommendation to the board that Cisco meet the child care needs of its employees directly. I think that that is a great example of our CEO's model of listening to employees. Now that the work–family agenda is actively supported, we also have programs such as adoption assistance, breastfeeding support programs, and baby gifts that came about as a result of HR initiatives, and we have some programs that even originated from employee interest groups such as a newly launching elder care education and resource program.

On Making a Business Case for Work–Family Programs. You have to look individually at each company to understand their point of need. It would be a mistake to assume that every company is going to look at work–life issues the same way, or that a single model is going to address the same issues for employees in different companies.

We have to start by finding out what it is that the business and its employees care about right now, as well as helping them understand what they are going to need to care about in the future—what their workforce is going to look like 3 or 5 years from now. We have to help them understand that by not implementing programs to address these needs, they may be "missing the boat." We also focus on the cost effectiveness of our programs. We are fortunate in that our particular child care center is based on a model that keeps the Cisco contribution quite low. The model works because the Cisco child care center is quite large. There are 18,000 Cisco employees, with an average age of 37, all on one campus—and they're having many, many babies. So we have a unique situation that has allowed us to run our center with low costs to the company. It's a child care model that fits with the Cisco fiscal model. But our model wouldn't work for companies with smaller centers.

On How to Maintain Work–Family Programs in an Economic Downturn. This has been a rough couple of years in the high-tech industry. Although we haven't eliminated any of our work–life programs in that time, we've certainly been creative in ways that we've looked at expanding such as using smaller pilots, etc. We've also found ways to take advantage of our own technology, for example creating some e-learning tools to extend the reach of some of the on-site courses we offer. An online version of our breastfeeding support class now makes it possible for employees out in the field to access course content that is offered at our major sites, plus it greatly increases the flexibility employees have to access the information when they most need it. So I think in these times you have to rise to the challenge to be creative and not allow your leaders to lose sight of the long-term work–family goals of the company.

Success Stories.   The recent celebration of the anniversary of the child care center had a wide-ranging effect on employees. We invited all the parents to attend, and CEO John Chambers walked from room to room and heard the stories of these parents and the experiences that they've had. This isn't something you could put on a ledger sheet, but it certainly contributes to the company's support of the child care center, and how employees perceive this benefit as extremely valuable. We taped that visit and use the footage strategically to share the power and impact of the center.

The title of our talk is *Sitting at the Corporate Table.* It is not that there is a single table you want to be at; you want to be at every possible table. I've taken the time to find out where the conversations are happening. I have developed relationships with people in all parts of the organization, and I couldn't have imagined the places my champions have come from or how people outside HR can influence decisions about work–family matters.

You can't just stay in the work–life box. You have to really open your mind up to leadership development, diversity, women's issues, facilities, fitness, wellness—any area that you can imagine—and then encourage each of the people in those areas, at those tables, to take as broad a view as possible of how we define an employee and how we define the employees' experience.

Chapter 7

Balancing Work and Family Demands in the Military: What Happens When Your Employer Tells You to Go to War?

David Bruce Bell
U.S. Army Research Institute

Walter R. Schumm
Kansas State University

Segal's (1988) research in work–family conflict looks at the fate of an "employee" who is caught between the demands of two very greedy institutions: the military and the family. The demands of the military seem, almost inevitably, to arise from the nature of the occupation itself. Although some civilian occupations contain one or more of the following features, few have all five—especially those that have a direct impact on the employee's family members. (The few that might qualify would be the following, relatively small, occupational groups: missionaries and career State Department/Foreign Service members.) These features are:

- Risk of injury or death to the service member;
- Periodic (and sometimes prolonged) separation from other immediate family members;
- Geographic mobility;
- Residence in foreign countries, and
- Normative role pressures placed upon family members because they are considered (associate) members of the employee's organization.

In this chapter, we discuss how the features of military life are different from what typically is seen in civilian life, how military families cope with problems commonly associated with these features, and what the Army specifically has done to help its families. We pay particular attention to the prob-

lems associated with long-term overseas deployments to potentially dangerous situations and/or locations. (A deployment occurs when a group of
soldiers leave their home station, *as a group*, to accomplish a specific mission.
Missions involve training for a task, maintaining the peace in a trouble spot,
or engaging in combat. The deployments that are most likely to be studied by
social scientists are those that involve at least 500 soldiers, are not routine
training missions, and involve time in some foreign country.)

FEATURES OF MILITARY LIFE

Risk of Injury or Death

Although differences in how records are kept make it difficult to draw direct conclusions, the Army appears to be a relatively safe place to work during peacetime. The main cause of death is automobile accidents while driving one's own auto on duty or while on leave. Accidents while operating
military equipment (e.g., trucks, tanks, or helicopters) are relatively rare.
Furthermore, we were unable to find any evidence that being in a military
family increases one's odds of injury or death.

What does seem to affect both the soldier and his or her spouse is how
rapidly and unpredictably the odds of being injured or killed change when
deployment to a potentially hostile place is ordered. We have researched
(or studied) spousal reactions to what might happen during routine deployments such as peacekeeping in the Sinai (Bell, Schumm, Segal, & Rice,
1996), potentially dangerous peacekeeping such as in Bosnia (Bell,
Bartone, Bartone, Schumm, Rice, & Hinson, 1997), dangerous peacekeeping missions such as Somalia (Bell & Teitelbaum, 1993; Bell, Teitelbaum, &
Schumm, 1996; Kerner-Hoeg, Baker, Lomvardias, & Towne, 1993); or the
first Gulf War (Bell, 1991; Peterson, 2002; U.S. Army Europe and Seventh
U.S. Army, 1991). The fear of potential harm was not related to the level of
danger actually experienced during these deployments. Rather, it appeared to be largely based on the lack of good information and a tendency
to fear the worst. (In the case of the first Gulf War, the fear of illness turned
out to be correct. However, usually the fear of what will happen to the soldiers far outweighs the reality.)

There have been many improvements since 1776 for both soldiers and
their families in the Army's manner of handling the inevitable injuries.
Medical care has greatly reduced death rates from injuries and diseases.
Also, modern tactics have reduced the percentage of soldiers (in a given engagement) who are either killed or wounded by enemy action. The system
for handling family affairs has vastly improved with the introduction of pensions for the spouses of fallen soldiers, casualty notification teams, and

chaplain assistance in handling the emotional fallout (Albano, 1994; Bell & Iadeluca, 1987; Bell, Stevens, & Segal, 1996). The Army has also reduced family fears through the introduction of post-wide spouse briefings, peer support groups, telephone trees, and improved communication with the deployed soldier via email, faxes, telephones, and videoconferencing.

Our research has demonstrated that one of the most powerful antidotes for spousal fear is reliable, credible information about what the soldier is experiencing, particularly that which comes from the soldier him- or her-self. The preferred mode of communication by both soldiers and spouses is the long distance telephone, since it provides current information in an interactive mode. However, the downside to this is that it is also the most expensive mode and therefore may cause financial problems for families with few financial resources or a large appetite for instant communications (Bell, Schumm, Knott, & Ender, 1999; Bell, Stevens, & Segal, 1996; Ender & Segal, 1996; Ender & Segal, 1998). It also helps when a spouse knows that the unit members are well trained and that the leaders care about the soldier's welfare (Rosen, Durand, & Martin, 2000). Concerned and caring leaders help soldiers support their families (Bell, Schumm, & Frost, 2003; Rosen et al., 2000) and also help families to adapt to the demands of Army life (Bourg, 1994; Bowen, 1998).

Periodic Separations

During 2001, 92% of spouses said that their soldiers had been away from home for at least a week during the last 12 months (Peterson, 2002). The length of time a given soldier is likely to be absent from his or her home station varies greatly by rank and military specialty. Thus officers, Special Forces units, military police, and infantrymen are absent a great deal, whereas soldiers in medical and administrative specialties are not. We were unable to find comparable civilian statistics, but we are quite sure that civilian families, in general, do not usually experience separations approaching the number of days that soldiers are away from home. The average number of weeks that enlisted soldiers, officers, and Special Forces soldiers were absent from their home stations during fiscal year 1998 was 2.8, 5.3, and 18, respectively (Bell, 2000).

Although the frequency and duration of military deployments are not always predictable for soldiers and their families, the consequences of frequent, unpredictable, and prolonged family separations are clear. Most spouses miss the companionship, intimacy, emotional support, and division of labor that is present when the soldier is at home. Spouses worry about the welfare of the soldier, particularly when the absence involves real or perceived danger. Fear of infidelity is also a common theme in separations, although the fear far outstrips the reality in these situations. The longer the separation, the more likely the family will need to change the way they get things done. For junior spouses, this change often involves relocating the family back to their or their soldier's family of origin to gain needed instrumental support and to reduce expenses. The more independent the spouses become, the better they adapt to the separation. However, the more the spouses change, the longer it will take for the couples to readjust once the soldiers return (Bell, Stevens, & Segal, 1996).

Divorce

Journalists, in particular, seem to be interested in whether long deployments "cause" divorce. Different researchers, using different methods, have addressed this question and reached different conclusions. Teitelbaum (1992) found that right after the Gulf War, the press focused on the increase in the number of soldiers wanting to get a divorce and suggested that the war had caused the increase. The legal records that Teitelbaum examined told a different story. There was a drop in the number of divorces during the war, but what the press was seeing was a "queuing problem" (i.e., soldiers who would have gotten out of their marriages earlier if the war had not intervened were now acting on their decisions). And, in fact, he found that the annual rate of divorce was no greater now than it had been before the war started.

According to our research (Schumm, Bell, Knott, & Rice, 1996), the best predictor of divorce among soldiers in intact marriages who deployed either to the Gulf War or as peacekeepers in the Sinai was the characteristics of the marriage before the deployment. That is, those whose marriages were "in trouble" before they left were much more likely to get a divorce upon returning than those whose marriage was stable before they left. Soldiers in marriages that they described prior to deployment as being in trouble had a 1300% greater chance of getting divorced when they returned than those who reported happy marriages. As expected, the physical arrangements mirrored what the soldiers said about their marriages. That is, soldiers who had separated from their spouses and/or obtained legal separations were much more likely to become divorced after the deployment than those still in intact marriages.

Specifically, a statistical analysis showed that active duty soldiers in intact marriages at the start of the Gulf War were more likely to get divorces upon their return if they were either in unstable marriages, female, deployed to the war, members of a racial minority, or relatively new to the Army (i.e., junior enlisted soldier or a junior officer). Additional analyses showed that being deployed was associated with higher divorce rates among female (7.0%) than male (3.1%) enlisted soldiers. Divorces were also more prevalent among male officers who did (1.6%), than those who did not, (0.6%) deploy.

Deployment Stages

Because deployments are visible and important, a good deal more work has been done in documenting the needs of families during deployment. Deployments present different problems as families prepare for the deployment (predeployment), experience the separation (the deployment), are temporarily reunited with the soldier while the deployment is still underway (rest and recuperation or R&R visits), and experience the soldier's eventual return (reunion). The needs for each phase are reviewed in more detail in Bell and Schumm (2000).

During *pre-deployment*, a family's main needs are for information about the deployment; getting one's affairs in order (e.g., wills and bank accounts); planning for ways to keep the family going while the soldier is away; learning about or verifying the availability of potential help during the deployment (e.g., Army agencies, friends, and relatives); and the problem of finding sufficient time to deal with the emotional upset that is part and parcel of any extended family separation. The Army attempts to meet these needs by holding family briefings about the pending deployment in which the unit commanders address family questions and representatives of various Army agencies are on hand to explain what types of assistance they can render. A short time later, the unit has each soldier meet with a series of agents and agencies that help the soldiers get their financial, legal, and child care affairs settled. The unit attempts to provide personal time for the soldiers to get their emotional affairs in order. However, the families often complain that the time provided is not sufficient (Bell & Schumm, 2000; U.S. Army Europe and 7th U.S. Army, 1991).

During deployments, the main needs for families are both emotional and instrumental. Not only do the spouses continue to be concerned about the soldiers, but they also are cast into the role of instant single parents with the resulting overload of tasks, many of which were previously shared with or attended to by the now missing partners. Thus, there are not only many tasks, but also many unfamiliar ones. Good information about the whereabouts and safety of the soldier may be hard to find or very expensive to come by in a timely manner. Rumors often become rampant, particularly about those topics the spouses care the most about: soldier safety and when the soldiers will return. Friends, neighbors, and relatives can and do provide what the spouses are most likely to need (e.g., respite child care, companionship, and advice on practical matters). Indeed, these are the sources that spouses most often turn to for help. The main help the Army offers is increased opportunities to "network" and thus gain friends and advisors through the unit-based Family Readiness Groups (FRGs), which are particularly active during major deployments (Schumm, Bell, Milan, & Segal, 2000). FRGs also assist with rumor control via their telephone trees, and they provide advice on additional sources of help (e.g., Army support agencies and programs) for those who may need it (Bell & Schumm, 2000; Bell, Stevens, & Segal, 1996; Schumm, Bell, & Knott, 2001).

The main problem with *Rest, Recuperation*, and *Reunion* is that the service member, the spouse, and even the children often fantasize about how perfect the reunion will be. It will be the most romantic moment for the couple; the children who have not seen the soldier for some time will be able to instantly relate to him or her; and miscommunications that have occurred throughout the deployment will magically disappear. However, in reality, children do misbehave, jet lag can take its toll, and unresolved issues can lead to arguments in both Rest and Recuperation visits and more permanent reunions. Furthermore, the military has long known that reunion can be very stressful (Boulding, 1950; Hill, 1949; McCubbin, 1980). During the first Gulf War, the Army devised new programs and media for helping both soldiers and spouses to cope with the stresses of reunion. What is less well known is that spouses experience an increase in depression following R&R, when the soldier goes back to his or her overseas assignment (Bell, Bartone, Bartone, Schumm, Rice & Hinson, 1997). (For details on the problems of R&R and reunions and how the Army handles them see: Bell, Bartone, Bartone, Schumm, Rice, & Hinson, 1997; Bell & Schumm, 2000; Durand, 1992; Rosen & Durand, 2000; Schumm, Bell, Milan, & Segal, 2000.)

Because the household has been operating without the soldier during deployment, most experts urge that during reunion the couple examine the changes that have occurred in how the family operates, and which changes they might wish to keep. Soldiers are urged to move slowly and to observe how things are working before they demand that things return to how they were before the current separation (Bell & Schumm, 2000; Rosen & Durand, 2000). For example, Durand (1992) reported that the most frequently mentioned areas of change that spouses reported in their soldiers following the Gulf War were a greater feeling of closeness, greater independence in the nondeployed spouse, and an increased participation in household chores and child care. However, as earlier research has shown, it is easier for the family to reintegrate when the family keeps the soldier as part of the family's emotional life during the absence (Hill, 1949).

Even with all of these potential stressors, most spouses adapt well to deployments. For example, the U.S. Army Europe and 7th U.S. Army's survey (1991) during the Gulf War found no differences between the spouses of deployed and nondeployed soldiers' reports of how well they met family, social, and Army demands. Jensen, Martin, and Watanabe (1996) found that the symptoms seen in children were generally mild and that they tended to mirror what was seen in their caregiver(s). The symptoms also tended to be a function of the presence (or absence) of social, community, and family supports. Those who have conducted follow-up studies from this and other deployments tend to reach similar conclusions (Bell & Frost, 2003; Peterson, 2002; Rosen & Durand, 2000; Schumm, Bell, & Gade, 2000).

However, some families seem to do a better job of coping with the stresses of deployment than others. These families are the ones that have the most resources (i.e., they are better educated, older, tuned into military channels of communication and are supportive of the Army's mission). They also tend to adopt positive attitudes about the deployment and concentrate upon those things they can control (Bell & Schumm, 2000). However, we must also note that these characteristics may be partially due to self-selection: Those who do not do well during deployments are more inclined to leave the military.

Geographic Mobility

In civilian life, relocating the family usually means finding different accommodations within the same city. Whether a move takes place at all, when it occurs, and where the family ends up is under the control of the family. Also, when civilian families move, they are moving in order to improve one or more aspects of their lives. In contrast, military families move because of the "needs of the service." In most cases, soldiers are going to move when and where the Army wants them to move. If a soldier is going to a location that allows the family to accompany him or her, the only choice that the family has is whether they are going to go with the soldier and if so, when. (Prior to the war in Iraq, the majority of civilian spouses [86%] were living with their soldiers. Most, 88% were living in the United States. However, only 39% of these spouses had lived at the same location for two or more years [Peterson, 2002].)

Although many spouses like the chance to live in different locations during the time the soldier is in service, 15% of the families experience severe relocation problems (Segal & Harris, 1993). The families that are most likely to have poor relocation adjustments are those who have fewer personal and social assets and perceived support for families among various Army leaders (Orthner, 2002). Army relocations are known to affect the following areas of military family life: spouses' adjustment to family, personal, and Army demands; the ability of spouses to locate outside employment; and school-related problems among many (44%) relocating high-school age children (Booth, Falk, Segal, & Segal, 1998; Scarville & Bell, 1992; Segal & Harris, 1993). The most common reported problems are unemployment, finances (e.g., nonreimbursed expenses), and finding available and affordable housing. Relocation, particularly if it occurs during a major deployment, can also have a large impact on the social networks that are so critical to adjusting well to the stresses of deployments (Bell et al., 1997; Bell &

Teitelbaum, 1993). Relocation problems can be reduced if the Army maintains vigorous "sponsorship programs" where unit soldiers, spouses, or whole families welcome and help the new families to adjust. It would also help if the Army would give families more control over when and where families move (Segal & Harris, 1993).

Residence in Foreign Countries

Currently, about half the combat force in the Active Army is serving overseas. Although families are not likely to accompany the soldiers to many of these locations (e.g., Iraq, Korea, Bosnia, Kosovo, and the Sinai), families can and do accompany their soldiers to Germany, Japan, and foreign embassies. In fact, the latest spouse survey shows that 10% of the spouses of active duty soldiers are currently living in Europe, and 2% are living elsewhere overseas (Peterson, 2002). Because virtually all soldiers with spouses eventually have a tour in Europe during a 20-year career, it is not unusual for families to spend part of that time overseas. Relatively little has been written since the 1980s about how living overseas affects Army families. Some reports were produced in the 1980s when the U.S. Army Research Institute for the Behavioral and Social Sciences had a field office in Germany. Then families complained about overcrowded housing, having to learn a foreign language, poor quality of post exchanges and commissaries, and adjusting to cultural differences (Girdler, Holz, Sanders, & Ozkaptan, 1984). Twiss (1999) also described overseas family housing as "difficult." Junior enlisted soldiers, probably because they had fewer resources, tended to have the most grievances overall (Ozkaptan, Sanders, & Holz, 1986).

Bowen (1989) found that the best predictor of adaptation to Germany was the extent to which the conditions met or exceeded the spouses' expectations and whether they felt they lived in a supportive community. When the Army downsized during the 1990s, it attempted to retain the best German accommodations that it had occupied previously. We do not know if the complaints diminished. However, in 1996 we noted that the families had a new complaint: The long distances they had to travel to use the family services that had been retained after the downsizing (Bell et al., 1997).

The Army made a genuine effort to provide additional services to the families of the soldiers that it sent to the first Gulf War and as peacekeepers to Bosnia. Army research shows that family use of Army services was much higher during the first Bosnia deployment than during the first Gulf War. Even though the Bosnia deployment was longer, there were fewer reports of financial difficulties or emotional problems. However, the percent of spouses of soldiers who deployed to Bosnia, Somalia, and the first Gulf War who said that they could cope with the demands of Army life (during the deployment) was essentially the same (71%, 73%, and 74%, respectively; Bell et al., 1997).

Normative Role Pressures

The Army exerts a strong direct and indirect influence on its families. It is much more involved with its families than are other employers. For example, for those who live on post, the Army is landlord, main "merchant" police force, and social service network. In 2001, 41% of Army families lived on post, in government owned housing (Peterson, 2002). In addition, Army families are likely to adversely affect their soldier's career if they engage in inappropriate behavior, because it is more likely that such behavior will be known to the Army (Segal & Harris, 1993). Even for those who do not live in the "company town," the Army still exerts pressure on the family through its control of working hours (which are long and often unpredictable) and its emphasis on certain norms and values (e.g., efficiency, hierarchy, dominance, power, and control of emotions), which may not always be compatible with family life (Segal & Harris, 1993). Although the Army has reduced its demands for volunteer and social contributions from its families (particularly those of higher ranks), it still treats families differentially based on the rank of the soldier (Durand, 2000; Segal, 1988).

Spouses need to learn how the military works, what it expects of family members and what consequences (real or imagined) there are for choosing (or not choosing) to behave as the military expects. Although many spouses experience the military pressure to behave in certain ways, spouses also benefit from being incorporated into the military social system with its recognizable roles and supportive social networks (Segal, 1988). The military family support system and family expectations are explicitly discussed in Army courses and manuals for spouses and through contact with older, more experienced Army spouses. The more one knows about the military, its services, and its benefits, the better one will be at coping with the stresses that are inherent in military life (Bell & Schumm, 2000; Campbell, Appelbaum, Martinson, & Martin, 2000; Military Family Resource Center, 2002; Schumm, Bell, Milan, & Segal, 2000; U.S. Army Community & Family Support Center, 1994a, 1994b).

IMPROVING WORK-FAMILY BALANCE IN THE ARMY

We have shown that that the Army is a different kind of employer. It demands much more of its "employees" and its families and thus creates real challenges in several areas of work–family balance. This employer determines when and how much its employees will travel, forces uncompensated "overtime," compels its employees to endure unsafe "working conditions" and strongly encourages the entire family periodically to relocate to places at times of its choosing. Furthermore, it is unusually active in prescribing what family behaviors are desirable (particularly for those living on post) and what responsibilities all, especially higher ranking, spouses should assume. Although much of what is being described here has been true of the Army from its inception 228 years ago, the Army has changed greatly in recent years in the amount of family separation that is present and the Army's attitude toward its families (Albano, 1994; Bell & Iadeluca, 1987; Shinseki, 2003).

Starting in the 1960s, particularly, there was a growing awareness that families made a major impact on both soldier retention and on the ability of the Army to accomplish its missions. This awareness, along with the sheer number of families—by then the Army had more "dependents" than soldiers—resulted in a movement to upgrade and professionalize Army family services. Army Community Service (ACS) provides assistance to military families through its information and referral services, budget and indebtedness counseling, household item loan closet, emergency food locker, information on other posts, and welcome packets to new arrivals. It also provides mobilization and deployment support, family employment services, and services for handicapped family members. The resulting services that have come on line for families since 1965 (e.g., Army Community Service [ACS], child care, youth services, family violence, and spouse employment) are not only outstanding but are also considered model programs for the nation (Bell, 1996; Hammonds, 1996; Campbell, Appelbaum, Martinson, & Martin, 2000; Military Family Resource Center, 2002). However, family support is not without its problems. As of 10 years ago, the majority of child care was still being provided in unlicensed homes (Segal & Harris, 1993); and it is still true that junior enlisted families often live far away from the installation based service system which they need (Wolpert, Martin, Dougherty, Rudin & Kerner-Hoeg, 2000). A recent review of programs concluded that the main improvements needed to reduce the number of family relocations are to invest more into preventing family problems; to consolidate the services that we have; and to move toward home basing (Shinseki, 2003). This is a system of basing soldiers and their families which repeatedly reassigns the soldier to the same installation throughout his or her career. For example, an infantryman may have a number of assignments (e.g. recruiter, drill sergeant, and service in a foreign country) that will require him (and possibly) his family to relocate. [All soldiers in infantry are males.] However, whenever he is serving as an infantryman in an infantry unit, he will be assigned to the same location (e.g., Fort Drum, New York). Others suggest that we simply expand existing services (e.g., serve more clients, expand hours of operations, or reduce fees; Military Family Resource Center, 2002).

Although improved service delivery and fewer relocations may help some families, these suggestions do not address the fundamental difficulties inherent in the military. Family separation is the third most frequent reason (after pay and benefits) why soldiers say they are considering leaving the Army. Home basing does reduce relocations and spouse unemployment. However, it does nothing to reduce family separations. Having fewer (or smaller) deployments or getting more soldiers into the military jobs (e.g., special forces, military police, and light infantry) that are the most likely to be associated with soldier deployments will provide the needed substitutes to give the currently deployed soldiers a chance to come home and be with their families. Since family separation is a large reason why soldiers leave the Army, having more soldiers in the frequently deployed occupations should also help with Army retention (Bell, 2000). The Army is at least tracking how much separation there is (Sticha, Sadacca, DiFazio, Knerr, Hogan, & Diana, 1999). However, world events have made it difficult to control the number of soldiers being deployed or to arrange for their families to accompany them on these missions (Cox, 2003; Kelly, 2003).

Policymakers would like to think there is a direct relationship between time separated from family and soldier retention. However, the research does not bear that out. It appears soldier retention is better if there are some deployments (rather than none) and that the problem is more a matter of what the soldier is being asked to do and how well the families are bearing up. What matters to the soldier is that the mission be meaningful, well-planned, and career-enhancing. It also helps if the deployment has a definite end date or at least that the family knows when their particular soldier will return. Having time between deployments to take care of family matters and leave to take care of family matters can also be very helpful (Bell, 2000). However, what seems to turn spouses against being in the military is that they experienced some kind of problem during the deployment (Bell, Schumm, & Martin, 2001). Thus, when it comes to family separation, it appears that policies and leadership play a role in helping soldiers and their families balance work and family demands. Family programs alone will not improve this area of Army life.

Home basing should help families as it will put more money in their pockets by eliminating many of the current relocations. It will also increase spouse employment by giving spouses more time to locate a job and a better probability that they will actually be hired, because they can promise potential employers that they will be available for work during longer periods of time. However, unlike the Navy's home-basing programs that are associated with major urban centers, the Army too often has its soldiers based in rural areas where jobs are scarce, and an oversupply of spouses who want jobs tend to not only keep unemployment up but also reduce wages (Booth et al., 1998). Moreover, because being unemployed and/or a discouraged worker (i.e., wanting a job but not looking for one) is negatively associated with soldier retention, the Army should take a more active role in trying to bring jobs to the sites where the Army is most concentrated. Unless there are more good jobs that the spouses can actually obtain, staying at the same location in a status that one does not want (i.e., unemployed or discouraged) may not yield the benefits that the Army is hoping for. Also, the Army needs to understand the role of homemakers, because that group is very likely to support making the Army a career (Schumm & Bell, 2002).

In the early 1980s, the Army made a quantum leap forward in helping Army families to balance the demands of family and work by establishing a pro-family philosophy (Wickham, 1983), significant family support programs (Shinseki, 2003), and a major research program (Segal & Harris, 1993) to help guide it. Now, 20 years later, we need to re-energize our family programs and policies to consolidate them and to bring them in line with the new realities of large, long deployments to dangerous places. We need a better model for how soldiers and families can cope with long, unpredictable deployments. Historically, the Army has allowed families to remain close to the soldiers; the Navy has just allowed the separations to take place. Is there a third way that could be developed? The combination of progressive programs and research was a win–win situation for the Army and its families during the 1980s. That combination can and should be brought to bear on the challenges we currently face (Shinseki, 2003).

REFERENCES

Albano, S. (1994). Military recognition of family concerns: Revolutionary War to 1993. *Armed Forces and Society, 20*(2), 283–302.

Bell, D. B. (1991, November). *The impact of Operations Desert Shield/Storm on Army families: A summary of findings to date.* Paper presented at the 53rd annual conference of the National Council on Family Relations, Denver, CO.

Bell, D. B. (1996). *Response to the CSA's inquiry on balancing work and family.* Unpublished manuscript. Alexandria, VA: U.S. Army Research Institute for the Behavioral and Social Sciences.

Bell, D. B. (2000). *Effects of deployments (and other military absences from home station) upon Army retention, readiness, and quality of life.* Unpublished manuscript. Alexandria, VA: U.S. Army Research Institute for the Behavioral and Social Sciences.

Bell, D. B., Bartone, J., Bartone, P. T., Schumm, W. R., Rice, R. E., & Hinson, C. (1997, October). *Helping U.S. Army families cope with the stresses of troop deployment in Bosnia-Herzegovina.* Paper presented at the 1997 Inter-University Seminar on Armed Forces and Society Biennial International Conference. Baltimore, MD.

Bell, D. B., & Frost, E. (2003, March). *Army children during dangerous deployments: What we know and what needs are still unmet.* Presentation at The National Consortium for Child & Adolescent Mental Health Services. Washington, DC.

Bell, D. B., & Iadeluca, R. B. (1987). *The origins of voluntary support for Army family programs* (Research Report 1456). Alexandria, VA: U.S. Army Research Institute for the Behavioral and Social Sciences.

Bell, D. B., & Schumm, W. R. (2000). Providing family support during military deployments. In J. A. Martin, L. N. Rosen, & L. R. Sparacino (Eds.), *The military family: A practice guide for human service providers* (pp. 139–152). Westport, CT: Praeger.

Bell, D. B., Schumm, W. R., & Frost, E. (2003, February). *On the Army's family support system for deployments: How the system came to be and how well it functions.* Paper presented to the 13th Annual Kravis-deRoulet Conference on Leadership in Work-Family Balance, Claremont McKenna College, Claremont, CA.

Bell, D. B., Schumm, W. R., Knott, B., & Ender, M. G. (1999). The desert fax: A research note on calling home from Somalia. *Armed Forces & Society, 25*(3), 509–522.

Bell, D. B., Schumm, W. R., & Martin, J. A. (2001, October). *How family separations affect spouse support for a military career: A preliminary view from the U.S. Army.* Paper presented at the 2001 Inter-University Seminar on Armed Forces and Society Biennial International Conference. Baltimore, MD.

Bell, D. B., Schumm, W. R., Segal, M. W., & Rice, R. E. (1996). The family support system for the MFO. In R. H. Phelps & B. J. Farr (Eds.), *Reserve component soldiers as peacekeepers* (pp. 355–394). Alexandria, VA: U.S. Army Research Institute for the Behavioral and Social Sciences.

Bell, D. B., Stevens, M. L., & Segal, M. W. (1996). *How to support families during overseas deployments: A sourcebook for service providers* (Research Report 1687). Alexandria, VA: U.S. Army Research Institute for the Behavioral and Social Sciences.

Bell, D. B., & Teitelbaum, J. M. (1993, October). *Operation Restore Hope: Preliminary results of a survey of Army spouses at Fort Drum, New York.* Paper presented at the Inter-University Seminar on Armed Forces and Society Biennial conference, Baltimore, MD.

Bell, D. B., Teitelbaum, J. M., & Schumm, W. R. (1996). Keeping the home fires burning: Family support issues. *Military Review, 76*(2), 80–84.

Booth, B., Falk, W. W., Segal, D. R., & Segal, M. W. (1998). The impact of military presence in local labor markets on the employment of women. *Gender & Society, 14,* 318–332.

Boulding, E. (1950). Family adjustment to war separations and reunions. *Annals of the American Academy of Political and Social Sciences, 60*(2), 59–67.

Bourg, M. C. (1994, August). *The effects of organizational support for families on work-family conflict and organizational commitment.* Paper presented at the Annual Meeting of the American Sociological Association, Los Angeles, CA.

Bowen, G. L. (1998). Effects of leader support in the work unit on the relationship between work spillover and family adaptation. *Journal of Family and Economic Issues, 19*(1), 25–52.

Bowen, G. L. (1989). *Family adaptation to relocation: An empirical analysis of family stressors, adaptive resources, and sense of coherence* (Tech. Rep. 856). Alexandria, VA: U.S. Army Research Institute for the Behavioral and Social Sciences.

Campbell, N. D., Appelbaum, J. C., Martinson, K., & Martin, E. (2000). *Be all that we can be: Lessons from the military for improving our nation's child care system.* Washington, DC: National Women's Law Center.

Cox, M. (2003). New chief: Army needs balance of skill, technology. *Army Times, 64*(3), 14–16.

Durand, D. B. (1992, August). *The redistribution of responsibilities and power in Army families following Operation Desert Shield/Storm reunions.* Paper presented at the Section on Sociology of Peace and War at the 87th annual meeting of the American Sociological Association, Pittsburgh, PA.

Durand, D. B. (2000). The role of the senior military wife—then and now. In J. A. Martin, L. N. Rosen, & L. R. Sparacino (Eds.), *The military family: A practice guide for human service providers* (pp. 73–86). Westport, CT: Praeger.

Ender, M. G., & Segal, D. R. (1996). (E)-mail to the foxhole: Isolation, (tele)communication, and forward deployed soldiers. *Journal of Political and Military Sociology, 24,* 65–81.

Ender, M. G., & Segal, D. R. (1998). Cyber-soldiering: Race, class, gender, and new media use in the U.S. Army. In Bosah Ebo (Ed.), *Cyberghetto or cybertopia?: Race, class, and gender on the internet* (pp. 27–52). Westport, CT: Praeger.

Girdler, K., Holz, R., Sanders, W., & Ozkaptan, H. (1984). *Families on the front: Army families in Germany* (USAREUR FU 84-1). Alexandria, VA: U.S. Army Research Institute for the Behavioral and Social Sciences.

Hammonds, K. (1996, September 16). Balancing Work and Family. *Business Week Online.* Available at http://www.businessweek.com/

Hill, R. (1949). *Families under stress: Adjustment to the crises of war separation and reunion.* New York: Harper & Row. Reprinted by Greenwood Press, Westport, CT, 1971.

Jensen, J. P., Martin, D., & Watanabe, H. K. (1996). Children's response to parental separation during Operation Desert Storm. *Journal of the American Academy of Child and Adolescent Psychiatry, 35*(4), 433–441.

Kelly, J. F. (2003, May). *How Army families fare in love and war: Military studies deployment impact on home front.* Washington, DC: Washington Post, p. A3.

Kerner-Hoeg, S., Baker, S., Lomvardias, C., & Towne, L. (1993). *Operation Restore Hope: Survey of Army spouses as Fort Drum, New York: Survey methodology and data book.* Fairfax, VA: Caliber Associates.

McCubbin, H. I. (1980, Winter). Coping with separation and reunion. *Military Chaplain's Review,* DA Pamphlet 165-124, 49–58.

Military Family Resource Center. (2002). *Overview of military child development system.* Retrieved January 30, 2003 from http://mfrc.calib.com/MCY/mm_cdc.htm

Orthner, D. K. (2002). *Relocation adjustment among Army civilian spouses.* 2001 Survey of Army Families (SAF) IV, U.S. Army community and Family Support Center. Retrieved December 18, 2002, from http://armymwr.com/corporateoperations/planning/surveys.asp

Ozkaptan, H., Sanders, W., & Holz, R. (1986). (Research Report 1428). *A profile of Army families in USAREUR: Results of the 1983 Families in Europe Survey.* Alexandria, VA: U.S. Army Research Institute for the Behavioral and Social Sciences.

Peterson, M. (2002). *Survey of Army families IV: Final executive summary Spring 2001.* Unpublished manuscript. Alexandria, VA: Army Personnel Survey Office, U.S. Army Research Institute for the Behavioral and Social Sciences.

Rosen, L. N., & Durand, D. B. (2000). Marital adjustment following deployment. In J. A. Martin, L. N. Rosen, & L. R. Sparacino (Eds.), *The military family: A practice guide for human service providers* (pp. 153–168). Westport, CT: Praeger.

Rosen, L. N., Durand, D. B., & Martin, J. A. (2000).Wartime stress and family adaptation. In J. A. Martin, L. N. Rosen, & L. R. Sparacino (Eds.), *The military family: A practice guide for human service providers* (pp. 123–138). Westport, CT: Praeger.

Scarville, J., & Bell, D. B. (1992, November). *Employment and underemployment among Army wives.* Paper presented at the 54th annual convention of the National Council on Family Relations, Orlando, FL.

Schumm, W. R., & Bell, D. B. (2002, February). *Homemakers and other working Army spouses: How work status influences Army and family outcomes.* Presented at The Persons, Processes and Places: Research on Families, Workplaces, and Communities Conference, San Francisco, CA.

Schumm, W. R., Bell, D. B., & Gade, P. A. (2000, November). *The impact of a military overseas peacekeeping deployment on marital stability, quality, and satisfaction.* Paper presented at the 2000 National Council on Family Relations, Minneapolis, MN.

Schumm, W. R., Bell, D. B., & Knott, B. (2001). Predicting the extent and stressfulness of problem rumors at home among Army wives of soldiers deployed overseas on a humanitarian mission. *Psychological Reports, 89,* 123–134.

Schumm, W. R., Bell, D. B., Knott, B., & Rice (1996). The perceived effect of stressors in marital satisfaction among civilian wives of enlisted soldiers deployed to Somalia for Operation Restore Hope. *Military Medicine, 161*(10), 601–606.

Schumm, W. R., Bell, D. B., Milan, L. M., & Segal, M. W. (2000). *The family support Group (FSG) leaders' handbook* (Study Report 2000-02). Alexandria, VA: U.S. Army Research Institute for the Behavioral and Social Sciences.

Segal, M. W. (1988). The military and families as greedy institutions. In C. C. Moskos & F. R. Wood (Eds.), *The military: More than just a job?* (pp. 79–98). Washington, DC: Pergaman-Brassey's International Defense Publishers, Inc.

Segal, M. W., & Harris, J. J. (1993). *What we know about Army families* (Special Report 21). Alexandria, VA: U.S. Army Research Institute for the Behavioral and Social Sciences.

Shinseki, E. K. (2003). *The 2003 Army Family White Paper*. Washington, DC: U.S. Army Center for Military History.

Sticha, P. J., Sadacca, R., DiFazio, A. S., Knerr, C. M., Hogan, P. F., & Diana, M. (1999). *Personnel TEMPO: Definition, measurement, and effects on retention, readiness, and quality of life* (Contractor Report 99-04). Alexandria, VA: U.S. Army Research Institute for the Behavioral and Social Sciences.

Teitelbaum, J. M. (1992, April). *ODS and Post-ODS divorce and child behavioral problems.* Paper presented at the office of the Secretary of Defense family research in-progress review, Pentagon, Washington, DC.

Twiss, P. C. (1999). The future of military housing. In P. McClure (Ed.), *Pathways to the future: A review of military family research.* Scranton, PA: Military family Institute of Marywood University.

U.S. Army Community and Family Support Center. (1994a). *Army Family Team Building—Family Member Training: Introduction and Intermediate.* Levels. Alexandria, VA: Author.

U.S. Army Community and Family Support Center. (1994b). *Army family team building—Family member training: Advanced level & camera ready art.* Alexandria, VA: Author.

U.S. Army Europe and 7th U.S. Army. (1991). *USAREUR Personnel Opinion Survey 1991: General findings report, Vol. 1 (Family).* (USAREUR Pamphlet 600-2). Heidelberg, Germany: Author.

Wickham, J. A., Jr. (1983). *Chief of Staff white paper 1983: The Army family.* Washington, DC: Department of the Army.

Wolpert, D. S., Martin, J. A., Dougherty, L. M., Rudin, B. J., & Kerner-Hoeg, S. (2000). The special case of the young enlisted family. In J. A. Martin, L. N. Rosen, & L. R. Sparacino (Eds.), *The military family: A practice guide for human service providers* (pp. 43–54). Westport, CT: Praeger.

Chapter 8

Understanding Burnout: Work and Family Issues

Christina Maslach
University of California, Berkeley

Burnout is a hot topic in today's workplace, given its high costs for both employees and organizations. What causes this problem, and what can be done about it? Conventional wisdom says that burnout is primarily a problem of individuals. But research argues otherwise. Burnout is not a problem of people but of the social environment in which they work. The structure and functioning of the workplace shape how people interact with one another and how they carry out their jobs. When that workplace does not recognize the human side of work, and there are major mismatches between the nature of the job and the nature of people, then there will be a greater risk of burnout. This framework of person–environment fit can also provide new insights into the relationship between the workplace and the home, thus yielding a better understanding of burnout and family issues.

WHAT IS BURNOUT?

Job burnout is a psychological syndrome that involves a prolonged response to chronic interpersonal stressors on the job. The three key dimensions of this response are an overwhelming exhaustion, feelings of cynicism and detachment from the job, and a sense of ineffectiveness and lack of accomplishment. This definition is a broader statement of the multidimensional model that has been predominant in the burnout field (Maslach, 1993, 1998; Maslach & Jackson, 1981).

The *exhaustion* dimension represents the basic individual stress component of burnout. It refers to feelings of being overextended and depleted of
one's emotional and physical resources. Workers feel drained and used up,
without any source of replenishment. They lack enough energy to face another day or another problem. The major sources of this exhaustion are
work overload and personal conflict at work.

The *cynicism* dimension represents the interpersonal context component of burnout. It refers to a negative, callous, or excessively detached response to various aspects of the job. It usually develops in response to the
overload of emotional exhaustion, and is self-protective at first—an emotional buffer of "detached concern." If people are working too hard and doing too much, they will begin to back off, to cut down, to reduce what they
are doing. But the risk is that the detachment can result in the loss of idealism and the dehumanization of others. Over time workers are not simply
creating a buffer and cutting back on the quantity of work but are also developing a negative reaction to people and to the job. As cynicism develops,
people shift from trying to do their very best to doing the bare minimum.
Their performance on the job can amount to "How do I get through, still
get my paycheck, and get out of here?" Cynical workers cut back on the
amount of time spent at the office or the job site and the amount of energy
they devote to their job. They are still performing, but doing it at the bare
minimum, so the quality of that performance declines.

The *inefficacy* dimension represents the self-evaluation component of
burnout. It refers to feelings of incompetence and a lack of achievement
and productivity in work. This lowered sense of self-efficacy is exacerbated
by a lack of job resources, as well as by a lack of social support and of opportunities to develop professionally. People experiencing this dimension of
burnout ask themselves, "What am I doing? Why am I here? Maybe I'm not
cut out for this job." This sense of inefficacy may make burned-out workers
feel they have made a mistake in choosing their career path and often
makes them dislike the kind of person they think they have become. Thus,
they come to have a negative regard for themselves, as well as for others.

Unlike acute stress reactions, which develop in response to specific critical incidents, burnout is a cumulative reaction to ongoing occupational
stressors. With burnout, the emphasis has been more on the process of
psychological erosion, and the psychological and social outcomes of this
chronic exposure, rather than just the physical ones. Because burnout is a
prolonged response to chronic interpersonal stressors on the job, it tends
to be fairly stable over time. In examining the three dimensions of burnout we find different factors in the workplace that are predictive of the
different dimensions of burnout, but all three dimensions should be examined to really get a good sense of what is going on when workers experience burnout.

The problem of burnout first surfaced in caregiving and human service occupations, such as health care, mental health, social services, the criminal justice system, religious professions, counseling, and education. All of these occupations share a focus on providing aid and service to people in need—in other words, the core of the job is the relationship between provider and recipient. This interpersonal context of the job meant that, from the beginning, researchers studied burnout not so much as an individual stress response, but in terms of an individual's relational transactions in the workplace. Moreover, this interpersonal context focused attention on the individual's emotions, and on the motives and values underlying his or her work with recipients. The therapeutic or service relationships that caregivers or providers develop with recipients require an ongoing and intense level of personal, emotional contact. Although such relationships can be rewarding and engaging, they can also be quite stressful. Within such occupations, the prevailing norms are to be selfless and to put others' needs first; to work long hours and do whatever it takes to help a client, patient, or student; to go the extra mile and to give one's all. Moreover, various social, political, and economic factors (such as funding cutbacks or policy restrictions), which result in work settings that are high in demands and low in resources, shape the organizational environments for these jobs.

Recently, as other occupations have become more oriented to "high-touch" customer service, the phenomenon of burnout has become relevant for these jobs as well (Maslach & Leiter, 1997). New research has utilized participant samples in this wider range of occupations, but the bulk of the research findings on burnout are still based on samples in health care, education, and human services (Maslach, Jackson, & Leiter, 1996; Schaufeli & Enzmann, 1998).

Although burnout has been identified primarily as a phenomenon in the world of work, the significance of the social context and interpersonal relationships for burnout suggests that burnout might be relevant to other domains of life. Indeed, several authors have applied the concept of burnout to the family. Burnout has been used to analyze the relationship between parents and children (Procaccini & Kiefaber, 1983), and the relationship between members of a marital couple (Pines, 1988, 1996).

HISTORY OF BURNOUT RESEARCH

Research on burnout has gone through distinct phases of development (for a more extensive discussion of this point, see Maslach & Schaufeli, 1993; Maslach, Schaufeli, & Leiter, 2001). In the first, pioneering phase, the work was exploratory and had the goal of articulating the phenomenon of burnout. This research was more qualitative in nature, utilizing such techniques as interviews, case studies, and on-site observations. What emerged from this descriptive work were the three dimensions of the burnout experience. The exhaustion dimension was also described as wearing out, loss of energy, depletion, debilitation, and fatigue. The cynicism dimension was originally called depersonalization (given the nature of human services occupations), but was also described as negative or inappropriate attitudes toward clients, irritability, loss of idealism, and withdrawal. The inefficacy dimension was originally called reduced personal accomplishment and was described as reduced productivity or capability, low morale, and an inability to cope.

The emergence of this multidimensional model of burnout occurred at the same time as a shift to the second empirical phase, which involved more systematic quantitative research. One of the first tasks of this new research phase was the development of standardized measures of the burnout experience. The only measure that assesses all three dimensions is the Maslach Burnout Inventory (MBI), therefore, it has been considered the standard tool for research in this field (see Maslach et al., 1996 for the most recent edition). The original version of the MBI was designed for use with people working in the human services and health care. A slightly modified version was then developed for use by people working in educational settings. More recently, given the increasing interest in burnout within occupations that are not so clearly people-oriented, a third, general version of the MBI was developed (the MBI-General Survey, or MBI–GS). The MBI–GS assesses the same three dimensions as the original measure, using slightly revised items, and maintains a consistent factor structure across a variety of occupations.

At first, the multidimensional quality of the burnout construct and its measure posed statistical challenges for researchers who wanted a single score that could be correlated with scores on other variables. With the development of more sophisticated methodology and statistical tools that could manage complex constructs, researchers were able to analyze the interrelationships between the burnout dimensions and other factors, and to develop structural models. As a result, researchers have been able to examine the contribution of many potential influences and consequences simultaneously, separating unique contributors from those that are redundant. More recently, a mediation model of burnout has been developed that links a set of organizational factors to experienced burnout, which in turn is linked to individual and social outcomes (Leiter & Maslach, in press).

Initial research on burnout was done in California, but eventually expanded beyond those local boundaries to other parts of the United States and to Canada. Carefully replicated research was conducted in Europe and Israel, and researchers have identified the same three dimensions of burnout in all of these locations. Currently, burnout research is being conducted in many other countries around the world, with the bulk of the work occurring in postindustrialized nations. Although the psychometric properties of the MBI are similar across cultures, there appear to be national differences in average levels of burnout. For example, Europeans show lower average scores than North Americans (Schaufeli & Enzmann, 1998), and other researchers have found cultural differences in multinational data sets (Golembiewski, Boudreau, Munzenrider, & Luo, 1996; Savicki, 2002). However, given that these studies were not designed to test cultural hypotheses, and did not use random and representative comparative samples, it is difficult to draw strong conclusions about the cultural implications of the findings.

A recent development in burnout research has been to expand the focus to the positive antithesis of burnout, rather than just focusing on the negative state that it represents. This positive state has been called job engagement, but it has been conceptualized in different ways. One approach has been to define engagement as the opposite of burnout; thus, it is comprised of the same three basic dimensions, but with the positive endpoints of energy, involvement, and efficacy (Leiter & Maslach, 1998). By implication, engagement is assessed by the opposite pattern of scores on the three MBI dimensions. A different approach has defined engagement as a persistent, positive affective-motivational state of fulfillment that is characterized by the three components of vigor, dedication, and absorption. Schaufeli and his colleagues have developed a new measure to assess this positive state, and the preliminary results show that while the scores are negatively correlated with burnout, they are most strongly related to the positive endpoint of efficacy (see Maslach, Schaufeli, & Leiter, 2001 for a more extensive comparison of these two approaches).

The significance of this focus on job engagement is not simply theoretical, but practical. To prevent or deal with burnout in organizations, it is important to frame interventions in terms of the positive goals to be achieved, and not just the negative problems to be fixed. Effective interventions need to include strategies for improving the organizational culture so that people have an increased sense of involvement and enthusiasm for their workplace and feel good about the work they are doing. Focusing on job engagement represents a new way of thinking about solutions to burnout (Leiter & Maslach, 2000b).

THE IMPACT OF JOB BURNOUT

Why should we care about job burnout? It is not uncommon for senior managers in organizations to downplay the negative effects associated with employees' feelings of stress and burnout (Maslach & Leiter, 1997). The general view is that if workers are having a bad day, then that is their own personal problem—it is not a big deal for the organization. However, the kinds of issues identified by both researchers and practitioners suggest that burnout should indeed be considered "a big deal" because it can have many costs, both for the organization and for the individual employee. Research has found that job stress is predictive of lowered job performance, problems with family relationships, and poor health (see Kahn & Byosiere, 1992; Sauter & Murphy, 1995), and studies have shown parallel findings with job burnout.

Of primary concern to any organization should be the possibility of poor work quality from a burned-out employee. When employees shift to minimum performance, minimum standards of working, and minimum production quality, rather than performing at their best, they make more errors, become less thorough, and have less creativity for solving problems. For example, one study found that nurses experiencing higher levels of burnout were judged by their patients to be providing a lower level of patient care (Leiter, Harvie, & Frizzell, 1998); another study found that burned-out police officers reported more use of violence against civilians (Kop, Euwema, & Schaufeli, 1999).

Burnout has been associated with various forms of negative responses to the job, including job dissatisfaction, low organizational commitment, absenteeism, intention to leave the job, and turnover (see Schaufeli & Enzmann, 1998, for a review). People who are experiencing burnout can have a negative impact on their colleagues, both by causing greater personal conflict and by disrupting job tasks. Thus, burnout can be "contagious" and perpetuate itself through informal interactions on the job. When burnout reaches the high cynicism stage, it can result in higher absenteeism and increased turnover. Employees suffering from burnout do the bare minimum, do not show up regularly, leave work early, and quit their jobs at higher rates than engaged employees.

The relationship of human stress to health has been at the core of stress research, ever since Selye (1967) proposed the original concept. Stress has been shown to have a negative impact on both physical health (especially cardiovascular problems) and psychological well-being. The individual stress dimension of burnout is exhaustion, and, as one would predict, that dimension has been correlated with various physical symptoms of stress: headaches, gastrointestinal disorders, muscle tension, hypertension, cold/flu episodes, and sleep disturbances (see Leiter & Maslach, 2000a for a review).

Burnout has also been linked to depression, and there has been much debate about the meaning of that link (see Maslach & Leiter, in press). A common assumption has been that burnout causes mental dysfunction—that is, it precipitates negative effects in terms of mental health, such as depression, anxiety, and drops in self-esteem. An alternative argument is that burnout is not a precursor to depression but is itself a form of mental illness. The most recent research on this issue indicates that burnout is indeed distinguishable from clinical depression, but that it seems to fit the diagnostic criteria for job-related neurasthenia (Schaufeli, Bakker, Hoogduin, Schaap, & Kladler, 2001). The implication of all this research is that burnout is an important risk factor for mental health, and this can have a significant impact on both the family and work life of the affected employee.

Given that most research on burnout has focused on the job environment, there has been relatively less attention devoted to how burnout affects home life. However, the research studies on this topic have found a fairly consistent pattern of a negative "spillover" effect. Workers who experienced burnout were rated by their spouses in more negative ways (Jackson & Maslach, 1982; Zedeck, Maslach, Mosier, & Skitka, 1988), and they themselves reported that their job had a negative impact on their family and that their marriage was unsatisfactory (Burke & Greenglass, 1989, 2001).

During the early phases of burnout research, interviews revealed two ways in which burnout affected family life (Maslach, 1982). On the one hand, families of burnout victims reported increased emotional volatility in their homes. Employees who are experiencing the exhaustion, cynicism, and inefficacy of burnout are likely to bring home a lot of emotional anger, hostility, and frustration. They are more easily upset by small disruptions, and serious arguments and conflicts erupt over mundane events in the home. On the other hand, family members also reported a self-imposed isolation and withdrawal of the burned-out individual from family life. The affected person may just want to get away from people for a while, and not hear another voice, or deal with another problem. There is a sense that the family is "living at the office," because this person is inaccessible, either emotionally or literally by being on call, or traveling or working much of the time. For example, the son of a minister said, "My father is a great man and does wonderful things for the community. But he's never there for me." In another case, a prison guard described how he tried to build a protective wall between his job and his family life, by refusing to discuss his work at home (and thus avoiding having to relive it). "I always say, 'don't ask me about my job, because I don't want to have to deal with it again'— but none of my three wives understood."

INDIVIDUAL RISK FACTORS FOR BURNOUT

Who are the people who are most likely to experience burnout? Are they distinctive in terms of their personality? Several personality traits have been studied in an attempt to answer this question, and although there is not a large body of consistent findings, there are some suggestive trends (see Schaufeli & Enzmann, 1998, for a review). Burnout tends to be higher among people who have low self-esteem, an external locus of control, low levels of hardiness, and a Type-A behavior style. Those who are burned-out cope with stressful events in a rather passive, defensive way, whereas active and confronting coping styles are associated with less burnout. In particular, confronting coping is associated with the dimension of efficacy. A more consistent trend has emerged from studies on the Big Five personality dimensions, which have found that burnout is linked to the dimension of neuroticism. Neuroticism includes trait anxiety, hostility, depression, self-consciousness, and vulnerability. People who score highly on neuroticism are emotionally unstable and prone to psychological distress; thus, it makes sense that such people would be more at risk for burnout.

Are there other personal characteristics that characterize the burnout-prone individual? Several demographic variables have been studied in relation to burnout, but the studies are relatively few and the findings are not that consistent (see Schaufeli & Enzmann, 1998 for a review). Age is the one variable that tends to show a correlation with burnout. Among younger employees the level of burnout is reported to be higher than it is among those aged over 30 or 40 years. Age is clearly confounded with work experience, so burnout appears to be more of a risk earlier in one's career, rather than later. The reasons for such an interpretation have not been studied very thoroughly. However, these findings should be viewed with caution because of the problem of "survival bias" (i.e., those who burn out early in their careers are likely to quit their jobs, leaving behind the survivors who have lower levels of burnout).

Do men and women differ with regard to burnout? According to popular opinion, the answer should be "yes" (e.g., women should be more stressed by the "double shift" of job and family responsibilities), but the empirical evidence tends to say "no." In general, the demographic variable of gender has not been a strong predictor of burnout. The one small but consistent sex difference is that males often score slightly higher on the dimension of cynicism. There is also a tendency in a few studies for women to score slightly higher on exhaustion. These results could be related to gender role stereotypes, but they may also reflect the confounding of sex with occupation (e.g., police officers are more likely to be male; nurses are more likely to be female). With regard to marital status, those who are unmarried seem to be more prone to burnout compared to those who are married. Singles seem to experience even higher burnout levels than those who are divorced. As for ethnicity, very few studies have assessed this demographic variable, so it is not possible to summarize any empirical trends.

SITUATIONAL RISK FACTORS FOR BURNOUT

Although there is some evidence for individual risk factors for burnout, there is far more research evidence for the importance of situational variables. Over two decades of research on burnout have identified a plethora of organizational risk factors across many occupations in various countries (see the reviews by Maslach, Schaufeli, & Leiter, 2001; Schaufeli & Enzmann, 1998). In other words, workplace features are far more predictive of burnout than are personality factors. However, this conclusion is responding to an "either/or" question ("is it the person *or* is it the job"), and it may well be that an "and" question is the better way to frame the issue. That is, there are both personal *and* situational variables that determine burnout, and the key issue is how best to conceptualize their combination or interaction. Building on earlier models of job–person fit (e.g., French, Rodgers, & Cobb, 1974), in which better fit was assumed to predict better adjustment and less stress, Maslach and Leiter (1997) formulated a burnout model that focuses on the degree of match, or mismatch, between the individual and key aspects of his or her organizational environment. The greater the gap, or mismatch, between the person and the job, the greater the likelihood of burnout; conversely, the greater the match (or fit), the greater the likelihood of engagement with work.

What are these key aspects of the organizational environment? An analysis of the research literature on organizational risk factors for burnout has led to the identification of six major domains (Maslach & Leiter, 1999, in press). These six areas of worklife are: workload, control, reward, community, fairness, and values. The first two areas are reflected in the Demand–Control model of job stress (Karasek & Theorell, 1990), and reward refers to the power of reinforcements to shape behavior. Community captures all of the work on social support and interpersonal conflict, while fairness emerges from the literature on equity and social justice. Finally, the area of values picks up the cognitive–emotional power of job goals and expectations.

Work Overload

The first of these six areas is the one that everybody thinks of first: work overload. With work overload, employees feel they have too much to do, not enough time to perform required tasks, and not enough resources to do the work well. There clearly is an imbalance, or mismatch, between the demands of the job and the individual's capacity to meet those demands. Not surprisingly, work overload is the single best predictor of the exhaustion dimension of burnout. People experiencing work overload are often experiencing an imbalance in the load between their job and their home life as well. For example, they may have to sacrifice family time or vacation time to finish their work.

Lack of Control

The second key area is a sense of lack of control. Research has identified a clear link between a lack of control and high levels of stress. Lack of control on the job can result from a number of factors. Employees who are micromanaged, and who are not allowed to use their own wisdom or experience to make decisions, will feel they do not have much personal discretion and autonomy in their work. They may feel they are being held accountable, and yet they do not have the ability to control what it is they are being held accountable for. In other cases, employees will feel a lack of control because working life has become more chaotic and ambiguous as a result of economic downturns. Many employees find themselves worrying about mergers, downsizing, layoffs, and changes in management. They will also feel out of control if they are in a situation where they might be called in to work, told to leave early, or sent off on a trip with little or no notice. These kinds of situations are very disruptive to personal relationships. Employees with little control may not be able to show up for a child's event they promised to attend because, all of a sudden, they are called in to work on an emergency. In all of these instances, the lack of control has an important impact on levels of stress and burnout.

Insufficient Rewards

The third critical area is insufficient rewards. This occurs when employees believe they are not getting rewarded appropriately for their performance. The standard rewards that most people think of are salary, benefits, or special "perks." However, in many cases the more important rewards involve recognition. It matters a great deal to people that somebody else notices what they do, and that somebody cares about the quality of their work. When employees are working hard and feel they are doing their best, they want to get some feedback on their efforts. The value of such concepts as "walk-around" management lies in its power to reward. There is explicit interest in what employees are doing, and the direct acknowledgment and appreciation of their accomplishments. Employee morale is heavily dependent on rewards and recognition.

As mentioned earlier, burnout was first identified in jobs in the human service professions. These jobs are often ones where positive feedback is almost designed out of the process. People come to the employee because they are in trouble, sick, having difficulties, or have broken the law. When the clients (or patients, or customers) are no longer in trouble, or are healthy or feeling happy, they go away—and are then replaced by somebody else who has problems, or is sick, or is in trouble with the law. In this scenario for human service workers, their "successes" always leave, and they have less of an opportunity to see the effect of their hard work. Human service professions deal with negative emotions and negative feedback on a regular basis; indeed, a "good day" is often one in which nothing bad happens. In other words, there is no positive reinforcement, just a lack of negative reinforcement. Positive recognition in this type of situation is very important in preventing burnout because it does not occur as a routine part of the job.

Breakdown in Community

The fourth area encompasses the ongoing relationships that employees have with other people on the job. When these relationships are characterized by a lack of support and trust, and by unresolved conflict, then there is a breakdown in the sense of community. Work relationships include the full range of people that employees deal with on a regular basis, such as the recipients of their services, their coworkers, their boss, the people they supervise, outside vendors or salespeople, or people in the larger community outside the organization.

If work-related relationships are functioning well, then there is a great deal of social support, and employees have effective means of working out disagreements. However, when there is a breakdown in community and there is not much support, there is real hostility and competition, which makes conflicts difficult to resolve. Under such conditions, stress and burnout are high, and work becomes difficult.

Absence of Fairness

The fifth area, an absence of fairness in the workplace, seems to be quite important for burnout, although it is a relatively new area of burnout research. The perception that the workplace is unfair and inequitable is probably the best predictor of the cynicism dimension of burnout. Anger and hostility are likely to arise when people feel they are not being treated with the respect that comes from being treated fairly. Even incidents that appear to be insignificant or trivial can, if they signal unfair treatment, generate intense emotions and have great psychological significance.

According to equity theories (Siegrist, 1996; Walster, Berscheid, & Walster, 1973), when people are experiencing the imbalance of inequity, they will take various actions to try to restore equity. Some actions might involve standard organizational procedures (e.g., for resolving grievances), but if employees do not believe there is any hope of a fair resolution, they may take other actions in areas that they can control. For instance, if employees think they are not being paid as well as they deserve, they may leave work early or take company supplies home with them, because "they owe it to me." It is possible that, in some extreme instances, employees will take action against the person (or persons) whom they may consider responsible for the inequity. Workplace violence often occurs around issues of perceived unfairness, but there has not been sufficient research on this topic.

Value Conflicts

Although there has not been much research on the impact of values, current work suggests that it may play a key role in predicting levels of burnout (Leiter & Maslach, 2004). Values are the ideals and goals that originally attracted people to their job, and thus they are the motivating connection between the worker and the workplace (beyond the utilitarian exchange of time and labor for salary). Value conflicts arise when people are working in a situation where there is a conflict between personal and organizational values. Under these conditions, employees may have to grapple with the conflict between what they want to do and what they have to do. For example, people whose personal values dictate that it is wrong to lie may find themselves in a job where lying becomes necessary for success. Successful job performance may require a bold lie, or perhaps just a shading of the truth (e.g., to get the necessary authorization, or to get the sale). People who experience such a value conflict will give the following kinds of comments: "This job is eroding my soul," or "I cannot look at myself in the mirror anymore knowing what I'm doing. I can't live with myself. I don't like this." If workers are experiencing this kind of mismatch in values on a chronic basis, then burnout is likely to arise.

To reiterate an earlier point, the key issue here is the fit, or match, between the person and the job, and not the specific type of person or type of job environment per se. For example, a Machiavellian individual, who believes that the end justifies the means, will have a better fit with a job in which lying is essential for success, and will probably not experience value conflict.

Other kinds of value conflicts may arise between conflicting values within the organization. For example, the organization may insist that the highest priority is the customer, and will encourage employees to go to any length to make customers happy. However, at the same time the company may judge employee performance on sales, which encourages the employee to sell at any cost, regardless of whether the customer wants it or not. Employees often feel they are caught between conflicting values in this common scenario.

Value conflicts within an organization are often found in the area of "family-friendly" policies. Organizations realize that to attract good people they need to offer such policies to their workers. They may espouse a corporate value about a balance between family and workload, but they do not always translate that corporate value into practice. In some cases, one policy may effectively prevent another one from being enacted (e.g., employees may be encouraged to attend their children's school events, but restrictive policies on rescheduling work hours may make that impossible). In other cases, there may be an implicit norm that stigmatizes taking advantage of certain policies (e.g., when someone who takes a parental leave is judged as less competent). Employees in this kind of situation may have many attractive policies available that are never used because of the underlying corporate culture and these unstated costs (see Hochschild, 1997).

Integration of the Six Areas

Now that these six domains of situational factors have been identified, more research needs to assess their interrelationships, as well as their role in predicting burnout. It seems clear that the six areas are not independent of each other. Problems in one area can be linked to problems in another area—for example, people who are working too hard (workload) may be dealing with many externally imposed tasks (control) or may be experiencing negative working relationships with colleagues (community). Initial research has confirmed these correlations between the six areas, and has also suggested that there is a consistent and complex pattern among them (Leiter & Maslach, 2004). Workload and control each play critical roles (thus replicating the Demand–Control model), but are not sufficient. Reward, community, and fairness add further power to predict values, which in turn is the area that is the critical predictor of the three dimensions of burnout.

Another intriguing possibility to explore in future research is that there may be individual differences in the weighting of the importance of these six areas. These differences could be a function of personality, but may also reflect differences in life-span development and family life. For example, an interview with some young women working as environmental consultants revealed some serious value conflicts between their ecological ideals and the realities of their job (assisting developers in getting permits to construct major shopping malls). For one of these women, the value conflict outweighed the advantages of the job in the other five areas, and the resulting stress led her to quit. However, for another woman, who was the mother of a young child, the advantages in the area of rewards (good salary, family health plan benefits, and on-site child care) outweighed the negative stress associated with the value conflict, so she stayed on the job.

Although the six areas were developed as a metric to describe the key dimensions of the workplace, they seem to be relevant to other domains as well. A number of people have commented on how well they capture critical aspects of family life, so the six-area metric may have more universal value for any meaningful domain of interpersonal relationships. This observation has yet to be explored and tested by researchers, but the shared relevance of this framework underscores the argument that work and family should not be conceptualized in terms that set up an "either-or" framework of balance between two separate spheres.

IMPLICATIONS FOR INTERVENTION

What can be done to alleviate burnout? One approach is to focus on the individual who is experiencing stress, and help him or her to either reduce it or cope with it. Another approach is to focus on the workplace, rather than just the worker, and change the conditions that are causing the stress. A focus on the workplace is the clear implication of the mediation model of burnout (Leiter & Maslach, in press), which posits that the six key areas of worklife affect people's experience of burnout or engagement, which, in turn, affect attitudes and behavior at work. Thus, an effective approach to intervention would be to change workplace policies and practices that shape these six areas. The challenge for organizations is to identify which of the areas are most problematic, and then design interventions that target those particular areas.

Assessment of these six areas, as well as assessment of burnout, is a key element in the organizational checkup survey (Leiter & Maslach, 2000b), which has proved to be a powerful tool for mobilizing both individual and organizational self-reflection and change. The process of the organizational checkup is designed to inspire the full participation of all the employees, and initial uses have yielded remarkably high response rates. The main intent of the survey is to generate a comprehensive profile of the organization's workforce, which can be used to inform decisions about intervention. Knowing which of the six areas are the critical "hot spots" can provide better understanding of the underlying core problems and can serve as a guide to solutions. Moreover, the participative nature of the checkup process can be viewed as an intervention in itself, which engages all employees in an organizational dialogue and prepares them to get involved in future change.

This organizational approach, which utilizes the six-area framework, makes a major contribution to making burnout a problem that can be solved in better ways than having employees either endure the chronic stress or quit their jobs. For the individual employees, the organizations for which they work, and the clients whom they serve, the preferred solution is to build a work environment that supports the ideals to which people wish to devote their efforts. This is a formidable challenge, but one that becomes more possible with the development of effective measures and a conceptual framework to guide intervention.

CONCLUSION

This analysis of the burnout phenomenon—what it is, what causes it, and what its effects are—points to an important bottom line in terms of the fit between people and their job. Employees need to have some choice and control over how they handle their workload, some sense of recognition and reward, support from the people they work with, and a sense of being treated with respect and fairness. There must be effective ways to resolve conflicts, and there should be clear organizational values that can mesh with employees' personal motives. All workers want to know that they are doing meaningful work that makes them proud. Burnout can be prevented and reduced when employers design workplaces that engage employees, and employees have the opportunity to make job choices that match their personal attributes. These guidelines may seem fairly simple and straightforward, but putting them into practice can be a complex process that requires continuous time and effort. However, the outcomes are well worth the commitment—healthier workers, happier families, and more productive organizations.

REFERENCES

Burke, R. J., & Greenglass, E. R. (1989). Psychological burnout among men and women in teaching: An examination of the Cherniss model. *Human Relations, 42*, 261–273.

Burke, R. J., & Greenglass, E. R. (2001). Hospital restructuring, work-family conflict and psychological burnout among nursing staff. *Psychology and Health, 16*, 83–94.

French, J. R. P., Jr., Rodgers, W., & Cobb, S. (1974). Adjustment as person-environment fit. In G. V. Coelho, D. A. Hamburg, & J. E. Adams (Eds.), *Coping and adaptation.* New York: Basic Books.

Golembiewski, R. T., Boudreau, R. A., Munzenrider, R. F., & Luo, H. (1996). *Global burnout: A world-wide pandemic explored by the phase model.* Greenwich, CT: JAI Press.

Hochschild, A. R. (1997). *The time bind: When work becomes home and home becomes work.* New York: Henry Holt.

Jackson, S. E., & Maslach, C. (1982). After-effects of job-related stress: Families as victims. *Journal of Occupational Behaviour, 3*, 63–77.

Kahn, R. L., & Byosiere, P. (1992). Stress in organizations. In M. D. Dunnette & L. M. Hough (Eds.), *Handbook of industrial and organizational psychology* (Vol. 3, pp. 571–650). Palo Alto, CA: Consulting Psychologists Press.

Karasek, R., & Theorell, T. (1990). *Stress, productivity, and the reconstruction of working life.* New York: Basic Books.

Kop, N., Euwema, M., & Schaufeli, W. (1999). Burnout, job stress, and violent behaviour among Dutch police officers. *Work & Stress, 13*, 326–340.

Leiter, M. P., Harvie, P., & Frizzell, C. (1998). The correspondence of patient satisfaction and nurse burnout. *Social Science & Medicine, 47*, 1611–1617.

Leiter, M. P., & Maslach, C. (1998). Burnout. In H. Friedman (Ed.), *Encyclopedia of mental health* (pp. 347–357). San Diego, CA: Academic Press.

Leiter, M. P., & Maslach, C. (2000a). Burnout and health. In A. Baum, T. Revenson, & J. Singer (Eds.), *Handbook of health psychology* (pp. 415–426). Hillsdale, NJ: Lawrence Erlbaum Associates.

Leiter, M. P., & Maslach, C. (2000b). *Preventing burnout and building engagement: A complete program for organizational renewal.* San Francisco: Jossey Bass.

Leiter, M. P., & Maslach, C. (2004). Areas of worklife: A structured approach to organizational predictors of job burnout. In P. L. Perrewe & D. C. Ganster (Eds.), *Research in occupational stress and well-being* (Vol. 3, pp. 91–134). Oxford, UK: Elsevier Science, Ltd.

Leiter, M. P., & Maslach, C. (in press). A mediation model of job burnout. In A. S. Antoniou & C. L. Cooper (Eds.), *Research companion to organizational health psychology*. Cheltenham, UK: Elgar Publishing, Ltd.

Maslach, C. (1982). *Burnout: The cost of caring*. Englewood Cliffs, NJ: Prentice-Hall. Reprinted in 2003; Cambridge, MA: Malor Books.

Maslach, C. (1993). Burnout: A multidimensional perspective. In W. B. Schaufeli, C. Maslach, & T. Marek (Eds.), *Professional burnout: Recent developments in theory and research* (pp. 19–32). Washington, DC: Taylor & Francis.

Maslach, C. (1998). A multidimensional theory of burnout. In C. L. Cooper (Ed.), *Theories of organizational stress* (pp. 68–85). Oxford, England: Oxford University Press.

Maslach, C., & Jackson, S. E. (1981). The measurement of experienced burnout. *Journal of Occupational Behavior, 2*, 99–113.

Maslach, C., Jackson, S. E., & Leiter, M. P. (1996). *Maslach Burnout Inventory Manual* (3rd ed.). Palo Alto, CA: Consulting Psychologists Press.

Maslach, C., & Leiter, M. P. (1997). *The truth about burnout*. San Francisco, CA: Jossey-Bass.

Maslach, C., & Leiter, M. P. (1999). Burnout and engagement in the workplace: A contextual analysis. *Advances in Motivation and Achievement, 11*, 275–302.

Maslach, C., & Leiter, M. P. (2005). Stress and burnout: The critical research. In C. L. Cooper (Ed.), *Handbook of stress medicine and health* (2nd ed., pp. 153–170). Boca Raton, FL: CRC Press.

Maslach, C., & Schaufeli, W. B. (1993). Historical and conceptual development of burnout. In W. B. Schaufeli, C. Maslach, & T. Marek (Eds.), *Professional burnout: Recent developments in theory and research* (pp. 1–16). Washington, DC: Taylor & Francis.

Maslach, C., Schaufeli, W. B., & Leiter, M. P. (2001). Job burnout. In S. T. Fiske, D. L. Schacter, & C. Zahn-Waxler (Eds.), *Annual Review of Psychology, 52*, 397–422.

Pines, A. M. (1988). *Keeping the spark alive: Preventing burnout in love and marriage*. New York: St. Martin's Press.

Pines, A. M. (1996). *Couple burnout: Causes and cures*. New York: Routledge.

Procaccini, J., & Kiefaber, M. W. (1983). *Parent burnout*. New York: Doubleday.

Sauter, S. L., & Murphy, L. R. (Eds.). (1995). *Organizational risk factors for job stress*. Washington, DC: American Psychological Association.

Savicki, V. (2002). *Burnout across thirteen cultures: Stress and coping in child and youth care workers*. Westport, CT: Praeger.

Schaufeli, W. B., Bakker, A. B., Hoogduin, K., Schaap, C., & Kladler, A. (2001). The clinical validity of the Maslach Burnout Inventory and the Burnout Measure. *Psychology and Health, 16*, 565–582.

Schaufeli, W. B., & Enzmann, D. (1998). *The burnout companion to study and practice: A critical analysis*. London: Taylor & Francis.

Selye, H. (1967). *Stress in health and disease*. Boston: Butterworth.

Siegrist, J. (1996). Adverse health effects of high-effort/low-reward conditions. *Journal of Occupational Health Psychology, 1*, 27–41.

Walster, E., Berscheid, E., & Walster, G. W. (1973). New directions in equity research. *Journal of Personality and Social Psychology, 25*, 151–176.

Zedeck, S., Maslach, C., Mosier, K., & Skitka, L. (1988). Affective response to work and quality of family life: Employee and spouse perspectives. *Journal of Social Behavior and Personality, 3*, 135–157.

Part IV

WORKING FAMILIES:
HOW WELL ARE THEY WORKING?

We tend to think of maternal employment as a recent phenomenon, but, throughout history mothers and fathers have divided the work needed to sustain a family, usually with mothers working closer to home, probably because they spent most of their adult years nursing or pregnant. The nature and place of work has changed, not the fact that mothers and fathers are both working.

In some ways, the manner in which mothers and fathers work today keeps them away from their children more than in the past, if you consider the distance to work, the time spent commuting, and number of nights away from home on business trips. Also, we would argue, although the jobs many working families hold today are still very demanding, it is in a different manner than the jobs on family farms and early industrial work. For some white-collar professionals, much work is brought home. Others who are employed to do intense physical labor are fatigued when they get home, leaving them with little energy to parent. Issues of technology have impinged on employees' home life with increased communication demands. Other subtle changes in working families come from recently evolving gender roles with more men wanting to spend increased time with their families than fathers of the 1950s to 1980s, and many working mothers finding the roles of work and motherhood complementary rather than contradictory.

In understanding the interplay between work and family, it is also important to understand how families support the transition from home to school to work. Various historical factors have served as barriers to African Americans' transitions. Thompson (chap. 9) traces the importance of education to transitions to work for African Americans. Being cognizant of these barriers and methods to overcome them will help these critical transition points.

Technology affects working families in a myriad of ways. It is difficult to stay current with the rapid expansion of electronic devices that keep us connected to home and our jobs. Pagers, PDAs, cellular phones, faxes, and email allow this connectivity 24 hours a day 7 days a week, year round. The manner in which these devices have affected the constant work and family interaction changes the way we think about relationship issues such as closeness and connectivity. Jackson's chapter portrays the changes families have seen with respect to technology and how families relate to one another and to their work.

The dual-earner couple has become a mainstay in the United States, but there are many remaining questions about the effects of this normative on families. Will it continue? What is the quality of life for these families? What about their children? In the final chapter in this section, Barnett offers research evidence to answer these compelling questions and in addition, provides a research agenda to continue to study family types.

Chapter 9

Home to School to Work— Transitions for African Americans: Eliminating Barriers to Success

Gail L. Thompson
Claremont Graduate University

The groundwork for a successful career is laid well before a young worker enters the workforce. In fact, the work ethic that is necessary to attain a successful career in the future is often established early on in the family environment that prepares children for successful transitions from home to school to work. Thus, there are not only "family-friendly" workplaces, but also "work-friendly families," where the critical importance of education and the work ethic are emphasized throughout childhood. We often wonder why some people succeed despite all odds, and others fail even when given many opportunities. An example of a strong work ethic can be seen in one of the poignant stories in *What African American Parents Want Educators to Know* (Thompson, 2003d), which is based on an interview with Francine, an African-American single parent. After being addicted to drugs for 15 years, at the time of her interview, Francine had been drug free for several years. In order to move her four children out of a crime-ridden public housing complex, she had to renovate a condemned house. In spite of the fact that they lived in an economically depressed city, instilling a strong work ethic in her children was one of Francine's main goals. She used three strategies to do this: assisting her children in creating and maintaining a family garden; modeling the importance of work through her fledgling florist business, as well as earning money from home by hairdressing; and stressing the importance of a good education as a means to socioeconomic mobility. Although she emphasized the importance of a good education to her children, ironically Francine had never graduated from high school. Many

117

years earlier, after her boyfriend was murdered—an act that became the primary catalyst for her subsequent drug addiction—Francine had dropped out of school in 10th grade. At the time, she was the teenage mother of her first child, a newborn baby girl. Consequently, during her interview, Francine stated that one of her personal goals was to return to school to earn a General Education Diploma (G.E.D.). Until then, her ultimate goal of becoming a drug-addiction counselor, a job that would improve her family's financial status, would remain elusive, and force her to continue to try to make ends meet through jobs that did not guarantee financial security.

A second story in *What African American Parents Want Educators to Know* (Thompson, 2003d) was based on an interview with May. Like Francine, May, who had two school-age children, was a single mother. Although May had not resorted to using illegal drugs to cope with personal problems, as Francine had, May had also dropped out of school. Peer pressure and a desire for material possessions were the main catalysts, according to May. After dropping out of school, May got a job, got pregnant, and then, found herself locked in a cycle of low-paying jobs. Like Francine, at the time of her interview, May was planning to earn a G.E.D. Despite the fact that she wanted her children to graduate from high school and have more opportunities than she had, May feared that her children, especially her daughter, a sixth grader who was already struggling academically, would follow in her footsteps and drop out of school. "I want them to get more. I want them to succeed," she stated (p. 174).

Francine's and May's stories are not unique. Millions of American parents are trapped in similar financially precarious predicaments, and African American and Latino single parents are disproportionately represented among these parents. Like Francine's and May's situations, often, a limited formal education remains one of the greatest barriers to their escape from poverty. However, the formal education system can also be a barrier that prevents many individuals, particularly African Americans and Latinos, from using the education system to improve the quality of their lives, and subsequently their children's. After describing the correlations between educational attainment and socioeconomic status, this chapter describes some of these barriers, and concludes with ways in which educators and policymakers can address some of these problems.

EDUCATIONAL ATTAINMENT, EMPLOYMENT RATES, AND SOCIOECONOMIC STATUS

A college degree can provide many benefits. For example, educational attainment is related to lower unemployment rates. According to the U.S. Census Bureau (2001), during 1992, 1995, 1999, and 2000, regardless of race/ethnicity or gender, college graduates were less likely than individuals who had not graduated from college to be unemployed.

Another benefit is that educational attainment is related to socioeconomic status. In general, more education is supposed to equate to higher salaries and more economic opportunities. For example, the U.S. Census Bureau (2001) reported that regardless of race/ethnicity, the average individual who had earned at least a bachelor's degree in 2000 had a substantially higher income than individuals who had less education. Moreover, in most cases, the average individual who had a master's degree earned more than an individual with a bachelor's degree and, on average, individuals who had a professional degree or a doctorate earned more than those with less education (see Table 9.1).

A third benefit is that a college education has traditionally been associated with more prestige. According to Thompson (2003d), "The procurement of jobs in the most highly respected professions, such as medicine, science, and law . . . not only requires college degrees, but this procurement tends to be equated with prestige and higher salaries as well" (p. 179).

Although education was supposed to become the "great equalizer," it has failed to live up to its full potential, especially for African Americans. In spite of the fact that countless African Americans from impoverished backgrounds have used the education system to improve their socioeconomic status, for countless others, the "American Dream" remains elusive (Thompson, 2002, 2003d). The Black middle class has grown considerably in recent decades (Cose, 1993; Thompson, 1999), but African Americans continue to be disproportionately represented among the unemployed class and among individuals who are underpaid or living below the poverty level (see Table 9.2). The U.S. Census Bureau (2002) reported that in 2001, the nation's poverty rate was higher than it was in 2000, and there was a decline in median household income. The median income declined and the poverty rate increased for several groups. Nevertheless, African Americans

TABLE 9.1

Educational Attainment—People 25 Years Old and Over, by Average Earnings in 2000, Work Experience in 2000

Race and Gender	H.S. Graduate	Bachelor's	Master's	Professional Degree	Doctorate
White Male	36,939	69,150	80,758	114,707	95,049
White Female	20,758	36,484	46,201	63,234	56,164
Black Male	30,306	53,756	52,338	59,606	65,455
Black Female	20,797	37,248	42,872	69,815	47,851
Hispanic Male	28,770	53,881	52,384	99,239	91,965
Hispanic Female	18,704	34,617	45,356	57,259	35,876

Source: U.S. Census Bureau 2001: Annual Demographic Survey March Supplement. Available online at http://www.census.gov/hhes/www/img/incpov01/fig08.jpg

TABLE 9.2
Three-Year-Average Median Household Income and Poverty Rate
by Race and Hispanic Origin: 1999–2001

	Income	Poverty Rate
All	$42,900	11.6%
Whites	$44,900	9.7%
Non-Hispanic Whites	$46,700	7.6%
Blacks	$29,900	22.9%
American Indians and Alaska Natives	$32,100	24.5%
Asians and Pacific Islanders	$55,000	10.3%
Hispanics (of any race)	$33,400	21.9%

Source: U.S. Census Bureau. Available online at http://www.census.gov/hhes/www/img/incpov01/fig08.jpg

and Hispanics continued to earn less on average than other groups and were disproportionately represented among individuals and families living below the poverty level. Moreover, when poverty rates were disaggregated by family status, African Americans and Hispanics were more likely than Whites, Asians, and Pacific Islanders to be living below the poverty level in 2000 and 2001 (see Table 9.3). Furthermore, as Table 9.3 indicates, for each of the four major racial/ethnic groups, African American and Hispanic females who had no husband present and who were heads of households were much more likely than other groups to be living below the poverty level.

The combination of poverty and single parenthood has traditionally been linked to numerous negative factors. In *Mothers Who Receive AFDC Payments,* the U.S. Census Bureau (1995) reported that on average, in 1993, mothers who received AFDC benefits were younger and had more children than mothers who did not receive AFDC. Characteristics of families in poverty are found in Table 9.3. Additionally, almost half of the AFDC mothers did not have a high school diploma, most were unemployed, they were more likely to live in "metro areas," and they were more likely to be earning very low incomes. For example, although less than 3% of non-AFDC mothers had a monthly family income of less than $500, 36% of AFDC mothers did, and while less than 7% of non-AFDC mothers had a monthly family income of $500–$999, 36% of AFDC mothers did. Finally, although 87% of non-AFDC mothers lived above the poverty level, only 18% of AFDC mothers did.

Two other reports from the U.S. Census Bureau described how single parenthood affected children. In *America's Children at Risk,* the U.S. Census Bureau (1997a) found that six factors placed children "at risk" as adolescents. Two of the factors—poverty and welfare dependence—were linked

TABLE 9.3
People and Families in Poverty by Selected
Characteristics: 2000 and 2001

Type of Family	2001 % Below Poverty	2000 % Below Poverty
Married Couple		
Non-Hispanic White	3.3	3.2
Black	7.8	6.3
Asian and Pacific Islander	6.6	5.9
Hispanic	13.8	14.2
Female Householder, no husband present		
Non-Hispanic White	19.0	17.8
Black	35.2	34.3
Asian and Pacific Islander	14.6	22.2
Hispanic	37.0	36.4
Male Householder, no wife present		
Non-Hispanic White	10.3	9.2
Black	19.4	16.3
Asian and Pacific Islander	9.1	5.4
Hispanic	17.0	13.6

Source: U.S. Census Bureau Current Population Survey 2001 and 2002 Annual Demographic Supplements Table. Available online at http://www.census.gov/hhes/www/img/incpov01/fig08.jpg

to children's economic status. Three factors—living in a home from which both parents were absent, living in a one-parent family, and living with an unwed mother—pertained to the type of household in which children lived. The last factor—having a parent who had not graduated from high school—pertained to parents' level of educational attainment. Children who experienced these risk factors were more likely at ages 16 and 17 years old to have dropped out of school and to be unemployed, and for girls to be mothers who were living with a child at ages 16 and 17.

In another report, *Children With Single Parents: How They Fare,* the U.S. Census Bureau (1997b) stated that "children living at home with both parents grow up with more financial and educational advantages than youngsters raised by one parent ..." (p. 1). However, the type of single-parent home made a difference for children. On average, children living with a divorced parent tended to have older, more educated parents and parents who earned higher incomes than children living with a parent who had never been married.

Because of disproportionately high rates of poverty and unemployment in their families, African American and Latino children are more likely than White, Asian, and Pacific Islander children to be labeled "at risk." For example, Hispanic and Black students have higher high school drop-out rates than Whites, but the rates for Hispanics are higher than the rate for Blacks. As noted previously, dropping out of high school increases the likelihood of unemployment, poverty, and earning a low income. "In addition, high school dropouts are more likely to receive public assistance than high school graduates who did not go to college" (U.S. Department of Education, 2001b, p. 43).

As the previous section illustrates, the groups that are most likely to be unemployed, living below the poverty level, or to be low wage earners—such as African Americans like Francine and May in the introduction of this chapter—are most in need of a good formal K–12 education, a high school diploma, and postsecondary education degrees. Because educational attainment has been positively correlated to socioeconomic advancement, it would appear that a simple solution to the problem would be for these individuals to take advantage of America's educational opportunities. However, this solution is simplistic, for it masks the fact that numerous barriers deter many African Americans and Latinos from using the education system to increase their socioeconomic opportunities. In fact, as the next section illustrates, like poor children and Latinos, African Americans are most likely to receive the most inadequate K–12 schooling and to be subjected to inequality of educational opportunity (Thompson, 2003a, 2003b, 2003c).

INEQUALITY OF EDUCATIONAL OPPORTUNITY: A MAJOR BARRIER TO SOCIOECONOMIC ADVANCEMENT FOR AFRICAN AMERICANS

The history of African Americans' formal education in the United States has been both positive and negative. Pivotal events in this history occurred both before and after the Civil War. A rudimentary knowledge of this history is essential to understanding why more African Americans have not been able to use the formal education system to attain socioeconomic mobility.

Although many African Americans wanted to become literate (Anderson, 1988; Davie, 1949; DuBois, 1935; Fleming, 1976; Greene, 1946; Johnson, 1938), during the slavery eras in both the northern and southern United States, laws were enacted periodically to prohibit slaves from learning to read and write, and to prohibit Whites from teaching them to read and write (Anderson, 1988; Woodson, 1933). In *Black Labor, White Wealth: The Search for Power and Economic Justice,* Anderson (1994) listed numerous "Boundary Safeguards and Restrictions in Southern States" that were designed to prevent African Americans from learning to read and write. Among these restrictions and safeguards were five antiliteracy laws, making it illegal for slaves to become literate.

According to Anderson (1988), "Between 1800 and 1835, most of the southern states enacted legislation making it a crime to teach enslaved children to read or write" (p. 2). Although slavery was abolished in the northern United States in 1818, there was little difference between the plight of African Americans in the North and African Americans in the South (Litwack, 1961). Fleming (1976) wrote, "Many northern states excluded free Blacks from their schools altogether, while those that offered some schooling to Blacks established separate facilities for them" (p. 24). Moreover, Black northerners' quest for access to a formal education often resulted in anti-Black riots and violence from Whites. Despite the fact that by the 1830s, most northern states permitted Black children to attend segregated schools, many attempts were made to destroy these schools. For example, Black schools were destroyed in Ohio, New York, Connecticut, and Washington (Litwack, 1961). Consequently, "by the end of the Civil War, it was readily apparent that the society as a whole, North and South, had successfully kept the majority of 4.5 million Blacks illiterate" (Fleming, 1976, p. 2).

After the Civil War, White philanthropists, the government-sponsored Freedmen's Bureau, and religious organizations started numerous schools for African Americans in the South. Although many philanthropic organizations were willing to provide funding for Black schools, their goal was to keep African Americans at a subordinate status in society, by funding schools that provided vocational and industrial training, instead of a liberal arts education. In fact, according to Anderson (1988), both White northerners and White southerners "insisted on a second class education to prepare Blacks for subordinate roles in the . . . economy" (p. 92). As Ferguson (2000) wrote, "Segregated schools were organized on the assumption that White students were entitled to a better education than Black students. Black students were not being educated to compete with Whites for jobs in the adult world of work" (p. 18). In spite of this fact, there was still opposition to Black schools.

After the Civil War, the Ku Klux Klan launched numerous attacks on Black schools and churches in the South (Fleming, 1976). Whereas White opponents did not succeed in destroying or shutting down all Black schools, they did succeed in ensuring that most African Americans would receive an inferior education through the curriculum, quality of school facilities, and materials, such as outdated and worn textbooks that were passed down from White schools that no longer needed them. As a result, during the 1930s, Carter G. Woodson, an African-American historian, concluded that most African Americans at that time were being "miseducated," because their formal education did not empower them to become independent thinkers, nor did it empower them religiously, politically, or economically. In *The Miseducation of the Negro* (Woodson, 1933), Woodson stated that the public school system taught African Americans that they were inferior to Whites, to despise their own race, and in the case of higher education, to separate them from the "masses" of African Americans. One of Woodson's greatest criticisms, however, was that the school system had failed to teach African Americans how to improve their socioeconomic status.

Twenty years after Woodson's indictment of the education system was published, the inferior status of Black schools received national attention. In 1954, the U.S. Supreme Court ordered the desegregation of public schools. In *Brown v. Board of Education of Topeka, Kansas,* the court ruled that separate but equal facilities for people of color were unconstitutional. Prior to this time, for the most part, African Americans and Latinos in urban communities and southern states had been relegated to segregated schools. These schools were not only separate from those that Whites attended, but they were unequal in many ways, including the quality of the school facilities, supplies, instructional materials, and textbooks. Hence, the court ruling held the promise of a better day for students of color. In fact, shortly after the ruling, the *Topeka Daily Capital* called it "a beacon of decency" and "the most important civil rights decision by the high court in this century" (Cray, Kotler, & Beller, 2003, p. 291). In *Simple Justice,* Kluger (1975) put it more bluntly, stating, "At a stroke, the Justices had severed the remaining cords of *de facto* slavery. The Negro could no longer be fastened with the status of official pariah" (p. 749).

Twelve years after the Supreme Court ruling in *Brown vs. Board of Education,* "The Coleman Report," a document that became widely quoted and that had far-reaching consequences, was published. The report that Coleman et al. produced, *Equality of Educational Opportunity,* revealed numerous important details about the public school system. One of the findings was that the majority of African American and White students were still attending "racially separate schools," despite the fact that "Blacks in desegregated schools did slightly better on . . . cognitive tests than Blacks in segregated schools" (Riordan, 1997, p. 115). The report also stated that school effects, such as curricula, teacher characteristics, and facilities, did not have a strong impact on how well students performed on tests, but "The one characteristic that displayed a consistent influence on test performance was the socioeconomic context of the school" (Riordan, 1997, p. 115). Two of the most surprising conclusions were that students' "home background and attitudes had the largest effects on their achievement . . . and very little difference was found between schools" (Riordan, 1997, p. 115). However, "among Blacks, Puerto Ricans, Indians, and Chicanos . . . the effects of school are actually greater than the effects of the home. Moreover, they are quite substantial. . . . It thus becomes clear that this between school difference is large for minorities" (Riordan, 1997, pp. 118–119).

In the aftermath of the "Coleman Report," numerous education reforms followed. However, the majority of those reforms failed to make widespread and comprehensive improvements in the schooling experiences of students of color. Today, a half century after the Supreme Court's historic ruling in *Brown vs. Board of Education*, the halcyon promises of equal education have eluded countless African American and Latino public school students. Inequality of educational opportunity continues to be pervasive in many schools, particularly those that are heavily attended by poor students of color.

One of the most obvious manifestations of the unequal schooling is the fact that the Black–White achievement gap persists. The National Assessment of Educational Progress (NAEP), the nation's oldest "report card," has repeatedly shown that African American fourth, eighth, and twelfth graders' reading, mathematics, science, and other scores trail those of their White counterparts, and often, even those of other students of color. For example, during 1998 and 2002, African American and Hispanic fourth graders had lower NAEP reading scores on average than White and Asian fourth graders. In 1998 and 2002, all non-White eighth graders in the major reporting groups had lower reading scores on average than White eighth graders, but African American and Latino students had significantly lower scores. There were similar reading results for twelfth graders. NAEP average reading scores for fourth, eighth, and twelfth grade as a function of race/ethnicity and year of test administration are shown in Fig. 9.1. In fact, for both years under review, African Americans had the lowest reading scores of any of the major racial/ethnic groups. NAEP mathematics (see Fig. 9.2) and science (see Fig. 9.3) scores revealed similar patterns for fourth, eighth, and twelfth graders, showing that African American and

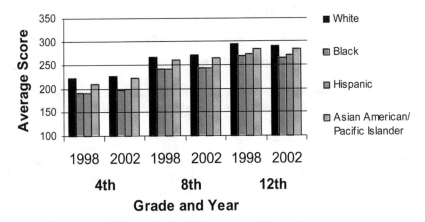

FIG. 9.1. 2002 and 1998 NAEP National Public Average Reading Scale scores by grade and race/ethnicity. *Source:* National Center for Education Statistics http://nces.ed.gov/nationsreportcard

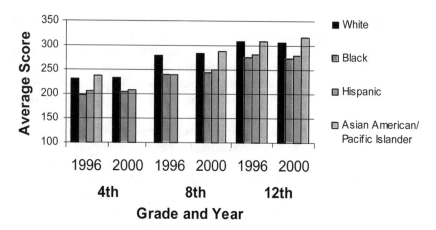

FIG. 9.2.   2000 and 1996 NAEP National Public Average Math Scale scores
by grade and race/ethnicity. *Source:* National Center for Education Statistics
http://nces.ed.gov/nationsreportcard

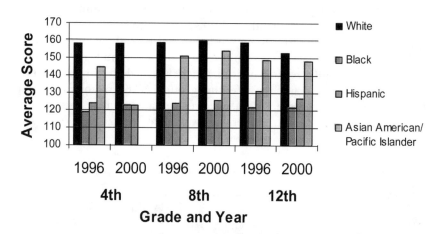

FIG. 9.3.   2000 and 1996 NAEP National Public Average Science Scale scores
by grade and race/ethnicity. *Source:* National Center for Education Statistics
http://nces.ed.gov/nationsreportcard

Hispanic students on average had lower scores than Whites and Asians, and
in several cases, African Americans had the lowest average scores of all
groups (National Center for Education Statistics, 2003).

   These NAEP results suggest that an alarmingly high percentage of African American and Latino students are already in danger of school failure
and of being relegated to impoverished or low-wage futures as early as
fourth grade. One reason is that good reading skills are a prerequisite for

success in all other academic subjects (Chall, 1967; Flesch, 1955; Thompson, 2000a, 2000b). A second reason is that mathematics and science are important "gatekeeping" subjects for college admission and socioeconomic advancement (Drew, 1996). In the case of African-American boys, the finding of early school failure has been reiterated in the research of Kunjufu (1985, 1990), who used the term "fourth grade failure syndrome" to describe their predicament.

Numerous theories have been offered to explain the causes of the Black–White achievement gap (Thompson, 2004). Many researchers have argued that the gap is caused by various school effects, such as teacher quality, tracking, the curriculum, teacher expectations, grade inflation (Thompson, 2002), overcrowded classrooms, and a lack of instructional materials and supplies (Oakes & Rogers, 2002). Research shows that there is a positive association between student achievement and teacher quality. In fact, the U.S. Department of Education (2000) found that teacher quality is the most important "in school" factor affecting student achievement. Independent researchers such as Chall (1967), Drew (1996), Haycock (1998), and others have found that "good teaching really does matter." In spite of this positive impact on student achievement, many students of color continue to attend schools in which their teachers are unqualified or underqualified (Ingersoll, 1999; Quality Counts, 2000; Thompson, 2000a, 2000b, 2004; U.S. Department of Education, 2000, 2002). In the report, *Meeting the Highly Qualified Teachers Challenge*, the U.S. Department of Education (2002) stated "Ever since the publication of the Coleman report, studies have consistently documented the important connection between a teacher's verbal and cognitive abilities and student achievement. Teachers' verbal ability appears to be especially important at the elementary level, perhaps because this is when children typically learn to read" (U.S. Department of Education, 2002, p. 7). The report also stated "More recent studies suggest that subject-matter background knowledge can also have a positive effect on student performance. Research has generally shown that high school math and science teachers who have a major in the subjects they teach elicit greater gains from their students than out-of-field teachers . . ." (U.S. Department of Education, 2002, p. 8). Despite the importance of having highly qualified teachers, the report concluded that students attending high poverty schools were more likely than those in low-poverty schools to have underqualified teachers. In other words, the students who were most in need of quality teaching in order to use the educational system for socioeconomic mobility, were the least likely to have highly qualified teachers.

The common practice of "tracking" students into high and low, and vocational, basic, and college preparatory academic tracks has also been implicated as a cause of the achievement gap and an example of inequality of educational opportunity for African American and Latino students (Ferguson, 2000; Hacker, 1992; Oakes, 1999; Oakes & Rogers, 2002; Thompson, 2002, 2003d, 2004). As a result, African Americans and Latinos are more likely to be overrepresented in Special Education courses and underrepresented in higher level academic tracks (Hacker, 1992; Kunjufu, 1985; Oakes, 1999; Thompson, 2002, 2003d, 2004). Lower level track students often receive an inferior curriculum and are often subjected to low teacher expectations. In *African American Teens Discuss Their Schooling Experiences,* Thompson (2002) used qualitative and quantitative data to present a comprehensive picture of the K–12 schooling experiences of African-American seniors in seven high schools. A recurring theme was that students who had been placed in Special Education classes tended to have more negative schooling experiences than those who were placed in Gifted and Talented Education (G.A.T.E.) classes during elementary school. Thompson said that "students who were placed in G.A.T.E. . . . appeared to be chosen for success" (Thompson, 2002, p. 163). Moreover, Thompson (2002) wrote:

> Being chosen for the G.A.T.E. program appears to benefit African American students in that they receive a better quality of instruction. . . . However, it is problematic because the low number of African American students who are in G.A.T.E., Advanced Placement, and College Preparatory classes at the high school level causes students to experience culture shock. (p. 163)

Because G.A.T.E. and other college preparatory courses are overtly designed to prepare students for college, the underrepresentation of African American and Latino students in these high-level academic tracks are directly related to their underrepresentation at four-year colleges and universities. A related problem is that in many predominantly Latino and African American high schools, there is a paucity of Advanced Placement courses (Dupuis, 1999). The converse tends to be true in predominantly White schools, resulting in what some researchers have found to be an unfair advantage for White students. For this reason, the American Civil Liberties Union (ACLU) has filed a lawsuit against the California Department of Education (Dupuis, 1999).

An issue related to academic tracking is the mathematics preparation that students receive. Mathematics course-taking patterns have been linked to college enrollment. Students who take higher level mathematics courses are more likely to be prepared for admission to four-year colleges and universities. The problem is that, as in many other cases, African American and Latino students are less likely than Whites and Asians to be enrolled in the higher level mathematics courses that are prerequisites for college (Drew, 1996). Thompson (2002, 2003d) described numerous complaints from African-American students and parents about negative messages that they inferred from mathematics teachers. These negative messages often served as deterrents to the students' mathematics achievement.

A third problem is grade inflation. Many students who earn high grades find that they have not been adequately prepared to pass standardized tests, such as the SAT and ACT, which are required for admission to many colleges and universities (Thompson, 2002, 2004). In *African American Teens Discuss Their Schooling Experiences*, Thompson (2002) wrote, "Students also said that in some classes all they had to do was show up to receive a passing grade" (p. 163). In describing a high school that she attended, Destiny, a senior who was interviewed for Thompson's study, stated, ". . . the education isn't that good . . . because I didn't try at that school and I still made a 3.8 gpa. The teachers know that the students don't do anything, but they'll still let them slide on by" (Thompson, 2002, p. 8). Several parents who were interviewed for *What African American Parents Want Educators to Know* (Thompson, 2003d) made similar comments. For example, Peggy, a mother of several school-age children, remarked, "A lot of Black kids don't succeed because of math. Do you know, I did not learn math until I went to a community college? Yet, I graduated from high school with a 3.3 grade point average" (Thompson, 2003d, p. 6). Another parent, Trishina, complained about the widespread grade inflation in middle schools and high schools. She said, "They're just letting them go through the system and not really working with them. . . . One teacher told me that my son wasn't comprehending what he was reading and didn't know what he was doing, but she gave him an 'A' " (Thompson, 2003d, p. 98).

Another example of how inequality of educational opportunity continues to be perpetuated in schools is that in high-poverty and high-minority schools, students often lack the materials and supplies that they need and are placed in overcrowded classrooms. The U.S. Department of Education (2001b) reported that high-minority and high-poverty schools are more likely than low-minority and low-poverty schools to be more than 25% overcrowded. Oakes and Rogers (2002) argued that a lack of instructional materials and overcrowded classrooms are among the reasons why many students of color underperform on standardized tests. Thus, instead of blaming "victims" for their poor academic performance, they blamed the system that perpetuates inequality of educational opportunity.

CONCLUSION

The attainment of a college degree or multiple degrees has been linked to more prestige and higher salaries. For many African Americans, especially those from lower socioeconomic backgrounds, a college degree can be a ticket out of poverty. *Getting Ready to Pay for College*, a report that was recently issued by the U.S. Department of Education (2003), indicated that the majority of sixth to twelfth graders from each major racial/ethnic group in the study and their parents believed the students would attend college. Among the African-American participants, 94% of the students and 96% of the parents stated that the students planned to pursue a postsecondary education. The report also revealed that African-American students "were more likely than White students to discuss such issues as academic requirements, college costs, and financial aid with their parents or teachers and counselors" (p. 54).

The strong desire of African-American students and parents for students to use higher education as a means of improving their lives also surfaced in two of Thompson's studies. In *African American Teens Discuss Their Schooling Experiences*, the majority of the students who participated in the interview phase of the study said that they planned to attend college. In *What African American Parents Want Educators to Know* (Thompson, 2003d), 91% of the parents and guardians who completed the questionnaire for the study said that their children planned to attend college and 74% said that they talked to their children regularly about the importance of attending college. For example, one mother said, "I try to let (my children) know how important it is to go to college. My daughter wants to be a lawyer. I try to let them know if they further their education they can be what they want to be" (p. 184). Another mother said, "I want them to have the best. I want them to be the best that they can be. My mom wanted me to have more than she had. I want my kids to have more than I have" (p. 180). A third mother said, "All of them better be going to college, because that is something I want them to do to educate themselves in order to get better paying jobs" (p. 185).

Like May and Francine—the single mothers who were described in the introduction of this chapter—many of the African-American parents believed that education would provide their children with more opportunities and options than they had had. Unfortunately, these parents seemed unaware that numerous problems with the K–12 education system itself could make the attainment of a college degree difficult, if not unlikely, for their children. In fact, in spite of these mothers' high hopes that their children would attain a postsecondary education, numerous deterrents decrease the likelihood that their dream will become a reality. The examples of inequality of educational opportunity that have been described in this chapter that are prevalent in countless public schools create formidable barriers for African American and Latino children throughout the nation. Moreover, there is a great probability that these mothers' children will end up not attending college at all or attending community colleges, which have extremely low transfer rates to four-year institutions. Lower academic track placements, a nonrigorous curriculum, underqualified teachers, inadequate instructional supplies and materials, and attending overcrowded schools result in a lack of adequate preparation for admission to four-year colleges and universities. Furthermore, often African-American students who are admitted to four-year institutions are placed in remedial courses, which increases the probability that they will never attain a degree.

Recently released data from the U.S. Census Bureau indicate that there is a pressing need for educational and societal barriers that are deterrents to the socioeconomic mobility of African Americans to be eliminated. A 2003 U.S. Census Bureau press release revealed several disconcerting details about poverty in the United States. The details included the facts that in 2002, income declined for all racial and ethnic groups except for non-Hispanic Whites, and although the poverty rate did not increase for most groups, it did increase for African Americans (U.S. Census Bureau, 2003). Because African Americans continue to be disproportionately represented among the families living in poverty, factors that inhibit their socioeconomic mobility must become national priorities for educators and policymakers. Both groups must make improving the public school system, and eradicating the "savage inequalities" in schools that Kozol (1991) described, major priorities.

The Bush Administration has already attempted to make closing the achievement gap a national priority with the passage of the No Child Left Behind Act (NCLB) (U.S. Department of Education, 2001a). One result has been that some school districts have already fired many noncredentialed teachers. However, although NCLB sounds good on paper, like previous education reforms it may be unsuccessful in helping the public school students who have traditionally been shortchanged academically. Systemic issues, such as tracking, grade inflation, insufficient and inadequate instructional materials, overcrowded classrooms, low teacher expectations, teacher apathy in predominantly minority schools, cultural mismatches between White teachers and students of color (Thompson, 2004), and NCLB's overreliance on standardized test scores are additional problems that must be tackled. Until these and other problems that contribute to inequality of educational opportunity are eradicated, countless African Americans and Latinos will remain unable to use the education system—one that continues to prepare them for second class citizenship and low wage futures—for socioeconomic advancement. Moreover, African American mothers like Francine and May will dream in vain that their children's financial futures will be better than their own.

REFERENCES

Anderson, C. (1994). *Black labor, White wealth: The search for power and economic justice.* Bethesda, MD: PowerNomics Corporation of America.

Anderson, J. D. (1988). *The education of Blacks in the South, 1860–1935.* Chapel Hill: University of North Carolina Press.

Chall, J. S. (1967). *Learning to read: The great debate.* New York: McGraw-Hill.

Cose, E. (1993). *The rage of a privileged class.* New York: HarperCollins.

Cray, E., Kotler, J., & Beller, M. (2003). *American datelines: Major news stories from colonial times to the present.* Chicago: University of Illinois Press.

Davie, M. R. (1949). *Negroes in American society.* New York: McGraw-Hill.

Drew, D. (1996). *Aptitude revisited: Rethinking math and science education for America's next century.* Baltimore, MD: Johns Hopkins University Press.

DuBois, W. E. B. (1935). *Black reconstruction in America: 1860–1880.* New York: Atheneum.

Dupuis, J. (1999). California lawsuit notes unequal access to AP courses. *Rethinking Schools Online, 14*(1). Available online at www.rethinkingschools.org

Ferguson, A. A. (2000). *Bad boys: Public schools in the making of Black masculinity.* Ann Arbor: University of Michigan Press.

Fleming, J. E. (1976). *The lengthening shadow of slavery.* Washington, DC: Howard University Press.

Flesch, R. (1955). *Why Johnny can't read and what you can do about it.* New York: Harper.

Greene, H. W. (1946). *Holders of doctorates among American Negroes.* Boston: Meador.

Hacker, A. (1992). *Two nations: Black and White, separate, hostile, unequal.* New York: Ballantine.

Haycock, K. (1998). Good teaching matters: How well-qualified teachers can close the gap. *Thinking K–16, 3*(2), 1–2.

Ingersoll, R. M. (1999). The problem of underqualified teachers in American secondary schools. *Educational Researcher, 28*(2), 26–37.

Johnson, C. (1938). *The Negro college graduate.* New York: Negro Universities Press.

Kluger, R. (1975). *Simple justice.* New York: Random House.

Kozol, J. (1991). *Savage inequalities.* New York: Harper Perennial.

Kunjufu, J. (1985). *Countering the conspiracy to destroy Black boys.* Chicago: African American Images.

Kunjufu, J. (1990). *Countering the conspiracy to destroy Black boys* (Vol. III). Chicago: African American Images.

Litwack, L. F. (1961). *North of slavery: The Negro in the free states, 1790–1862.* Chicago: University of Chicago Press.

National Center for Education Statistics. (2003). Available online at http://nces.ed.gov/nationsreportcard

Oakes, J. (1999). Limiting students' school success and life chances: The impact of tracking. In A. Ornstein & L. Behar-Horenstein (Eds.), *Contemporary issues in curriculum* (2nd ed., pp. 224–237). Needham Heights, MA: Allyn & Bacon.

Oakes, J., & Rogers, J. (2002). Diploma penalty misplaces blame. *Los Angeles Times,* October 8, M2.

Quality Counts. (2000). *Education Week,* XIX(18).

Riordan, C. (1997). *Equality and achievement: An introduction to the sociology of education.* Reading, MA: Longman, Addison Wesley.

Thompson, G. (1999). What the numbers really mean: African-American underrepresentation at the doctoral level. *Journal of College Student Retention Research, Theory & Practice, 1*(1), 23–40.

Thompson, G. (2000a). California educators discuss the reading crisis. *The Educational Forum, 64, Spring,* 229–234.

Thompson, G. (2000b). Stories from the field: What prospective and beginning secondary teachers learned from working with struggling third and fourth grade readers. *Educational Horizons,* Fall, 19–25.

Thompson, G. (2002). *African American teens discuss their schooling experiences.* Westport, CT: Bergin Garvey-Greenwood.

Thompson, G. (2003a). For children of color, business cannot continue as usual in schools. *Urban Review, 35*(1), 1–6.

Thompson, G. (2003b). No parent left behind: Strengthening ties between educators and African American parents. *Urban Review, 35*(1), 7–23.

Thompson, G. (2003c). Predicting African American parents' and guardians' satisfaction with teachers and public schools. *Journal of Educational Research, 96*(5), 277–285.

Thompson, G. (2003d). *What African American parents want educators to know.* Westport, CT: Praeger-Greenwood.

Thompson, G. (2004). *Through ebony eyes: What teachers need to know about African American students.* San Francisco, CA: Jossey-Bass.

U.S. Census Bureau. (1995). *Mothers who receive AFDC payments: Fertility and socioeconomic characteristics.* Washington, DC: U.S. Department of Commerce, Economics and Statistics Administration.

U.S. Census Bureau. (1997a, September). *America's children at risk.* Washington, DC: U.S. Department of Commerce, Economics and Statistics Administration.

U.S. Census Bureau. (1997b, September). *Children with single parents: How they fare.* Washington, DC, U.S. Department of Commerce: Economics and Statistics Administration.

U.S. Census Bureau. (2001). *Statistical abstract of the United States.* Available online at http://www.census.gov/hhes/www/img/incpov01/fig08.jpg

U.S. Census Bureau. (2002). *United States Department of Commerce News.* www.census.gov/pressrelease/www/2002/cb02-124.html

U.S. Census Bureau. (2003). *Poverty, income see slight changes.* Washington, DC: U.S. Department of Commerce, Economics and Statistics Administration.

U.S. Department of Education. (2000). *Eliminating barriers to improving teaching.* Washington, DC.

U.S. Department of Education. (2001a). *No child left behind.* Washington, DC: Office of the Secretary.

U.S. Department of Education. (2001b). *The condition of education.* Washington, DC: National Center for Educational Statistics Office of Educational Research and Improvement.

U.S. Department of Education. (2002). *Meeting the highly qualified teacher challenge: The secretary's annual report on teacher quality.* Washington, DC: Office of Postsecondary Education.

U.S. Department of Education. (2003). *Getting ready to pay for college: What students and their parents know about the cost of college tuition and what they are doing to find out.* Washington, DC: Institute of Education Sciences.

Woodson, C. G. (1933). *The miseducation of the Negro.* Washington, DC: Associated Publishers.

Chapter 10

The Limits of Connectivity:
Technology and 21st-Century Life

Maggie Jackson
Columnist, New York City

Tricia Shiland, owner of a maternity evening wear company in New York City, routinely gets messages at her office about teen pop stars, No. 2 pencils, and Beanie Babies. But it isn't spam. Sitting in a sunlit office crammed with sparkling dresses and boxes of fabric samples, Shiland carries on a running high-tech conversation with her 10-year-old daughter after school, on the evenings that Shiland works late, and on the weekends Devon spends with her dad. Using fax, email, instant message and phone, they catch up on the day or on Devon's current wish list, and make plans—sometimes just for a face-to-face talk later. "It's become such a central part of our existence, the computers, the IM," says Shiland. "It's changed our lives."[1]

The technology revolution is changing the way we work and play, and how we relate to others and to the wider world. We can make cell phone calls on the beach, on the ski lift—or from the office. We work at home, from any room in the house, and we eat, play, shop, exercise, and make most of our friends at work. In an age when families spend much of their day apart, spouses trade emails, and then call each other's cell phones on the commute home to cobble together supper menus. Traveling parents read a good-night book by phone to children tucked in bed thousands of miles away, or, like Tricia Shiland, instant message their children when they come home from school. The changes wrought by technology are so rapid

---

[1]Parts of this chapter were adapted from the author's book (2002) and April 2003 article in *Working Mother* magazine. Unless otherwise noted, quotations are from author interviews.

and so deep that we are often left marveling—and wondering. What are we gaining and losing as we move into this new era? How can we best use technology to improve our lives, and ensure that we control our gadgets—and not allow them to control us? How does technology affect the balance between work and home?

Undoubtedly, the impact of mobile technology on 21st-century life will not be thoroughly understood or even realized for decades, perhaps generations. In the early days of the telephone, some people assumed that it was an English-language device (Fischer, 1992). Perhaps in 100 years, the notion of parent–child togetherness via instant message will seem equally naïve. Still, it is crucial that we begin to study the social impact of technology to better understand and control its consequences. New technologies tend to usher in as many problems as they solve, according to historian Howard P. Segal. "If, as in the significant case of the automobile, modern technology solved a number of problems, social as well as technical, from the outset it *simultaneously* (italics added) bred or helped breed several others, social and technical alike"(Segal, 1994, p. 30). Just as Americans once struggled to come to terms with the railroad, the telegraph, automated factories, and the telephone, so must we seek to comprehend the power and the limits of the technologies of our day.

Consider our experience of place. What we do does not necessarily connect anymore with where we are. Our homes are being transformed into permeable workplaces, while the comforts of home are often found at work. Who can say "where" Tricia Shiland's daughter is? She is both physically at home on her computer, and intellectually at her mother's office, bubbling with after-school chatter. Mobility is the landscape of 21st-century life, the new stage upon which our days are played. Technology changes our relationship to boundaries and to place.

Moreover, technology is beginning to alter our relations to others. Wired families, for instance, are living out more of their lives *via* technology—on-air so to speak—and in so doing, creating a kind of "separate togetherness." Technology is the tool for building a new room in the house, but a moveable, multilevel space. "It really does add a layer of electronic space that becomes very, very real and very vibrant," says Andrea Saveri, director of the Emerging Technologies Program at the Institute of the Future in Menlo Park, California. "Anywhere families go, they can jump into a shared space."

Again, the ultimate repercussions are not clear, but the implications and possibilities are enormous. Most families do not see high-tech connections as replacing face-to-face togetherness—what MIT professor Sherry Turkle calls the "gold standard" of human relations. But how much do virtual relations "count"? The fact that families are living out more and more moments "on-air" means they are concluding, at least implicitly, that virtual relations are a valued alternative to face-to-face. Still, the issue is muddied by the fact that virtual ties co-exist alongside face-to-face, and the delicate balance between them is evolving, even as the boundaries between them blur. For example, if you are chatting with your son by cell phone while he is instant-messaging his friends, does that count as family time? Our ability to be in multiple places at once redefines togetherness and the notion of "paying attention" in unexpected ways. The "always-on" nature of virtual relationships adds another variable to the mix.

ISSUES OF PLACE: BLURRING HOME AND WORK

Today, mobile technologies are helping to create a new room in the house, a flexible, accessible, mobile space for relations. Family life is becoming as portable as the gadgets that drive this trend. Just as we have erased our tethers to *place*, so are we able to tear down boundaries between *people*. The potential for togetherness and closeness is compounded. At the same time, the limits of connectivity begin to emerge. Togetherness is not only disembodied, but fragmented. Although this chapter focuses on family life, the implications for work relationships are enormous. Trends surrounding mobile technology will shape the future of both work and private life, and the growing integration between them. But to begin to understand these changes, it is important to take a look at our evolving experience of place.

There is an apartment in New York City owned by a foreign currency trader, who follows the markets night and day (Jackson, 2002). He has installed more than a dozen video monitors in his 1500-square-foot space. There are monitors in the kitchen, the bedroom, the living room. One is set in the arm of a sofa, so the trader can lift a pillow and have a peek at the yen or franc as soon as he wakes up from a nap. Another monitor hangs upside down and inverted in the bathroom, so he can watch while shaving in the morning. His home, in other words, is a high-tech trading room, a home office writ large.

This home seems futuristic, or at the least reminiscent of cutting-edge Manhattan or Los Angeles spaces. But the trader is not all that ahead of his time, and he is not really that different from many Americans. Workers from secretaries to CEOs are checking email on Sunday nights, doing telework and turning their homes into workplaces. They are rapidly tearing down the boundaries of work and home, largely through the adoption of mobile technology. This is all too apparent in the design and furnishing of homes today.

The most popular piece of home office furniture is the computer armoire, a resurrection of the large chests and cupboards used in homes before built-in closets became standard. Two hundred years later, we are re-adopting a symbol of domestic portability, this time for our work. Philippe Starck has designed a sofa that helps bring work into the living room: it can be ordered with side and back tables replete with electrical outlets and a phone jack (Shaw, 1999). With the growth in wireless networks, more people are toting their work from bedroom to kitchen, perching almost anywhere to work and connect. The function of a room may not have much significance in the future, just as the boundaries between home and office are disappearing.

In coming decades, the lines will only blur further. Few people will worry about hiding PCs in armoires or which sofa has the laptop plug. Closets and clothing, eyeglasses and kitchen counters, all will *be* computers. Intel is working on a program to incorporate a tiny radio into every microprocessor the company ships in 7 years—a plan that could turn personal computers, cars, digital cameras, even clothing and plants into objects that send and receive data (Bolande, 2002). Scientists at MIT's Media Lab, which has more than 170 corporate sponsors, are working on innovations that will allow people to work or surf wherever they are sitting, walking, or eating. In this new era, will our shoes and tables, along with our pagers and cell phones, beep and ring at us each evening?

This way of life not only changes our relationship to place, it changes the perimeters of private time. In pre-Industrial times, farmers and craftsmen worked most everyday of the week, blending home and work in the same spaces. Yet the natural rhythms of sun and season, along with religious and community dictates, gave people shared cues to rest. As work moved away from home, machines and electric light severed people from these natural cues, but in the past century we gradually adopted weekends and vacations as times of rest. Now technology is chipping away at weekends and vacations, yet the sun and seasons hold little sway over our lives. There is no unanimity on when to rest, no set day of the week, no annual ritual of the work-free summer vacation. Seventy percent of employees must be accessible to their jobs at least sometimes during their off-hours (Galinsky, Bond, & Kim, 2001).

Furthermore, work is not the only portable sphere of our lives. Home is a moveable feast. We have evolved from the occasional personal phone call snatched at our desks, the occasional Christmas card posted in the office mailbox, to a sort of wholesale importation of domestic life into the workplace. Thanks to a range of perks and benefits in recent years, many corporations have evolved into a kind of new American neighborhood where you can eat, play, shop, exercise, meet your future spouse, and make most of your friends. Workers turn to their employer for the comforts of home, and keep their noses to the grindstone on weekends from their back deck. This does not mean that work and life have neatly switched places. Rather, home and work are becoming truly portable. There is no longer a place for everything and everything is no longer in its place.

But what happens when we are not only working at home, and "homeing" at work and doing it all on the road, on vacations, anywhere we go? In many ways, in loosening our connections to place, we are becoming increasingly nomadic. The work of anthropologist Peter Wilson, who has studied modern hunter–gatherer societies, deserves consideration as a way of understanding our present shift toward a mobile life (Wilson, 1988). Nomadic societies navigate the world primarily through the prism of focus, writes Wilson in *The Domestication of the Human Species*. Boundaries are hazy and relationships are flexible and fluid, with a great deal of individual self-sufficiency expected. Relationships are often personal, not formal or rule-governed. In contrast, the creation of permanent settlements, starting about 15,000 years ago, radically changed people's outlook. Such settlements created repetitive experiences of time. Crops were planted, harvested, replanted. Comings and goings happened again and again. The house was an anchor of the universe. In ancient Greece, a man who did not own a house could not take part "in the affairs of the world because he had no location in it which was properly his own," writes Hannah Arendt (1998, pp. 29–30).

Our society looks more and more like a system based on "focus," not boundaries. Our relationships at work, home, and in the community are increasingly fluid, in large part due to the influence of technology. Think of the demise of the traditional family, and the rise in free agent careers and mobility in work. In the Internet age, you can work with, love, learn about, and relate to people without even knowing where they live. No matter where you are, your day is likely to be increasingly shaped by what you focus on: the TV, pager, email, cell phone, the road ahead, a cubicle-mate. Industrialization marked the zenith of a society of boundary-making, while the Computer Age propels us into a world navigated by focus.

This mobility helps shatter old stereotypes of home and work. After all, boundaries that cannot be crossed are prisons. Today, good workers can be trusted to do the job, even out of sight of their boss. The locale matters less and less. Work and private life are becoming integrated. Yet this new boundary-less, nomadic life has its costs. When the home becomes a permeable workspace, we risk losing home as a place of intimacy and refuge. When the workplace becomes our primary source of friends and emotional support, we forget that *power* colors such relationships, not unconditional caring. In making home and work portable, we gain flexibility, yet risk making ourselves "homeless" in an emotional sense. We gain freedom, but risk cutting ourselves adrift.

MAINTAINING FAMILY CONNECTEDNESS

It is wonderful to be *at* home in a world that is growing less local and comprehensible—to cuddle up in an armchair at Starbucks, to grab a nuked dinner in the car on the way to an exercise class, to count on the workplace for support. Maybe someday society will be completely nomadic and mobile. But for now, I do not believe that we are ready for a boundary-less society defined by "focus," where home and private life are just a series of moments snatched along the road—in the office, the hotel room, the car. We still need to preserve times and places for stability and privacy by redrawing some boundaries around our closest relations and ourselves. We need to be anchored in a mobile world, especially as our relationships become increasingly place-less. Just as work and home are becoming portable, so are relationships becoming both virtual and "anytime-anywhere." Increasingly, we are bumping up against both the potential rootlessness and facelessness of life in the Information Age.

Lisa Ross, a public relations executive, arrived at her 4-year-old son's preschool class one Friday to watch his class participate in a candle-lighting ceremony, only to get a call about a client crisis. She contacted her husband, who rushed over to take her place in the audience. "Without technology, I might not have been able to reach him so quickly, and my client might not have been able to reach me so quickly," says Ross, president of RBB Public Relations in Miami, Florida.

Last-minute solutions and other logistics comprise the bulk of the communications that many families share via technology, says Charles Darrah, an anthropology professor at San Jose State University who has studied wired families for more than a decade. While seemingly trivial in nature, the chats allow "just in time" family management. "They would check in with each other all through the day," says Darrah, describing the families he has studied. "It wasn't about planning. The planning occurred face to face. It was more to make sure that the plans were still on."

As well, many wired parents find instantaneous connectivity highly comforting. They not only feel that technology provides a safety net when things go awry, but it gives them a quick dose of family life in an era when families are separated routinely from dawn to dusk and longer. Regular business travelers, who make up 20% of adults, average six nights away from home a year, according to the Travel Industry Association of America (2001). In an age of political and economic upheaval, a note of uncertainty invariably accompanies such separations.

Teresa Dunn-Thordarson, the chief financial officer for Alvaka Networks, a Huntington Beach, California computer networking company she founded with her husband Oli Thordarson, prizes being able to reach her husband when they are on the go. "It's not so much what you say, it's knowing that you're connected, that gives me peace of mind," says Dunn-Thordarson, mother of a 3-year-old, a 6-year-old, and an 8-year-old who carries a walkie-talkie when he's bicycling in the neighborhood. She regularly emails her husband by Blackberry when he is traveling for business. "I love you too!," she once wrote. "We miss you. What time do you get home tomorrow? The kids had a good first day of school. I'm sure they will have lots to tell you. Teresa. XOXO."

In forging this connectedness, wired families are doing far more than just checking in and trading grocery lists. Families are sharing important moments, and in so doing, living out more of their lives *via* technology—on-air so to speak. Life takes place in the new virtual room. Mara G. Aspinall, a biotechnology executive, and her two sons went over their final report cards last spring—by fax and phone. She was away on a business trip, and the boys, ages 9 and 10, faxed the grades to her hotel and then called her to discuss them. "That was an important milestone, sharing your end-of-the-year report card," says Aspinall, who travels several days a month as president of two operating divisions of Genzyme Corp., based in Cambridge, Massachusetts. "You wouldn't want to miss that, or hear about it later."

In future, the ease and allure of this "separate togetherness" will be greatly increased by the spread of such technologies, and because innovations will boost the depth and visual power of the virtual experience. About 51% of American adults, or 143 million people, have cell phones, compared with 20% in 1997. Partly thanks to the introduction of family calling plans late last year, nearly 40% of children ages 12 to 19 have cell phones, about double the number than in 1999, according to Teenage Research Unlimited. About 11% of American adults—or more than 20 million people—own a PDA (Personal Digital Assistant), cell phone, and a computer or laptop, according to the Consumer Electronics Association. Wired families are in the minority, but their numbers are growing.

In just a few years, the clunky web of communications of today will give way to a cyber-environment that is complex, portable, individually controlled, and easily shared. Microsoft Corp. just introduced shared browsing that allows people to navigate the Web interactively, and the company is working on an Internet feature that plays back pictures, music, and conversation exchanged by participants in an instant-message conversation. Meanwhile, advances in Internet-based telephoning will change how people communicate, notes sociologist Barry Wellman (2000) of the University of Toronto. Soon people will be able to make multiple phone calls at one time, easily integrate phone, email, and fax, and check an incoming caller's stress level, background, and sincerity levels, he writes.

TECHNOLOGICAL RELATIONSHIP CHALLENGES

Innovations in technologies, however, demand new protocols, a revelation that former Xerox chief scientist John Seely Brown says that people are slow to realize. "The problem is that we think the virtual should have all the same protocols as the physical, as opposed to inventing new types of social cues," says Brown, author of *The Social Life of Information*. "If you do a tremendous amount of teleconferencing, you can't just ask if people agree. You also have to ask if anyone disagrees. In virtual space, the absence of opinion isn't obvious" (Southwick, 2002, p. 46).

Through much trial and error, families are testing what kinds of emotions they want to share "on-air," and exploring how best to use the new tools of family life, just as early users of the telephone worried about whether or not to interrupt family meals to answer a call. They are discovering, just as office workers are, that bare-bones email or text messages easily can be misconstrued. Oli Thordarson once emailed Teresa to ask if she'd mailed a certain check, but unwittingly used language—"What's going on with this?"—that offended her. "We've had some spats that have grown out of email," he recalls.

Sometimes, however, the absence of voice tone or body language turns email and other virtual communications into a preferred medium. Divorced parents, for instance, appreciate the facelessness of electronic exchanges. "Exchanging information through email is a neutral zone," says Dawn Johnston, a trainer with the Texas Department of Health, and a mother and stepmother to five children, ages 10 through 20. Companies that run online family calendars report a loyal client base from divorced families, who use the sites to exchange information from a distance. "These people don't want to talk, and we've provided them with a safe ground where they don't make it ugly for the rest of the family," says an executive from Familytime.com, an online calendar company.

Teens also gravitate to virtual space when uncomfortable topics must be discussed. One in 10 teens, for instance, think that email is the best way to break up with a boyfriend. Virtual apologies and confidences, especially to parents, flow more easily via email from adolescents who are awkward with eye contact and spoken sentiment. "Email has an intimacy and yet some distance," notes MIT professor Sherry Turkle. "It allows a certain distance and privacy and boundaries that sometimes help open up avenues."

Jeffrey S. McQuillen (2003) compares computer-mediated communications to interactions at a costume party. Relations via computer are characterized by "highly selective self-presentation, the manipulation of one's perceived self, and the highly restricted nature of one's self-disclosure clues," writes McQuillen, an assistant professor at the University of Texas. He describes newly formed Internet relationships. Still, his and others' observations on the veiled nature of the Internet help raise important questions about the nature of virtual relations. Are virtual moments pale substitutes or important replacements for face-to-face interactions? Does a string of increasingly "rich" electronic communications help users grow closer over time? At issue is the *quality* of virtual relations.

Just as home and work have not neatly traded places in the Information Age, so face-to-face togetherness is not likely to be entirely eclipsed by virtual communications. People will always come together, for meetings, meals, play, and work. "Technology is simply another tool in a toolbox we use to communicate with each other," says Oli Thordarson. Still, the more we use cell phones and the like to communicate with others, the more we are effectively *assuming* that virtual relations bring us closer, that they have heft, and thus a role in our lives. The question is, do our new tools fulfill those promises? This debate is being carried out quietly in one corner of American life: the divorce courts. In a handful of cases around the country, judges have ordered virtual custody visits, which provide parents with a video-conferenced session with their children (Gardner, 2002). Such experiments imply that virtual visits carry the same weight as face-to-face. Yet the rulings are being fiercely debated, especially by the parents involved. Paul Cleri, a divorced father of three from Massachusetts, took a highly publicized stance on the issue in 2002 when he contested a custody arrangement that includes twice-weekly "virtual visits" with his 5-year-old son and 3-year-old twin daughters. The visits via Webcam are in addition to twice-monthly in-person visits Cleri has with his children, who live in New York state. "It falls very short of a real visit," says Cleri. "I like to pick up the kids and give them hugs and pat Nathanial on the back, that type of thing, put the kids on my shoulders. It's hard to do that with a computer."

Little research exists on the impact of technologies on relationships, but a few initial studies of on-line communications provide some clues to the strengths and pitfalls of this particular type of media. A summary of research, compiled by Cummings of Carnegie Mellon University and others in 2000, concludes that computer-mediated communication, and especially email, "is less valuable for building and sustaining close social relationships than other means, such as face-to-face contact and telephone conversations" (Cummings, Butler, & Kraut, 2002, pp. 103–104). The paper drew from studies of employees at a bank, college students, and new home Internet users.

One interesting finding from the home Internet study was that the frequency of communication was a "significant predictor" of psychological closeness with a non-Internet partner, but not with an Internet partner. "Online relationships are characterized by less communication and are weaker than offline relationships," concludes Cummings and his co-authors, noting that their research does not answer the question of whether online relationships add to or substitute for other connections in life (Cummings et al., 2002, p. 106). Other research shows that extroverts and those with strong social supports increase their face-to-face interactions with friends and family while using the Internet, yet introverts with few social supports decrease such ties (Kraut et al., 2002). Do online relations bring us closer? Early evidence suggests that they sometimes do, but often, they are a pale substitute to face-to-face togetherness.

Yet such direct comparisons of the physical and virtual, especially in relation to just one form of virtual connection, tell only part of the tale. That is because the multitude of tools that create virtual space give us a profound new ability to be in multiple contexts at once. In other words, the new room in the house is not only portable and faceless, but it has no walls. For instance, a mother driving her son across town to baseball practice might be on her cell phone during the trip. Mother and son are technically face-to-face for that half-hour or hour, but are they *together*? Or picture a Dad who is using instant messaging to catch up with his son, who has just returned from school. They are having a real-time, on-line conversation, sharing a moment while physically apart. Now, what if the son is instant messaging two other friends at the same time, while talking to his Dad? What if the Dad is listening to his voicemail, while instant messaging his son? Are they together? Which family is more "together" in these two examples?

CHANGING NATURE OF SOCIAL RELATIONSHIPS

Virtual ties simultaneously co-exist with other connections, both face-to-face and electronic. We can not always assume that an online, real-time conversation *or* a face-to-face, real-time chat takes place one-on-one. The boundaries between physical and virtual togetherness are blurring. "There's a weird notion about how many people you're having in your social agenda, not all of whom are sharing your social milieu," says Naomi Baron (2000), a linguistics professor at American University and author of *Alphabet to Email: How Written English Evolved and Where It's Heading.* This will "radically change our notion of what it means to be 'present' in a social relationship."

As well, mobile technologies inspire a proliferation of social relationships that demand increasing amounts of attention and time. A culture centered on the local involves far fewer social ties than today's global, 24-hour lives, which potentially include thousands, if not millions, of contacts. In the past, people's intercourse with others remained rooted in their neighborhood, notes Barry Wellman (2000). He writes, "They were limited by their footpower in whom they could contact" (Paragraph 7.2). In this century, people gained the ability to travel and communicate across cities and neighborhoods. Then, technologies such as the cell phone detached people from place. British researcher Sadie Plant, founder of the Cybernetic Culture Research Unit at Warwick University in England, notes that numerous contacts lead to fluid relationships in Japanese cell phone users. "The more contacts people have in their phones, the looser those relationships are," says Plant. "People even 10 years older (than the mobile generation) remember having fewer friends but stronger friendships" (Moseley, 2002, p. 32).

In this crowded, permeable, multidimensional virtual world, relationships are increasingly based on snapshots of each other. That is partly because our presence in each other's lives will be narrow and specialized, according to Wellman (2000). "Specialized communities often will afford permeable, shifting sets of participants, with more intense relationships continued by private communication," writes Wellman, echoing Wilson's description of a nomadic society with fluid relationships (paragraph 7.18). This way of life allows people to increase the number and diversity of their social relationships. But there are costs. "The compartmentalization of role-to-role interpersonal life—within the household and workplace as well as within the community—may (mean) that no one knows anyone entirely anymore, breeding alienation and insecurity," writes Wellman (paragraph 7.19). "A person becomes nothing more than the sum of her role-parts." (paragraph 7.19). Togetherness means connecting a slice of a person with a slice of another, all while those people are potentially connecting with others.

As a result, mobile technologies redefine not only what it means to be together, but what it means to *pay attention* to others. Cell phones, instant messaging, email, and other tools allow us to multitask communication with each other, not just the activities of daily life. This national attention deficit syndrome perhaps occurs when a mobile society based on *focus* is mixed with technological tools that produce multidimensional, simultaneous and ever-accelerating snowstorms of communications. "Without boundaries and without *the concept* of the permanent boundary, people are not conceptually locked into their relationships or surroundings," writes Wilson (1988, p. 50). Mobile technologies push the fluidity of nomadic cultures to extremes by liberating people from demands to focus on anyone or anything purely or for more than a bit of time. The implications for relationships are chilling.

Teenagers, for instance, describe their IM conversations as substantially less enjoyable than face-to-face visits or phone calls, yet report that they enjoy instant-messaging in part because it allows them to multitask. "Personally, I like talking to a lot of people at a time," says Amelia, a Pittsburgh-area teen. "It kind of keeps you busy . . . It's kind of boring just talking to one person cause then like . . . you can't talk to anyone else" (Boneva et al., in press). A similar paucity of attention spans can be seen among adults. In the corporate world, business executives are increasingly banning cell phones from meetings, only to find that workers are distracted by wireless laptops or Palm Pilots (Jackson, 2003b). It has become common to see people fiddle with gadgets during performances, presentations, college classes and even while dining with friends. A *Wall Street Journal* film critic attributed declining attendance at foreign films, which are often slower-paced and thoughtful, to Americans' shrinking attention span. U.S. cinema-goers now routinely pull out *and use* cell phones during slow parts of films, noted Joe Morgenstern (2003). In this distractible culture, relationships are likely to be based on knowing very small slivers of each other.

Perhaps that's why technology-users are so reluctant to turn their gadgets off. Could it be that relationships carried out "on-air" are so thin and fragmented that disconnecting (i.e., separating) seems unbearable, particularly when loved ones are involved? Just as the freedom of anytime–anywhere work easily morphs into the mandate of all-the-time work, so the portable family is shifting into an always-on relationship. Wired families, for instance, fire little bursts of communication back and forth so often during the day that they seem bored when they reconnect face-to-face, says Charles Darrah. "In a way, they can never get away from their family. People are always 'on'," he says. "In a strange way, it brings a kind of immediacy to family. They never know when they're going to be 'in' their family."

The yearning for always-on connectivity is prompting many sleepaway camps to get wired—a trend that may change the definition of "leaving" home. No one tracks how many of the country's 2,300 accredited camps allow parents to email children, but a growing number do, printing out the missives and distributing them like letters. (Few camps allow children to email back, mainly due to a scarcity of computers.) Nearly 70% of camps have Web sites, where many camps post up to 100 digital photos daily, according to the American Camping Association. Late postings prompt calls, say camp directors, who are also beginning to see—or rather, hear—cell phones smuggled into care packages. "I've had closing day ceremonies where I'll introduce the person who cooked three meals a day for 70 days and they'll get polite applause," said Steve Baskin, co-owner of Camp Champions, based in Marble Falls, Texas. "I'll introduce my Webmaster, and they'll get a standing ovation. . . . They think, 'This is the person who gave me my child back.'"

Jennifer Seavey is one fan. An English teacher at Thomas Jefferson High School for Science and Technology in Alexandria, Virginia, she became "addicted" to scanning the snapshots posted daily on the Web site of her 17-year-old daughter's camp, Heart O' the Hills in Hunt, Texas. "It was like having a window on her life," said Seavey. "I felt as if I was a part of that day, that I was there with her." Camp director Steve Baskin compares the technology to a "one-way mirror" that allows worried parents to comfort themselves with glimpses of their child's experiences away from the family nest. But the technologies do more than provide parents with an anonymous peek into their child's camp life. Emails, Web photos, and cell phone calls keep connections between parents and children open, almost as if they have never been apart. Increasingly, camp directors are forced to juggle parents' demands for connectedness, with the main aim of camp: providing an experience *away* from home. Roger Popkin, co-owner of Blue Star

Camps in Hendersonville, North Carolina, says most parents do not want to sabotage the sense of independence that children gain at camp, yet parents' desire for connectivity is mounting. "There are a great number of parents who don't use the Web site, who think as we did 30 years ago, who want to hear the stories after the child comes home, but there are fewer and fewer of those," says Popkin, former president of the American Camping Association, "Parents have never been out of the loop. It's that the loop is at a different level of intensity."

Still, families that expect limitless connectivity, in the name of togetherness, ultimately risk threatening the creation of trust and independence, just as employers that applaud high-tech accessibility often wind up leashing employees to work in the name of flexibility. In coming years, the issue will increasingly resonate as families split up to go their separate ways—to camp, on business trips, for jobs that require long-distance commuting, or just for the day—and as technologies grow more rich and more persistent. Satellite navigation technologies, such as GPS, will enable people to both check in with and check *on* their family. Oli Thordarson, for instance, intends to use high-tech advances such as GPS-equipped cell phones to keep a close virtual eye on his son. "He may not be home, but I'll know where he is," says Thordarson. "We'll be able to replicate the route that he took to get there." Thordarson is convinced that technology will enable him to give his son freedom as he grows. Yet his son's independence will certainly come with strings attached.

SUMMARY AND CONCLUSIONS

Today, relationships are increasingly fluid, flexible, and portable, thanks to mobile technologies. Parents track and contact children to a degree unimaginable a generation ago. Husbands and wives make plans and catch up on each other's news all day, anywhere in the world. Employees take work home or on the road and stay fully connected to the information channels of the office. Technology has freed us from the constraints of being in one place or another, and given us a mobile, accessible, and increasingly "rich" virtual space where we gather. We no longer have to sit down, plug in, dial up, and stay put to be connected.

Yet virtual relationships are also potentially fragmented and multidimensional. Carrying out relationships "on-air" perhaps can be likened to watching television in the appliance section of a department store. With 10 screens or more in front of you, the strength of your attention to any one show is diluted. Mobile technologies connect us to many more people at once, and give us the ability to be present in many contexts, effectively blurring the boundaries between face-to-face and virtual moments. In this new room, relationships are based on snapshots of one another. Togetherness and attention to one another are redefined.

In a world of quick and easy communications, limitless connectivity begins to become the norm. Perhaps because togetherness is increasingly experienced in snippets, the idea of a real separation is too frightening to contemplate. High-tech accessibility to the office slides into expectations of anywhere–anytime work. Families apart only for hours communicate incessantly. Parents maintain virtual umbilical cords with children at sleepaway camps and college. Trust and independence, the values inherent in strong relationships, are shelved when separations and togetherness begin to meld.

As we struggle to learn how to use the powerful new technologies of the Computer Age to our best advantage, we are in danger of dragging old ideals of togetherness into a new era, and hobbling technology's potential to give us more flexible and ultimately fulfilling lives. Strict ideals of family togetherness in recent centuries were ultimately impossible to live up to at home, as were rigid expectations of face-time in the Industrial Age workplace. Nor did efforts to live out such ideals guarantee close families or good workers. In turning to always-on connectivity to nurture relationships, we risk using our most powerful new communications tools to uphold outdated ideals. Instead, we should ask whether rigid ideals of togetherness— virtual or face-to-face—are the right yardsticks of success at home or work. Some families can be emotionally close while living apart. Others can suffocate each other—by email.

As well, our first glimpses into the impact of connectivity on 21st-century living clearly show the limits of integrating work and home. By enabling us to live in multiple, simultaneous contexts, technology blurs the boundaries between separation and togetherness, potentially fragmenting and diluting relationships. At the same time, technology equips us to live both at work and at home simultaneously, diluting and fragmenting our attention to either world. Once-rigid boundaries between home and work, self and others, created a world that often lacked flexibility. Yet a boundary-less world is potentially a muddle. Technology fools us into thinking that apartness and togetherness, and that work and home, can be *simultaneous*. But they can't. We must remember that we often need a purity of focus on one world or the other or one person or another, in order to truly *be there* for either.

Finally, a caveat about technology and society: We have much to learn. When you buy a cell phone, no one at Radio Shack takes you into a back room for a bit of counseling. Yet that gadget changes your experience of space and time, remaps your connections to others and gives a jolt to your work–life balance. Today, we are only beginning to learn how the portability of home and work changes our lives and how virtual connectivity impacts relationships.

Yet we will learn best if we keep in mind what technology is not: inert and a panacea. In 1902, the Times of London newspaper wrote: "An overwhelming majority of the population do not use the telephone, and are not likely to use it at all" (Baron, 2000, p. 223). When first introduced, the telephone was assumed to be a business tool, nothing more. The changeability of technology puts us in the petri dish, yet gives us a license to use our new tools with creativity and innovation. We are both experiment and experimenter in the Information Age, and which role we play first and foremost will decide our destiny. At the same time, we must forsake the age-old temptation to assume that technology will solve our problems. Increasingly, we expect technology and science to constantly make us happier, and blame them if they don't, notes Howard Segal (1994). In the long run, however, it is up to us to keep issues of our humanity from slipping into second place behind our machinery. If we cannot, the wonders of technology will be squandered. The marvels of connectivity will prove costly in time.

REFERENCES

Arendt, H. (1998). *The human condition* (2nd ed.). Chicago: University of Chicago Press. Introduction by Margaret Canovan, Originally published in 1958.

Baron, N. (2000). *Alphabet to email: How written English evolved and where it's heading.* London, New York: Routledge.

Bolande, H. A. (2002). In the chips: By putting a radio into every one of its chips, Intel hopes to rewrite the rules of the wireless world. *The Wall Street Journal,* September 23, R10.

Boneva, B. S., Quinn, A., Kraut, R., Kiesler, S., & Shklovski, I. (in press). Teenage communication in the instant messaging era. In R. Kraut, M. Bryin, & S. Kiesler (Eds.), *Information technology at home.* Oxford: Oxford University Press.

Business travel market overview. (2001). *Business and convention travelers* (p. 7). Washington, DC: Travel Industry Association of America.

Cummings, J., Butler, B., & Kraut, R. (2002). The quality of online social relationships (pp. 103–108). *Communications of the Association for Computing Machinery, 45,* 7.

Fischer, C. (1992). *America calling: A social history of the telephone to 1940.* Berkeley: University of California Press.

Galinsky, E., Bond, J. T., & Kim, S. S. (2001). *Feeling overworked: When work becomes too much.* New York: Families and Work Institute.

Gardner, M. (2002). Turn on the computer for a visit from dad. *The Christian Science Monitor,* July 17, p. 14.

Jackson, M. (2002). *What's happening to home? Balancing work, life and refuge in the information age.* Notre Dame, IN: Sorin Books.

Jackson, M. (2003a). Ping! Always-on technology is redefining togetherness and changing the boundaries of family life. *Working Mother,* April, 44–47, 98.

Jackson, M. (2003b). Turn off that cell phone: It's meeting time. *The New York Times,* March 2, BU12.

Kraut, R., Kiesler, S., Boneva, B., Cummings, J., Helgeson, V., & Crawford, A. (2002). Internet paradox revisited. *Journal of Social Issues, 58*(1), 49–74.

McQuillen, J. S. (2003). The influence of technology on the initiation of interpersonal relationships. *Education, 123*(3), 616–623.

Morgenstern, J. (2003). Subtitles, please: What young fans are missing. *The Wall Street Journal,* June 4, D10.

Moseley, L. (2002). Lords of the ring: A British researcher looks at the global impact of mobiles phones. *Newsweek, 139*(23), 32.

Segal, H. P. (1994). *Future imperfect: The mixed blessings of technology in America.* Amherst: University of Massachusetts Press.

Shaw, D. (1999). Domestic bliss: Laptop of luxury. *House & Garden*, September, pp. 63–64.

Southwick, K. (2002). Back in touch: John Seely Brown puts the human factor back into technology. *Forbes, 169*, 7, 46.

Wellman, B. (2000). Changing connectivity: A future history of Y2.03K. *Sociological Research Online.* 4, 4. http://www.socresonline.org.uk/4/4/wellman.html

Wilson, P. J. (1988). *The domestication of the human species.* New Haven, CT: Yale University Press.

Dual-Earner Couples: Good/Bad for Her and/or Him?

Rosalind Chait Barnett
Brandeis University
Women's Studies Research Center

The dual-earner couple is here to stay. Indeed, it is the modal American family. All indications are that it will be the dominant family form for the foreseeable future (Coontz, 1997). This demographic fact has been a reality in the United States for the past 30 years, but it is still not widely acknowledged as such, at least by policymakers and, perhaps, by most Americans (Skolnick, 1993). Much has been written about this family form. Sadly, most of what we know, or think that we know, is based on media reports, many of which are nothing more than sensationalized anecdotes: The frenzied, high-powered, New York lawyer who suddenly realizes that she cannot manage her 80-hour-a-week job and rear her 2-year-old daughter. The head of a huge multinational corporation who quits because she wants to spend more time at home. These figures are now staples of the media coverage of dual-earner families. As a result of this kind of reportage, many people have a one-sided and often negative view of the dual-earner family form and its effects on the women, men, and children in them.

In this chapter, we offer a different view. Relying on systematic studies across a number of disciplines, we present a more balanced and scientifically accurate picture of life in the dual-earner family. First, we present data indicating that the dual-earner family will remain a substantial demographic presence. Second, we share research findings that provide an up-close look at how these families are doing. Third, we inquire into the well-being of children reared by two working parents. Fourth, we suggest some directions for future research. Finally, we discuss the theoretical implications of these new insights into the lives of men, women, and children in dual-earner families.

THE DUAL-EARNER FAMILY IS HERE TO STAY

The Present

As of 2002, 78% of all employees were in dual-earner families, compared to 66% in 1977 (Bond, Thompson, Galinsky, & Prottas, 2003). In 1998, women constituted 46% of the labor force, and that percentage is also projected to increase (Bond et al., 2003; Padavic & Reskin, 2002). Evidence suggests that women's labor force participation is catching up with that of men. Women are increasingly working a full-time, full-year pattern, whereas not long ago the typical female labor-force pattern was part-time, part-year. Indeed, women's and men's labor force participation steadily converged throughout the 20th century, and experts project that this trend will continue into the 21st (Barnett & Hyde, 2001; Bond et al., 2003; Fullerton, 1999). The percentage of full-time employed dual-earner couples with children is also on the rise. Almost 70% of all dual-earner couples had children as of 2002, compared to roughly 62% in 1995 (Reeves, 2002).

More and more women are combining full-time employment with marriage and children. And, on average, women take short maternity leaves. Today, the majority of mothers in the United States who return to work after having a child do so before that child's first birthday. In the National Institute of Child Health and Human Development (NICHD) Study of Early Child Care, the overwhelming majority of mothers who were employed in their infants' first year returned to work and placed their children in some kind of routine nonmaternal care arrangement before the child was 6 months of age (Hofferth, 1996; NICHD Early Child Care Research Network, 1997a, 1997b). Data from 1998 to 1999 indicate that 55% of all women with infants under 1-year-of-age are in the labor force (U.S. Bureau of Labor Statistics, 2000); comparable rates in 1970 and 1984 were 24% and 53%, respectively (Hofferth, 1996; Hoffman, 1989). As of 1997, the majority of children in the United States had mothers and fathers who were employed full-time (Bond, Galinsky, & Swanberg, 1998). In 2002, 67% of dual-earner couples had a child under 18 in the home (Bond et al., 2003).

Future Trends

Several demographic and attitudinal trends suggest that the dual-earner family will continue to be the dominant American family form. The trends that lead to this conclusion include:

- Rising age at first marriage for both women and men over the course of the past five decades
- Declining average number of children per household
- Increasing life span for both women and men
- Women now constituting a majority of enrollment at all levels of postsecondary education
- Increasing prevalence of egalitarian gender-role attitudes; and
- A couple's capacity to maintain a middle-class standard of living now being dependent largely on the wife's earnings.

Since the 1950s, there has been a steady increase in age at first marriage for both women and men. As of 2002, the median age at first marriage was 25.3 years for women and 26.9 years for men; in 1950, the comparable ages were 20.5 years for women and 23.7 years for men (U.S. Census Bureau, 2003, Table MS-2). In part, this trend reflects women's increasing educational attainment. As of 2000, women in the United States earned 56% of bachelor's degrees, 55% of master's degrees, and 41% of doctorates. These figures reflect a sharp and steady increase from 1950, when the comparable percentages were 25%, 26%, and 10% (Caplow, Hicks, & Wattenberg, 2001). The increasing median age at first marriage may also reflect changes in earning patterns for men. Men tend to postpone marriage until they can adequately provide for a family; therefore, when men's wages stagnate or decline, their age at first marriage tends to increase (Oppenheimer, 1997).

Finally, the trend toward increasing age at first marriage also reflects women's increasing commitment to the labor force and expanding control over fertility. As of 1999, U.S. fertility was hovering around 2.1 children per couple, barely replacement level (Caplow et al., 2001). Another indicator of women's commitment to the workforce is the percentage of women who are employed and who have dependent children. In 1990, 58.9% of married women with children under age six were in the labor force, as compared to 63.6% in 1998 (U.S. Census Bureau, 1998). Of married women with older children (6 to 17 years of age), 73.6% were in the labor force in 1990 and 77.6% were in the labor force in 1998 (U.S. Census Bureau, 1998). It is instructive to see the low fertility figures in the context of the lengthening life span for women and men. As of 1999, women lived an average of 79.4 years, compared to 73.9 years for men (Anderson & DeTurk, 2002). Thus, today fewer children are being born and reared in a narrower band of years within a longer life span. As a result of these trends, it is less likely that today's women will center their long lives solely around rearing one or two children. As the maternal role has been compressed, the employee role has been expanding.

There is convincing evidence that women's and men's gender-role ideology is increasingly supportive of women's new social roles. Although measures assessing gender-role ideology vary, most contain the following two items: "It is usually better for everyone involved if the man is the achiever outside the home and the woman takes care of the home and family"; and "A working mother can establish just as warm and secure a relationship with her children as a mother who does not work." Four studies suggest increasing alignment of egalitarian gender-role attitudes. One study reports on the responses of high-school seniors between 1980 and 1997 who were asked the first of these two items. A clear trend emerged. For both males and females, the percentage endorsing "traditional" (i.e., role-segregated) attitudes declined 17% over this period of time (Cornell Employment and Family Careers Institute, 1999). A similar trend was reported among college freshmen: Between 1970 and 1995, men's and women's attitudes became more egalitarian, with men's attitudes showing the more dramatic change (Twenge, 1997). A 2000 survey reported that, for the first time, a higher percentage of men between the ages of 21 and 39 endorsed the importance of work schedules that allowed them to spend more time with their families (82%) than endorsed such traditionally male values as having: challenging work (74%), a high level of job security (58%), a high salary (46%), or high job prestige or status (27%) (Radcliffe Public Policy Center, 2000). Surprisingly, the percentage of men endorsing the importance of family was close to that for women (85%). In a sample of 300 full-time employed men and women in dual-earner couples, although wives were more likely to be egalitarian than their husbands, in 42.3% of the couples, the husband was either more egalitarian than his wife or both spouses were equally egalitarian (James, Barnett, & Brennan, 1998). Lastly, the most recent *National Study of the Changing Workforce* (Bond et al., 2003) revealed a 32% decline in traditional gender role attitudes among men over the course of the previous 25 years: 42% of men surveyed in 2002 felt that women's "appropriate" role was to tend the home and children while men earned money for the household, down from 74% of male respondents in 1977 (Bond et al., 2003). Taken together, these studies suggest widespread and growing acceptance of egalitarian social roles for women and men.

A similar trend appears in data on men's and women's actual behavior. Between 1977 and 2002, in two nationally representative samples, full-time employed men significantly increased the time that they spent on household and child-care tasks, whereas women's time on these chores remained the same or decreased (Bond et al., 2003). Specifically, the gap between the time that women and men each spent in household tasks during non-workday time decreased from 3.0 hours to 1.0 hour, and the gap on workdays narrowed from 2.5 hours to 1.0 hour (Bond et al., 2003). With respect to child-care tasks, the gap on non-workdays decreased from 2.1 to 1.9

hours, and on workdays, it decreased from 1.4 to 0.8 hours. One effect of these changes is that, in 2002, children in dual-earner families spent more time with their parents than they did in 1977 (Bond et al., 2003).

Changes in workforce participation among married men and women have affected median family income for more than a generation. The gap between the median household incomes for families with and without a mother in the workforce increased steadily between 1967 and 1999. In 1967, the gap was about $10,000; in 2001, it was approximately $30,000 (U.S. Census Bureau, Table F-7, 2002). Moreover, a significant proportion of married women are now earning as much as or more than their husbands. As of 1998, 40% of White college-educated women earned more than their husbands (Freeman, 1998). The prevalence of this pattern was underscored in the summer of 2003 by a cover story in *Newsweek* (Tyre & McGinn, 2003).

The confluence of these trends toward continued support for women's labor force participation and increasingly egalitarian attitudes toward gender roles within family structures suggests that dual-earner couples are likely to retain their dominance in the demographics of families for the foreseeable future.

INSIDE THE DUAL-EARNER FAMILY

How do dual-earner couples manage their various work and family roles? This is an issue of pressing concern. Our interest is in understanding variations within this family form, rather than in comparing it with other types of families. Accordingly, we rely most heavily, but by no means exclusively, on a study that we did with a random sample of 600 full-time employed men and women in dual-earner couples. This study, funded by the National Institute of Mental Health, was the first longitudinal study of such a sample. The study was conducted in two suburban towns with broadly defined middle-class populations in greater Boston. The 300 couples were interviewed extensively at three times over a 2-year period. The aim of the study was to relate subjective experiences in three major social roles—worker, partner, and, when appropriate, parent—to both physical- and mental-health outcomes.

Before turning to the study proper, there are several important points to consider. First, not all dual-earner couples are alike. Some adopt this pattern in response to economic needs; still others come to embrace this family form because it meets the needs of both partners. Others choose this family form for ideological reasons. In tough and uncertain economic times, couples often have to decide between one partner working long overtime hours or taking a second job and having both partners work a standard full-time schedule. Today, increasingly, both enter marriage with similar credentials and aspirations. Under such conditions, fulfilling their career aspirations may be key to the well-being of both partners. Finally, many survivors of failed traditional marriages choose not to replicate that pattern if and when they remarry (Schwartz, 1994). Given this variety, one must exert caution in drawing conclusions about dual-earner couples as a group. Also, the families in this study were middle-class, heterosexual, primarily White, and residing in close proximity to an urban center. Thus, the findings may not generalize to men and women in other family forms, such as single-parent families, gay and lesbian families, non-White or multiracial families, sole-breadwinner families, two-earner couples that are either younger or older, or those at the very low or very high ends of the income range.

Second, analyzing data from couples poses several major methodological and conceptual challenges. Within a couple, partners' outcomes are correlated. For example, her psychological distress is related to his, and his marital-role quality is related to hers. In other words, the husbands and wives in the sample do not constitute independent samples, which violate a key assumption of regression analysis. Therefore, research on couples requires an analysis strategy that can accommodate correlated outcomes and retain the couple membership of the participants. Hierarchical linear modeling (HLM) is the strategy we use to handle this challenge in both cross-sectional and longitudinal analyses.

Third, one has to create couple-level variables from individual-level data. As an example, consider income. Imagine that you have data on his income and her income at three time points and you want to create a couple-level variable. You could compute the couple average. You could also compute a variable that reflects the within-couple magnitude and direction of the difference from the average at each time point. Suppose that you have two couples, both with mean incomes of $60,000. In the first couple, she earns $40,000 and he earns $80,000. The male–female difference would be +$40,000 and the female–male difference would be –$40,000. In the second couple, she earns $70,000 and he earns $50,000. Here, the male–female difference would be –$20,000 and the female–male difference would be +$20,000. You would want to use both the couple average and the female–male and male–female gaps as couple-level variables to estimate the relationship between change over time in earnings and change over time in an outcome of interest (such as marital-role quality). With these variables, it is possible to model the relationships between the time-invariant couple-level variables (e.g., the couple average) and the time-varying couple-level variables (e.g., changes in the direction and magnitude of the female–male and male–female difference). It is then possible to ask questions about the linkages among the couple average income, the change over time in the magnitude and direction of the gap between his and her earnings, and such outcomes as psychological distress and marital-role quality.

Lastly, having a sample of full-time employed men and women in dual-earner couples offers a rare opportunity to study gender differences. In contrast to many studies of gender differences in the relationship between social-role experiences and health and well-being outcomes, the participants in this study are matched on many variables often unmeasured or otherwise confounded with gender elsewhere. In our study, the man and woman in each couple have the same household income, and the same number and ages of children; they have been married the same length of time, live in the same neighborhood, have the same access to health care, and if they have a difficult child or a sick parent, they have that dependent in common as well. Moreover, they are both employed full-time, and we have data on their occupational prestige and individual salaries.

Because we are able to control for this large array of gender-related factors, we can ask about the effects of gender, stripped of many of its covariates, on the relationships of interest. HLM permits one to conduct an explicit test for the effect of gender. Thus, we are uniquely able to test the effect of a disaggregated gender construct on the relationships under study, thereby challenging many widely held assumptions about gender differences in the relationship between social-role experiences and both health and quality-of-life outcomes.

THE STUDY

We drew a random sample of two-earner couples from the publicly available annual town voting lists in the two communities. These couples were sent a letter describing the study and explaining that participation would require each partner to be interviewed in person three times over the next 2 years. Eligible and willing couples were contacted by trained interviewers who completed the screening questionnaires and scheduled separate 90-minute interviews with each partner. The interviews covered many aspects of their work and family lives as well as self-reports of physical and mental health. In addition, each participant was sent a questionnaire to be completed and returned prior to each interview. Each couple was paid $25.00 at each wave of data collection.

The response rate in the first wave was excellent, as was the retention rate. Even with the criterion that both members of a couple had to agree separately to participate in the study, 68% of the eligible couples agreed to participate, and over the three data collections, only 8% of the sample dropped out.

We assessed experiences both at one point in time and over time in their three major social roles—partner, employee, and, if applicable, parent. The measures that we used all have well-established psychometrics, with high internal consistency, reliability, and test-retest stability over a 1- to 3-month period. Although we assessed many outcome variables, in this chapter we focus on psychological distress, defined as self-reported frequency of symptoms of anxiety and depression over the preceding week. Here, too, we used a well-researched instrument with excellent psychometric properties (Derogatis, 1975).

What did we learn? The simple answer is that we learned a great deal. The data have been reported in more than 30 peer-reviewed articles and in the book *She Works, He Works* (Barnett & Rivers, 1996). The data are still being analyzed, thanks to the Murray Research Center at Harvard University, where the data are archived. The more complex answer requires that we discuss the findings in some detail. For ease of presentation, we discuss the results by topic, starting with job and marital experiences and ending with parenting experiences. We augment the discussion of the findings with other research as appropriate.

First, a description of the participants is in order. As noted earlier, the sample was overwhelmingly White, reflecting the communities from which they were drawn. The sample was also stratified on parent status, with 60% being parents at the first data collection. The men and women were between the ages of 25 and 40 at Time 1. On average, they had had at least 16 years of education, although there was wide variation in educational attainment; roughly one-third had not completed college and another one-third had had some graduate education. In addition, there was considerable overlap in the types of jobs the men and women occupied. For example, 68% of the men and 71% of the women were employed in managerial and professional occupations.

RESEARCH QUESTIONS

Did these couples report high levels of stress-related mental and physical-health problems? Did they report high levels of concerns about their jobs? Did they describe their marital and parenting relationships as troubled? The answer to all of these questions is NO. On average, the men and women in this sample reported low levels of psychological distress and of stress-related physical health problems. Moreover, they reported high levels of satisfaction with their job-role, marital-role, and parent-role experiences.

The next set of questions concerned the relationship between the quality of experiences in each of these social roles and reports of symptoms of anxiety and depression. Are experiences in the roles of employee, partner, and parent related to reports of psychological distress? And, do these relationships differ by gender?

Based on current theoretical writings, we tested three major hypotheses:

H1: Job-role quality will have a greater impact on men's than women's psychological distress.

H2: Marital-role quality will have a greater impact on men's than women's psychological distress.

H3: Parent-role quality will have a greater impact on women's than men's psychological distress.

Hypothesis 1

Job-Role Quality. Job-role quality was, on average, high for both husbands and wives. However, wives' scores were significantly more positive than their husbands' (Barnett, Marshall, Raudenbush, & Brennan, 1993); women indicated that their jobs were, on average, *considerably* rewarding, whereas men indicated that their jobs were between *somewhat* and *considerably* rewarding. With respect to job concerns, both men and women reported that, on average, their jobs were between *somewhat* and *considerably* a concern. As expected, the quality of experience on the job was related to psychological distress: The better the job, the lower the distress.

With respect to the effect of gender, however, the data offered no evidence that the effect of job-role quality on psychological distress was different for women and for men. In other words, subjective experiences on the job were significantly associated with psychological distress for both men and women, and the magnitude of this effect depended little on gender.

Specific Job Conditions. Beyond overall job-role quality, are there specific job conditions that are more closely related to men's than women's psychological distress? Among the items of the job-role quality scale, we identified scales assessing seven job conditions. We focused on two aspects of job control that have received substantial research attention—skill discretion (also referred to as substantive complexity, challenge, and underutilization of skills and abilities), and decision authority (also referred to as autonomy and task control). Results showed that both higher average skill discretion and increasing skill discretion were associated with lower levels of distress, while higher average job demands and increasing job demands were related to higher levels of distress. The magnitude of these relationships was not affected by gender. More specifically, increasing concerns about having to do dull, monotonous work and having to work under the pressures of time and conflicting demands were both associated with increasing psychological distress, and this was equally true for full-time employed women and full-time employed men dual-earner couples (Barnett & Brennan, 1995, 1997). These findings provide no support for Hypothesis 1.

It was especially interesting that pay adequacy and job security were unrelated to distress in this sample. The findings might have differed in a sample of couples in which household income was dependent solely or largely
on the salary of only one partner. Pay adequacy and job security may also be
more potent predictors of distress in less affluent and more racially/ethi-
cally diverse populations.

The absence of any significant effect of gender warrants comment. Explicit tests for the effect of gender on the association between each of the
seven job conditions and psychological distress found no case in which
the gender effect was significant. These findings are consistent with evidence that, after controlling for appropriate covariates (e.g., occupational prestige); gender has little effect on the relationship between job
stressors and psychological distress (Barnett & Hyde, 2001; Lowe & Northcott, 1988).

The absence of gender differences flies in the face of firmly held cultural
beliefs that "the workplace and its events . . . more closely regulate the psychological fate of men than of women" (Pearlin, 1975, p. 202). Instead,
however, evidence supports the argument that positive and negative job experiences appear to have similar influences on men's and women's mental
health. These findings suggest that the previously assumed sex differences
in the relationship between job-role stress and psychological distress may be
artifacts of the segregated worlds in which men and women once operated.
When, as in this study, it is possible to hold constant the social-role patterns
of men and women (a crucial aspect of gender), then there is no significant
residual effect of the remaining gender construct.

Hypothesis II

Marital-Role Quality. More than 90% of the study participants were in
their first marriage; 9.3% of the women and 7.3% of the men had been
married previously. On average, the couples had been in their current partnership for 8.25 years (SD = 5.23 years).

On average, women experienced essentially the same levels of rewards
and concerns in their marriages as did men. That is, men and women indicated that their marriages were between *considerably* and *extremely* rewarding,
and between *not at all* and *somewhat* a concern. Thus, on average, men's and
women's marital-role quality scores are virtually identical. For both men and
women, marital-role quality was significantly negatively related to psychological distress, and the magnitude of this effect depended little, if at all, on gender. Women were not more vulnerable to ongoing family role strains than
were men. In addition, this relationship did not depend on parental status
for women or for men. In other words, being a parent did not buffer women
or men in dual-earner couples from the mental health consequences of a

troubled marital relationship (Barnett, Brennan, Raudenbush, & Marshall, 1994). These findings lend no support to Hypothesis II.

Hypothesis III

Parent-Role Quality. On average, the 180 couples who had children had an average of 1.76 children (range 1–4, *SD* = 0.72). Most (88.3%) of the couples were rearing preschool or school-age children: 66.1% had at least one preschooler in the home; 39.4% had at least one school-aged child in the home. In contrast, only 26.1% had at least one teenage child in the home.

As with marital-role quality, women's and men's mean scores on parent-role quality were essentially identical, as were their levels on the subscales representing parent rewards and parent concerns (Barnett, Brennan, & Marshall, 1994). On average, women and men in dual-earner couples indicated that their relationships with their children were between *considerably* and *extremely* rewarding. Conversely, they indicated that, on average, their relationships with their children were between *not at all* and *somewhat* a concern.

In a series of HLM analyses, we found that (a) For both men and women, the parent role was a significant predictor of psychological distress; (b) This relationship did not depend on the number of children in the household; and (c) The effect of parent-role quality on psychological distress was similar for women and for men. If parent–child relationships were negative, employed mothers were no more or less likely to report high distress than were employed fathers. Conversely, if parent–child relationships were positive, mothers and fathers were equally likely to report low levels of distress. Of course, with cross-sectional data, it was not possible to rule out the alternative interpretation—that individuals who experience low psychological distress report high parent-role quality.

These findings lend no support for Hypothesis III. The absence of gender differences challenges earlier findings that "children . . . have less effect on the mental health of fathers" (Kessler & McRae, 1982, p. 218). As with job-role experiences, positive and negative relationships with children appeared to have similar influences on men's and women's mental health.

These findings also contrast with previous findings indicating a relationship between parent strain and distress among employed mothers but not among employed fathers (Cleary & Mechanic, 1983). The discrepancy might be due to both sampling and methodological differences. For example, the married men in prior studies were not all married to women who were employed full-time, and the employed women were not all employed full-time. There are indications that, as the role patterns of men and women converge, gender differences in the associations between role quality and distress disappear (Barnett et al., 1993; Barnett, Brennan, & Marshall, 1994; Barnett, Brennan, Raudenbush, & Marshall, 1994; Gore & Mangione, 1983). Thus, findings from studies of unrelated employed men and women or of married men and women not employed full-time may not be generalizable to full-time employed dual-earner couples.

Indeed, dual-earner couples may be different from other couples. Employed fathers married to full-time employed women may be more highly invested in the parenting role and therefore more likely than other employed fathers to be affected by its emotional tone. Stated differently, it may be that the parenting role is equally salient for men and women in dual-earner couples, rendering them equally vulnerable to the affective tone of their relationships with their children (Simon, 1995). These men may also participate more heavily in child-rearing tasks and may have more egalitarian sex-role attitudes, both of which have been reported to affect the relationship between parent stressors and mental-health indicators (Cleary & Mechanic, 1983).

Findings from this set of analyses suggest strongly that subjective quality of experiences in their jobs, marriages and parent–child relationships are similar for men and women in dual-earner couples, and that the quality of these role experiences has similar effects on mental health outcomes for men and women in dual-earner couples (Barnett & Hyde, 2001). It appears that as the role patterns of men and women become increasingly similar, we need to rethink our ideas about gender differences.

These findings add to the growing consensus that work and family roles have similar psychological significance for men and women (Pleck, Bowen, & Pittman, 1995; Thoits, 1991, 1992). Taken together, these findings provide compelling evidence that, contrary to popular assumptions, there appear to be no gender differences in the associations between job-role and family-role quality and psychological distress. However, it is important to note that with less advantaged couples and with other mental-health indicators, gender differences might be found.

The familiar caution against affirming a null hypothesis applies here. Failure to reject our null hypothesis that the effect of social-role quality on distress is of greater magnitude for women than for men does not imply that these effects are identical for men and women. Interpretation depends on the power of the test. However, after performing the appropriate power analyses, we are confident that we had adequate power to detect differences if they were present.

In addition to asking research questions about the impact of social role experiences on distress outcomes for each member of the marital dyad, it is also possible to ask about crossover effects. Specifically, how do events in her life affect his outcomes, and vice versa?

CROSSOVER EFFECTS WITHIN COUPLES

At present, no theory formally links events in one partner's social experience with events in the other partner's social experience, quality of life, or stress-related outcomes (Barnett, 2003). Yet evidence is amassing that such crossover effects do occur and need to be incorporated in future theories.

We now discuss two within-couple crossover effects that provide insights into the dynamic and intertwined lives of women and men in dual-earner couples. Specifically, we present findings on the relationships among (a) the distribution of child-care responsibilities, each partner's evaluation of the marriage, and each partner's psychological distress; and (b) changes over time in the magnitude and direction of the salary gap within couples and each partner's psychological distress.

When His Involvement in Child Care Approaches Hers. How does a husband's involvement in child care impact his and his wife's psychological distress and his and his wife's evaluation of the marriage? To answer these questions, we ran a series of HLM models in which psychological distress was treated as the primary outcome and marital-role quality was treated as the mediator (Ozer, Barnett, Brennan, & Sperling, 1998). When we considered the main-effects relationship between each partner's relative child-care contribution and each partner's psychological distress, we found a different pattern for the husbands than for the wives. The more child care he did relative to her, the fewer symptoms of anxiety and depression he reported. Thus, he received a mental-health benefit from his child-care involvement.

She, in contrast, did not appear to benefit in the same way. For her, there was no meaningful association between her relative child-care involvement and her level of well-being. However, when we introduced her evaluation of the marriage into the model, the picture became more complicated and interesting. The lack of an association between her relative child-care involvement and her well-being actually masked conflicting results from two separate and buffering processes. When she did more than he did, there was a direct positive effect on her mental health (just as there is for him), *and* an indirect negative effect due to her reduced marital-role quality. Thus, his participation in child care has crossover effects on her evaluation of the marriage.

It is worth noting that there was no evidence to suggest that these women were acting as gatekeepers, limiting their husbands' involvement in this previously female-gendered preserve. However, we do not know whether these findings would differ among women who varied in the traditionality of their gender-role beliefs.

When She Earns More Than He Earns. In our sample, 31.5% of the wives earned as much as or more than their husbands (Brennan, Barnett, & Gareis, 2001). Among the couples in which the wife earned more than the husband, she earned, on average, 59% of the household income. In terms of actual earnings, these wives earned between $1,000 and $75,000 more than their husbands (*Mean* = $14,111.51, *SD* = $14,318.78, *Median* = $10,000).

Previous research (Ono, 1998) shows that the likelihood of divorce is lower in couples in which the wife is an earner. But what about the quality of their marriages? Are women's earnings critical to their own and their husbands' evaluations of their marriages? They should be, if what several theorists say is true (Becker, 1981; Parsons, 1949).

In our sample, however, wives' relative earnings had no appreciable effect on their evaluations of their marriages (Brennan et al., 2001). Those who earned more than their husbands were no more or less likely to devalue their marriages than were those who earned less. Similarly, change over time in the magnitude of the female–male salary gap had no significant effect on her evaluation of the quality of the marital relationship.

But the men's story revealed a sharp contrast, especially among those men with certain ideas about their "proper" role in the family. When their wives made more than they did, men's beliefs about their own earnings; specifically, a construct that we label "salary affect," determined how men felt about their marriages. The components of salary affect are: (a) how important the men's earnings were to them; and (b) how important it was to the men to make more money than others in their field.

Men in full-time employed dual-earner couples who placed a high value on their breadwinner role were particularly vulnerable to marital unhappiness if their wives' earnings were greater than their own—or if their wives' earnings continued to increase over time relative to their own. If you think you ought to be bringing home most of the bacon, but your wife earns nearly as much or more than you do, this can spell trouble (Melzer, 2002). The findings were quite different for men who held egalitarian views, and who did not strongly identify with the breadwinner role. They did not have problems when their wives earned as much as or more that they did.

Combining the results of these two analyses, it appears that, in this sample, employed wives were far less concerned about their husbands' relative financial resources than some theorists, especially the evolutionary psychologists (e.g., Buss, 1989) would have us believe. These full-time employed women did not seem to obsess over their husband's financial status. In fact, it was the husbands, not the wives, who were more concerned about relative earnings. These findings support the conclusions Eagly and Wood (1999) drew from their meta-analysis of mate selection. They found that non-employed women were far more attracted to a potential mate's earnings than were employed women. Indeed, the full-time employed wives in our dual-earner sample seem more reactive to their husbands' child-care involvement than to their earnings.

WHAT ABOUT THE CHILDREN?

How are children faring in the new American family? Are they insecurely attached to their mothers? Do they feel abandoned and rejected? Do they feel that their parents do not spend enough time with them? Are their parents shortchanging them?

These are pressing questions for today's dual-earner families—questions that require careful research. Fortunately, there are several well-designed studies that provide at least partial answers to these questions. Before going into detail, it is fair to say that, overall, the children in these families are doing well and their parents are giving them adequate attention.

A rich source of answers to these questions comes from a large-scale longitudinal study sponsored by NICHD of 1,300 children and their mothers. The study is being conducted at 10 major research institutions across the country and is led by a team of 25 child psychologists. Participants were recruited into the study when the target children were born and have been followed intensively since then; the children are now in the fifth grade.

As babies, the children received different types of care: Some received routine maternal care, while others received one of five forms of nonmaternal care: father care, nonparent relative care, in-home nonrelative care, home-based care, or child-care center-based care. The first, and perhaps most important, question the researchers addressed concerned the security of the mother–child bond. Were babies whose mothers were not their primary caregiver less securely attached to their mothers than babies who were routinely cared for by their mothers?

For employed mothers, there could be no more critical question. Happily, the answer was that the type of care was unrelated to the security of the mother–child bond. The overwhelming proportion of children (roughly 60%) was securely attached to their mothers at 5 months and when assessed again at 14 months (NICHD Early Child Care Research Network, 1997c). This proportion did not vary with the type of care, the age at which the child was put into nonmaternal care, or the number of hours that the child was in such care. Instead, the mother–child bond was impacted by the mother's sensitivity and responsiveness to the child, with insensitive mothers more likely than sensitive mothers to have insecurely attached children.

Recent media attention has focused on the linkage between time in child care and bullying behavior among preschoolers. Is it possible that the real harm to children in routine nonmaternal care is not in terms of the security of their attachment to their mothers but in terms of their antisocial behavior? You would certainly think so from the rash of headlines reading "Connecting the Dots Between Day Care and Bullies" (Parker, 2001) and "Day Care Turns Out Bullies" (*Ottawa Citizen*, 2001), and the flurry of articles in such wide-circulation magazines as *People* (Fowler, 2001). In fact, only 17% of the children in non-maternal care fell into the "aggressive" category; 83% did not (NICHD Early Child Care Research Network, 2003). First, 17% is the same rate of aggression as is found in the population at large of children that age. Moreover, the 11-item scale used to assess "aggression" included such ambiguous items as "stubborn," "loud," "brags," and "talks too much." It is unclear whether such items assess aggression or independence, self-confidence, or any of a number of other personality characteristics.

The real, but much less publicized, story is that children in high-quality childcare scored higher on cognitive skills—language, memory, and other skills—than children cared for at home (NICHD Early Child Care Research Network, 1997d). And children of working parents did not seem to be any more aggressive than children of nonworking parents.

Research tells us that, despite a sharp increase in the number of dual-career families, today's children actually spend significantly more time with their parents than children did two decades ago (Bond et al., 1998). This increase is largely the result of fathers spending more time with their children in 1997 than they did in 1981, with mothers' time with children remaining stable over that period of time.

How is it possible that employed mothers spend as much time with their children as nonemployed mothers? Sandberg and Hofferth (2001) conducted a time-diary study from two nationally representative samples of about 2,500 children and found that, "contrary to popular belief, structural changes in the population have not diminished the time that children in the United States spend with their parents"(Sandberg & Hofferth, 2001, p. 434). The authors note that fathers appear to be taking up the slack in families in which both parents are employed. Although working mothers in their study spent about 5 hours per week less time with children than nonworking mothers, total parental time increased, suggesting that "fathers may have taken more responsibility for childcare when mothers worked in 1997 than in 1981" (Sandberg & Hofferth, 2001, p. 429).

As described in more detail in Galinsky's chapter 14 (this volume), Suzanne Bianchi (2000) elaborates on these themes. Based on her research, she concludes that "the increase in female employment outside the home has occurred with less reallocation of time away from child rearing among parents than would first appear" (p. 402). She buttresses her conclusion with four arguments:

1. We tend to exaggerate the amount of a mother's time in the home that is actually available for interaction with her children;

2. We overestimate how much paid work takes mothers away from their children;

3. Mothers now have fewer children and are more likely to enroll them in a preschool setting outside the home, thereby minimizing differences in maternal time with children based on the mother's employment status;

4. Fathers, especially those in dual-earner families, are doing more child care, thereby enhancing overall parental time with children.

The fact that the overall time that parents spend with their children has risen significantly over the past 20 years gives the lie to the notion that today's parents are so harried or otherwise absorbed that they slight their children. One intriguing fact to emerge from the Bond et al. (1998) study was that today's working mothers spend as much time with their children as did nonworking mothers did with their children 20 years ago. In an era when mothers were less likely to work outside the home, they also spent less time with their kids. Given these data, it is hard to make a case that we currently have a nation of selfish, absentee parents.

Other research tells a similar story. In a groundbreaking study, a team at Penn State (Crouter, MacDermid, McHale, & Perry-Jenkins, 1990) looked at the quality of the relationship between kids and parents. The research involved 152 families with children ages 9 to 12, equally divided into three groups: those in which the mother was not employed and was at home; those in which the mother worked part-time outside the home; and those in which the mother worked full-time outside the home. The researchers wanted to know how "tuned in" parents were to their kids: To what extent did they know about who their children's friends were, what was happening at school, and what their children's day-to-day problems and joys were?

The Penn State team was surprised by what it found. There was no difference among these groups of women. The nonworking mothers were no more "tuned in" to their kids than the working mothers. It seems that working parents do indeed find ways to be very close to their children.

Good news about fathers is also on the rise. For the first time, fathers are spending more time with their children than on their own personal interests and pursuits, reports the *National Study of the Changing Workforce* (Bond et al., 2003). And younger men, it seems, are focused on fatherhood more than were men in the past. As discussed earlier, a national survey by the Radcliffe Public Policy Center (2000) found that men between the ages of 21 and 39 gave family matters top billing over career success. Some 82% endorsed the importance of work schedules that allowed them to spend more time with their families, and 71% said they would sacrifice part of their pay to have more time with their families.

CONCLUSION

The study of dual-earner families presents both challenges and opportunities. The results of the analyses reported in this chapter call into question some broadly accepted theories of within-couple dynamics. The findings also contradict traditional notions of gender differences in the roles of worker, partner, and parent for women's and men's psychological well-being. The consensus that children in these families do not suffer emotionally, cognitively, or behaviorally should force reconsideration of widely held beliefs.

With respect to the findings from the within-couples analyses, it appears that older theories predicting significant gender differences are no longer a good fit with today's realities. For example, the psychological well-being of full-time employed women in dual-earner couples is as reactive as that of their husbands to their job-role quality. And men's psychological well-being is as reactive as that of their wives to the quality of their marital and parent–child relationships. Older theories relating salary differences and child-care involvement to marital disruption and satisfaction need to be better aligned with present realities.

It is time to retire the "selfish parent" stereotype from our national debate about the dual-earner American family and the purported consequent decline of family life. It is not now—nor has it ever been—easy to raise kids and keep a family on an even course. But today's dual-earner parents do it just as well today as American parents ever did in the past. It appears that older theories relating gender-specific social role experiences to distress outcomes are no longer a good fit with present realities (Barnett & Hyde, 2001).

REFERENCES

Anderson, R. N., & DeTurk, P. B. (2002). United States life tables, 1999. *National Vital Statistics Reports, 50*(6). Hyattsville, MD: National Center for Health Statistics

Barnett, R. C. (2003, September). *An expanded model of the job stress-illness relationship.* Paper presented at the 17th Annual Conference of the European Health Psychology Society, Kos, Greece.

Barnett, R. C., & Brennan, R. T. (1995). The relationship between job experiences and psychological distress: A structural equation approach. *Journal of Organizational Behavior, 16,* 259–276.

Barnett, R. C., & Brennan, R. T. (1997). Change in job conditions, change in psychological distress, and gender: A longitudinal study of dual-earner couples. *Journal of Organizational Behavior, 18,* 253–274.

Barnett, R. C., Brennan, R. T., & Marshall, N. L. (1994). Gender and the relationship between parent-role quality and psychological distress. *Journal of Family Issues, 15*(2), 229–252.

Barnett, R. C., Brennan, R. T., Raudenbush, S. W., & Marshall, N. L. (1994). Gender and the relationship between marital-role quality and psychological distress. *Psychology of Women Quarterly, 18,* 105–127.

Barnett, R. C., & Hyde, J. S. (2001). Women, men, work, and family: An expansionist theory. *American Psychologist, 56*(10), 781–796.

Barnett, R. C., Marshall, N. L., Raudenbush, S., & Brennan, R. (1993). Gender and the relationship between job experiences and psychological distress: A study of dual-earner couples. *Journal of Personality and Social Psychology, 64*(5), 794–806.

Barnett, R. C., & Rivers, C. (1996). *She works/he works: How two-income families are happier, healthier, and better-off.* San Francisco: Harper.

Becker, G. S. (1981). *A treatise of the family.* Cambridge, MA: Harvard University Press.

Bianchi, S. M. (2000). Maternal employment and time with children: Dramatic change or surprising continuity? *Demography, 37*(4), 401–414.

Bond, J. T., Galinsky, E., & Swanberg, J. E. (1998). *The 1997 national study of the changing workforce.* New York: Families and Work Institute.

Bond, J. T., Thompson, C., Galinsky, E., & Prottas, D. (2003). *Highlights of the 2002 national study of the changing workforce* (No. 3). New York: Families and Work Institute.

Brennan, R. T., Barnett, R. C., & Gareis, K. C. (2001). When she earns more than he does: A longitudinal study of dual-earner couples. *Journal of Marriage and the Family, 63,* 168–182.

Buss, D. M. (1989). Sex differences in human mate preferences: Evolutionary hypotheses tested in 37 cultures. *Behavioral and Brain Sciences, 12,* 1–49.

Caplow, T., Hicks, L., & Wattenberg, B. J. (2001). *The first measured century: An illustrated guide to trends in America, 1900–2000.* Washington, DC: AEI Press.

Cleary, P. D., & Mechanic, D. (1983). Sex differences in psychological distress among married people. *Journal of Health and Social Behavior, 24,* 111–121.

Coontz, S. (1997). *The way we really are: Coming to terms with America's changing families.* New York: Basic Books.

Cornell Employment and Family Careers Institute. (1999, Winter). *Facts about the demographics of working families.* Ithaca, NY: Cornell University Press.

Crouter, A. C., MacDermid, S. M., McHale, S. M., & Perry-Jenkins, M. (1990). Parental monitoring and perceptions of children's school performance and conduct in dual-earner families. *Developmental Psychology, 26*(4), 649–657.

Day care turns out bullies. (2001). *The Ottawa Citizen,* April 20, p. A10.

Derogatis, L. R. (1975). *The SCL-90-R.* Baltimore: Clinical Psychometrics.

Eagly, A., & Wood, W. (1999). The origins of sex differences in human behavior: Evolved dispositions versus social roles. *American Psychologist, 54*(6), 408–423.

Fowler, J. (2001). Kiddie conundrum. *People Weekly,* Vol. 55, issue 21, May 28, pp. 75–76.

Freeman, R. B. (1998, January–February). Unequal incomes: The worrisome distribution of the fruits of American economic growth. *Harvard Magazine, 100,* 62–64.

Fullerton, H. N. (1999). Labor force projections to 2008: Steady growth and changing composition. *Monthly Labor Review,* 19–32.

Gore, S., & Mangione, T. W. (1983). Social roles, sex roles, and psychological distress: Additive and interactive models of sex differences. *Journal of Health and Social Behavior, 24*(4), 300–312.

Hofferth, S. L. (1996). Effects of public and private policies on working after childbirth. *Work and Occupations, 23*(4), 378–404.

Hoffman, L. W. (1989). Effects of maternal employment in the two-parent family. *American Psychologist, 44*(2), 283–292.

James, J. B., Barnett, R. C., & Brennan, R. T. (1998). The psychological effects of work experiences and disagreements about gender-role beliefs in dual earner couples: A longitudinal study. *Women's Health: Research on Gender, Behavior, and Policy, 4*(4), 341–368.

Kessler, R. C., & McRae, J. A. (1982). The effect of wives' employment on the mental health of married men and women. *American Sociological Review, 47,* 216–227.

Lowe, G. S., & Northcott, H. C. (1988). The impact of working conditions, social roles, and personal characteristics on gender differences in distress. *Work and Occupations, 15,* 55–77.

Melzer, S. A. (2002). Gender, work, and intimate violence: Men's occupational violence spillover and compensatory violence. *Journal of Marriage and Family, 64,* 820–832.

NICHD Early Child Care Research Network. (1997a). Familial factors associated with the characteristics of nonmaternal care for infants. *Journal of Marriage and the Family, 59*(2), 389–408.

NICHD Early Child Care Research Network. (1997b). Child care in the first year of life. *Merrill-Palmer Quarterly, 43*(3), 340–360.

NICHD Early Child Care Research Network. (1997c). The effects of infant child care on infant–mother attachment security: Results of the NICHD Study of Early Child Care. *Child Development, 68*(5), 860–879.

NICHD Early Child Care Research Network. (1997d). *Mother–child interaction and cognitive outcomes associated with early child care: Results of the NICHD study.* Paper presented at the biennial meeting of the Society For Research in Child Development, Washington, DC.

NICHD Early Child Care Research Network. (2003). Does amount of time spent in child care predict socioemotional adjustment during the transition to kindergarten? *Child Development, 74*(4), 976–1005.

Ono, H. (1998). Husbands' and wives' resources and marital dissolution. *Journal of Marriage and the Family, 60,* 674–689.

Oppenheimer, V. K. (1997). Women's employment and the gain to marriage: The specialization and trading model. *Annual Review of Sociology, 23,* 431–453.

Ozer, E. M., Barnett, R. C., Brennan, R. T., & Sperling, J. (1998). Does child care involvement increase or decrease distress among dual-earner couples? *Women's Health: Research on Gender, Behavior, and Policy, 4*(4), 285–311.

Padavic, I., & Reskin, B. (2002). *Women and men at work* (2nd ed.). Thousand Oaks, CA: Sage.

Parker, K. (2001). Connecting the dots between day care and bullies. *Denver Post,* April 25, pp. B-07.

Parsons, T. (1949). The social structure of the family. In R. Anshen (Ed.), *The family: Its function and destiny* (pp. 173–201). New York: Harper.

Pearlin, L. (1975). Sex roles and depression. In N. Datan & L. H. Ginsberg (Eds.), *Life-span developmental psychology: Normative life crises* (pp. 191–207). New York: Academic Press.

Pleck, J. H., Bowen, G. L., & Pittman, J. F. (1995). Work roles, family roles, and well-being: Current conceptual perspectives. In *The work and family interface: Toward a contextual effects perspectives* (pp. 17–22). New York: National Council on Family Relations.

Radcliffe Public Policy Center. (2000). *Life's work: Generational attitudes toward work and life integration.* Cambridge, MA: Harvard University, Radcliffe Institute for Advanced Study.

Reeves, R. (2002). *Dad's army: The case for father-friendly workplaces.* London: The Work Foundation.

Sandberg, J. F., & Hofferth, S. L. (2001). Changes in children's time with parents, United States. 1981–1997. *Demography, 38*(3), 423–436.

Schwartz, P. (1994). *Peer marriages: How love between equals really works.* New York: Free Press.

Simon, R. W. (1995). Gender, multiple roles, role meaning, and mental health. *Journal of Health and Social Behavior, 36*(2), 182–194.

Skolnick, A. (1993). Changes of heart: Family dynamics in historical perspective. In P. A. Cowan, D. Field, D. A. Hansen, A. Skolnick & G. E. Swanson (Eds.), *Family, self, and society: Toward a new agenda for family research* (pp. 43–68). Hillsdale, NJ: Lawrence Erlbaum Associates.

Thoits, P. A. (1991). On merging identity theory and stress research. *Social Psychology Quarterly, 54*(2), 101–112.

Thoits, P. A. (1992). Identity structures and psychological well-being: Gender and marital status comparisons. *Social Psychology Quarterly, 55*(3), 236–256.

Twenge, J. M. (1997). Attitudes toward women, 1970–1995. *Psychology of Women Quarterly, 21,* 35–51.

Tyre, P., & McGinn, D. (2003). She works, he doesn't. *Newsweek,* May 12, *44.*

U.S. Bureau of Labor Statistics. (2000). *Employment characteristics of families in 2000* (News Release, April 19, 2001). Washington, DC: Author.

U.S. Census Bureau. (1998). *Statistical abstract of the United States* (118th ed.), Tables 84, 654. Washington, DC: U.S. Government Printing Office.

U.S. Census Bureau. (2002). *Historical Income Tables-Families. Table F-7. Type of family (all races) by median and mean income: 1947 to 2001.* Washington, DC: Retrieved October 22, 2003, from http://www.census.gov/hhes/income/histinc/f07.html

U.S. Census Bureau. (2003). *Table MS-2. Estimated median age at first marriage, by sex: 1890 to present* (Annual Demographic Supplement to the March 2002 Current Population Survey, Current Population Reports No. Series P20-547). Washington, DC: Author.

Part V

THE CHILDREN:
HOW ARE *THEY* DOING?

As the percentage of working mothers in the United States doubled from the 1970s to the present, politicians, policy analysts, and other opinion leaders questioned the effects that this change would have on the country's children. Early research studies attempted to assess the impact of working mothers on their children and there was a time when it seemed as though every other study that was released attempted to "prove" one side of the argument over the other. The research asked such questions as: Was day care bad for children? Were working mothers depriving their children of maternal love? Were families with working mothers more stressed than families with stay-at-home mothers? Not surprisingly, given the complexity of variables like "working mother" and "day care" that vary along multiple dimensions, the research literature was soon jumbled with mixed results. A single study might provide answers to only part of a question, because multiple variables affect the study outcome. For example, to answer the question, "do working mothers negatively affect their children?", research might say that the prevalence of negative effects might depend on whether the mother bonded with the child in infancy, or if the stress of her current job spills over into the home. It is only when a number of studies investigate the questions of interest in this field that we gain clear answers.

In this section, four chapters trace the effects of mothers' and fathers' employment on children by providing comprehensive reviews of the relevant research evidence. The first, Riggio and Desrochers describe the effects of maternal employment on attitudes children have toward gender roles, and how they plan to combine work and family. Children learn their lessons about work and balancing work and family from their parents and very early through their own experience. According to the Bureau of Labor Statistics, about 40% of 15-year-olds hold a job with a regular employer sometime during the year, mostly in service, sales, or laborer jobs. Other attitudes that are formed early are related to how they will combine work and family and seem to be strongly affected by their mothers' employment status. One study showed that the number of young women expecting to work when they became mothers was greater than the number of young men who expected their wives to work outside the home. Riggio and Desrochers' chapter presents results of a study that looked at the effects of the various work–family attitudes of young adults and the influence of maternal employment.

The history of research on maternal and dual-earner employment and children's development presented in chapter 13 gives the reader important insight into what is known in this area. Gottfried traces the types of questions and paradigms used since the 1980s in studies assessing the effects of working parents on children. She proposes that to assess these effects it is necessary to understand the network of family and contextual factors such as fathers' involvement, maternal attitudes toward parenting and employment, and parental occupational status.

Galinsky's chapter builds on the previous chapter by focusing on four specific public debates: Is having an employed mother good or bad for children?; What about an employed father?; What are the effects of child care?; Is it quality time or quantity time that is important with children? These are sensitive questions that get at the core concerns that many people hold about the changing nature of work and family. These questions are answered by asking the children of working parents. In her research she finds that children do have strong opinions, but have positive opinions about working parents. But these positive attitudes are affected by the type of job their parents hold. For the most part, if the jobs are reasonably demanding and challenging and the workplace environment is supportive this helps improve family life immensely. Galinsky leaves us with an agenda to guide future research in the area.

In chapter 15, Wohl looks at the problem of child care using an innovative lens. In the summer of 2001, as part of the Child Care Action Campaign, she worked with a group who attempted to "un-stick" the national dialogue on child care by considering the pertinent issues for child care in the year 2020 under a number of different possible futures. The focal question was, "How do we best influence societal priorities in American life in a way that values both care and equality, to achieve a better, more caring future for children, families and society for the next generation?" The provocative question resulted in four different futures that extrapolated current events and trends.

In the final chapter, we assess what we now know and still need to know about work–family interaction to make it a reality for a majority of working families. We present a vision for the future and delineate the role of employers, government, families, and researchers.

Chapter 12

The Influence of Maternal Employment on the Work and Family Expectations of Offspring

Heidi R. Riggio
Stephan Desrochers
Claremont McKenna College

The work and family roles of middle-class women in the United States changed dramatically during the late 20th century as women with children, especially young children, continued to enter the workforce in increasing numbers (Barnett & Hyde, 2001; Bond, Galinsky, & Swanberg, 1998). As of 2000, almost 73% of women in the United States with children under age 18 years participated in the labor force (Bureau of Labor Statistics, 2000). Not surprisingly then, the influence of maternal employment on children was the original focus of the "work and family" field that emerged in the 1960s, and it continues to be one of the major themes of the work and family literature today (Perry-Jenkins, Repetti, & Crouter, 2000). Extensive reviews of empirical studies have not shown consistent negative effects of maternal employment on child development (Armistead, Wierson, & Forehand, 1992; Harvey, 1999). Although much research has focused on consequences for childhood and early adolescence, comparatively less research has examined the consequences of earlier maternal employment for offspring in later adolescence and adulthood (Ahmad-Shirali & Bhardwaj, 1994; Bridges & Etaugh, 1996). This is particularly important because important decisions about school to work transitions are made during these years. Identity formation is a crucial developmental task during adolescence and young adulthood, including the development of gender roles and personal ideals toward work and personal relationships, with parents in particular serving as crucial role models of what it means to be an "adult" (Jackson & Tein, 1998; Eccles, 1993).

Most research examining consequences of maternal employment for adolescents and young adults has focused on the development of gender role ideology, particularly how mothers' employment and role satisfaction influence offspring endorsement of nontraditional versus traditional gender roles (Kiecolt & Acock, 1988; Parcel & Menaghan, 1994). Less research, however, has focused explicitly on the work and family attitudes and expectations of adolescents and young adults with working mothers (Bridges & Etaugh, 1995; Castellino, Lerner, Lerner, & von Eye, 1998; Trent & South, 1992). Given that the number of young adults with mothers who worked during their entire childhoods is increasing, understanding the long-term consequences of maternal employment for the development of work and family attitudes and expectations by offspring is becoming increasingly important. This chapter briefly reviews research examining consequences of maternal employment for offspring gender roles and work and family attitudes, and presents new research examining relations between maternal employment and young adult work and family expectations.

MATERNAL EMPLOYMENT
AND OFFSPRING GENDER ROLES

Studies of adolescent gender role development consistently indicate that cross-nationally, boys are more traditional than girls in their attitudes toward women's roles (Helms-Erikson, Tanner, Crouter, & McHale, 2000; Tuck, Rolfe, & Adair, 1994). Additional research indicates that "dual-earner" families in which both parents work are likely to be characterized by more egalitarian views on gender roles, with the distribution of home and work roles between parents likely to be more symmetrical compared to families in which mothers are not employed (Perry-Jenkins, 1993). Both Zuckerman (1981) and Lamb (1998), in extensive reviews of research on children, concluded that both boys and girls with employed mothers report less traditional, more egalitarian gender-role attitudes than children of nonemployed mothers. These results are consistent with the view that a primary function of maternal employment for offspring is mothers' modeling of the occupational role (Barber & Eccles, 1992; Hoffman, 1989).

The findings of studies investigating how maternal employment relates to adolescent and young adult gender roles have been less consistent (Jackson & Tein, 1998). Several studies have indicated that maternal employment is related to increasingly liberal, nontraditional sex-role attitudes, particularly among daughters (Kiecolt & Acock, 1988; Schulenberg, Vondracek, & Crouter, 1984). In contrast, findings from other studies have suggested that maternal unemployment is not related to the sex-role attitudes of adolescents and young adults (Keith, 1988; Starrels, 1992). O'Neal Weeks, Wise, and Duncan (1984) reported that maternal career status was unrelated to the gender-role attitudes of female high school students. Willets-Bloom and Nock (1994) found little support for relations between maternal work status and the gender-role attitudes of college students. However, they also found that young adults with working mothers expressed more favorable attitudes toward working women, a finding that suggests a more direct influence of maternal employment on the development of ideas about women's occupational roles than on the development of broad gender roles. Other recent research indicates that maternal employment per se is unrelated to adolescents' gender roles, but that qualities of mothers' work, including occupational prestige and mothers' role satisfaction and attitude, mediate relations between maternal employment and gender roles of offspring. As such, adolescent development of nontraditional gender roles has been found to be more likely when mothers hold more prestigious jobs, view themselves as equally responsible as fathers for providing for their families, and are satisfied in their multiple roles (Helms-Erickson et al., 2000; Perry-Jenkins, Seery, & Crouter, 1992).

Developmental researchers have repeatedly found that the same-sex parent has a greater influence on adolescent gender roles and attitudes, and is more likely to serve as a role model for educational and career attainment, than the opposite-sex parent (Huston, 1983). Indeed, much research on maternal employment effects on adolescent and young adult gender roles suggests that the strongest, most meaningful effects are for daughters of working mothers. Daughters of employed mothers have been found to be more self-confident, independent, and well-adjusted, to achieve better grades in school, and to exhibit more egalitarian gender-role attitudes than daughters whose mothers are homemakers (Betz & Fitzgerald, 1987; Tsuzuki & Matsui, 1997). As previously mentioned, however, positive effects of maternal employment for daughters are most likely when daughters perceive their mothers as satisfied and happy in their occupational roles (Willetts-Bloom & Nock, 1994). When mothers view their occupations as less central to their identity than mothering, maternal employment is less likely to be influential in the development of sons' and daughters' gender roles (Helms-Erickson et al., 2000). As for negative effects, other research indicates that maternal employment is associated with lower achievement by adolescents when the mothers' work attitudes were inconsistent with their employment status (Paulson, 1996). This finding suggests that a mother's employment is more likely to have a negative impact on children's achievement when she is working but would rather not be.

INFLUENCES ON WORK–FAMILY ATTITUDES
OF YOUNG MEN AND WOMEN

During adolescence and young adulthood, individual self-concept and identity take shape and become consolidated (Tuck et al., 1994). Major features of the consolidation process include the development of specific images of possible future selves that influence occupational and family planning (Markus & Wurf, 1987), and the development of and commitment to specific educational, occupational, marital, and parental goals (Barber & Eccles, 1992). Individual ideas about gender roles are clearly tied to young people's decisions about careers and family, both of which are characterized by distinct gender-role prescriptions in our society, despite the women's movement (Eccles, 1987). As children move into adolescence and adulthood and engage in self-concept and identity formation, their ideas of appropriate occupational choices for themselves are likely to be consistent with their ideas about appropriate gender roles (Gottfredson, 1981), and parents play a primary role in shaping adolescents' career aspirations (Eccles, 1993).

The career aspirations and family plans of adolescents and young adults are also likely to be influenced by the nature of the linkages between gender, work, and family that they observe in the world around them. Among married couples in the United States, wives are more likely than husbands to have jobs characterized by the particularly stressful combination of high demands and low control (Menaghan, 1994); they are likely to be paid less than husbands, giving them less bargaining power at home (Rosenfield, 1989); and they are likely to have a greater share of the responsibility for housework (Hochschild, 1989). Not surprisingly then, employed women tend to have greater combined work and family demands than employed men (Duxbury, Higgins, & Lee, 1994; Shelton, 1990). Together, these conditions result in women being more likely to make work-related sacrifices to accommodate family needs than men.

Empirical findings on work–family tradeoffs are somewhat mixed. Demographic research using large, representative samples of U.S. residents show that moving is more financially costly for married women than for married men, which suggests that husbands' careers are typically the reason for moving, with wives more commonly losing their jobs or taking lower paying jobs as a result of moving (Jacobsen & Levin, 1997). Pixley and Moen (2003) found that both husbands and wives place the husband's career above the wife's career in making decisions that influenced work and family lives, including moving to another residence. In addition, men were more likely than women to have encountered career opportunities that required spouses to make a major change, such as move or change jobs. Furthermore, among those who encountered opportunities, men were more likely than women to have taken advantage of them. In contrast, a recent study by Milkie and Peltola (1999) found that men and women were equally likely to make career sacrifices, including turning down promotions, refusing to work overtime, and cutting back on work. Thus it may be that the data are beginning to show a trend that reflects a much greater commitment to work by many working women. It seems likely that men and women may differ in the types of career sacrifices they are willing to make for their families, but that once engaged in their jobs, women are just as committed to work as are men. It is within this larger social context of work, family, and gender relations that young people are socialized to form expectations and plans regarding their future work and family lives.

If young adults observe a tendency among married couples for husbands' careers to take priority over those of their wives, it seems likely that their own work and family plans for the future might be affected. The results of studies comparing the work and family plans of male and female adolescents and young adults have also been quite mixed (Barber & Eccles, 1992). Two seemingly contradictory finding coexist: Some findings suggest that young women are increasingly expressing more interest in less traditional occupations (Koski & Subich, 1985), and that young men and women are becoming increasing similar in their occupational values, with women placing increasing importance on status-attainment goals (Fiorentine, 1988). On the other hand, other research indicates that stereotypes about women are deeply held and resistant to change (Heilman & Martell, 1986), and that young men's views of housework and child care are still fairly traditional, with most responsibility attributed to wives (Shelton, 1990). Similarly, Thornton (1989) found that young men believed it is most beneficial for families if husbands work outside the home and wives focus on home and family matters. Additional studies have reported large sex differences in occupational plans and values (Herzog & Bachman, 1982), with the work plans of college students and adolescents still largely based on gender-role stereotypes (Eccles, 1987). Barnett's recent study of dual-earner middle-class couples, reported in chapter 11 (this volume), clearly found greater endorsement of egalitarian attitudes and values than any of the earlier studies, again suggesting an increasing trend in this direction.

Past research has also investigated young adults' expectations of combining work and family life. Some researchers have argued that the occupational choices of young women, more so than those of young men, are inextricably tied to their marriage and family plans (Spade & Reese, 1991). Most college women aspire toward both a career and motherhood (Murrell, Frieze, & Frost, 1991; Schroeder, Blood, & Maluso, 1992), and regardless of the status of their planned occupation, young women are still likely to report higher expectations than men for earlier marriage and childbearing (Barnett, Gareis, James, & Steele, 2003). Although some young women report a preference for role-sharing, dual-career families characterized by symmetrical relationships between husbands and wives (Spade & Reese, 1991), other young women report a preference for more conventional dual-career families, where the female spouse maintains primary responsibility for parenting and home life (Hallett & Gilbert, 1997). Additional research has indicated that the majority of college women express a preference for interrupted employment, where they do not work outside the home while their children are very young (O'Connell, Betz, & Kurth, 1989). Baber and Monaghan (1988) found that while 70% of female college students planned to establish careers prior to childbirth, only 30% reported planning to work full-time soon after the birth of children. Other research indicates that the ability to successfully re-enter a career field after taking time off work for childrearing is an important consideration for college women's career selection (Bridges, 1989).

More recent studies suggest that young men and women are expressing increasingly similar concerns about work–family balance issues in their adult lives. Although research indicates that young women report greater expectations of work–family conflict and greater difficulty in career planning because of concerns for marriage and family than men (Novack & Novack, 1996), recent research suggests that employed men now experience as much work–family conflict as women (Bond et al., 1998), a reality that may eventually influence the work and family expectations of young adults. In addition, although previous research indicated that young women expressed greater willingness to modify work roles for family's sake than men (Herzog & Bachman, 1982), recent studies indicate that men and women are equally likely to make career sacrifices, including turning down promotions, to accommodate family responsibilities (Milkie & Peltola, 1999). Young men are expressing an increasing preference for marriage to women who are educated and financially independent (Oppenheimer, 1997), and some research suggests that both young men and women are increasing likely to prefer dual-earner families for themselves, where both partners share economic duties (Moen, 1999). Although there is disagreement in the literature, it seems clear that the work–family expectations of young men and women are different, but that they are also changing as women's participation in the workforce increases and the dual-earner family becomes the modal family form in the United States (Hayghe, 1990).

MATERNAL EMPLOYMENT AND OFFSPRING WORK–FAMILY ATTITUDES

Several studies have examined the influence of maternal employment on the occupational and family aspirations of adolescents, and results are again somewhat mixed. Some findings suggest that younger adolescents with employed mothers are less likely to view a woman's career as having a negative effect on marriage and family than younger adolescents from families with nonworking mothers (Jackson & Tein, 1998), and that daughters of working mothers expect their pattern of participation in homemaking and paid employment to be similar to that of their mothers (Falkowski &

Falk, 1983). Stephan and Corder (1985) found that adolescents raised in dual-career families were more likely to aspire to dual-career families themselves compared to those raised with nonemployed mothers. Tuck and colleagues (1994) found that adolescents with employed mothers expressed more egalitarian attitudes toward work and family roles, attributing equal responsibility for housework, child care, and income to men and women. Additional research suggests that maternal employment, combined with maternal work-role satisfaction, job prestige, and educational attainment, is related to higher and more nontraditional career aspirations of young adolescents (Castellino et al., 1998).

In contrast, other findings reflect less positive effects of maternal employment on work and family attitudes, with older adolescent boys with working mothers being less likely to endorse gender-role equity in spouses' housework and parenting responsibilities than boys with nonworking mothers (Jackson & Tein, 1998). Keith (1988) found similar sex differences in effects of maternal employment, with sons of women in high-status occupations viewing the prospect of a dual-earner family more negatively than sons of nonworking mothers, and daughters' work–family plans unaffected by maternal employment. Still other research indicates that maternal employment has no influence on adolescent occupational aspirations (Davey & Stoppard, 1993; O'Neal Weeks et al., 1984). That these findings are also inconsistent with previous research documenting a liberalizing effect of maternal employment on offspring gender roles provides further evidence that additional investigations of adolescent work and family aspirations in relation to maternal employment are warranted.

Compared to studies focusing on adolescents, relatively more research has focused on the consequences of maternal employment for the work and family expectations of young adults. Many studies have indicated that daughters of employed mothers are more career-oriented and are more likely to pursue nontraditional occupations than daughters of homemaker mothers (cf. Betz & Fitzgerald, 1987). Similarly, with a sample of Japanese college women, Tsuzuki and Matsui (1997) found that maternal employment was related to egalitarian sex-role attitudes, which in turn were related to greater intentions to continue working across the life span. Other studies of young African American and White women in the United States indicate that maternal employment is associated with greater intentions to resume employment after childbirth and intentions to resume employment earlier after the birth of children (Bridges & Etaugh, 1996). Similarly, Willetts-Bloom and Nock (1994) found that young women expressed greater approval of maternal employment when their own mothers were employed for longer periods of time during respondents' childhood. Additional findings are consistent with research suggesting that mothers' satisfaction with occupational roles is critical in determining the influence of maternal employment on young women's gender roles (Helms-Erickson et al., 2000), indicating that young women express greater and more positive work orientations and greater perceived rewards from work when they perceive their mothers to be satisfied in their occupational roles (Matsui, Tsuzuki, & Onglatco, 1999).

The findings of research investigating the influence of maternal employment on the work–family attitudes of young men are less consistent. One study indicated no effects of maternal employment on the work and family role expectations of young men (Thorn & Gilbert, 1998). Other studies indicate that maternal employment is related to more nontraditional attitudes toward marriage, including more positive attitudes toward divorce and nonmarital childbearing (Trent & South, 1992), and more egalitarian views toward division of household labor (Cunningham, 2001), of both male and female college students. One study found that college students with mothers who were employed less during their childhoods reported greater concerns about their marriage and spouses' careers interfering with their own careers. Interestingly, maternal employment during a child's earlier life (before age 12 years) was found to have a much greater influence on expected work–family conflict than maternal employment during adolescence, with earlier maternal employment associated with lower offspring expectations of work–family conflict (Barnett et al., 2003).

THE CURRENT STUDY

Although previous research does provide relatively strong support for the notion that maternal employment affects offspring work and family attitudes, given the growing population of young adults raised by full-time, continuously employed mothers (U.S. Bureau of the Census, 1994), and the inconsistency apparent in some of the research findings, an exploratory study was conducted by the authors to determine differences in specific work–family attitudes of college students with employed and homemaker mothers. A Website-based self-report survey was used to assess male and females students' work and family expectations and plans. A total of 495 young adults (23% men, 77% women, mean age = 21 years) from all over the United States participated.[1] Approximately 81% of participants were White, with 19% reporting non-White or Hispanic ethnicity.

In addition to demographic information, five categories of variables were assessed:

1. *information about parents*, including parents' occupations, annual salary, hours worked per week, and so on;

---

[1]The size of the sample that participated in various analyses varied due to incomplete data.

2. *marriage and family plans*, including plans to marry, have children (including number of children), planned time with spouse and children per week, opinions about responsibilities for housework/child care, opinions about marriage before having children, importance of a happy family to life goals, and so on;

3. *job plans*, including age at first job, expected income during first year and after 20 years in the workforce, age at retirement, desired number of sick/vacation days, desired number of workdays per week and work hours per day;

4. *importance of job features*, including job rewards (salary, promotion, travel, fame/recognition, task variety, teamwork, etc.), and the importance of a good job to life goals;

5. *importance of family–job issues*, including job flexibility (setting one's own schedule, freedom, weekends off, etc.), as well as questions about working from home, switching jobs to spend more time with family, and so on.

Several comparisons were made based on participant sex and whether or not mothers were employed. The main analysis examined the effects of sex, the effects of maternal employment, and the combination of the two in affecting young adults' job and family plans, attitudes about the importance of job features and family–job issues, and attitudes about work–family balance. Three hundred fifty-one participants provided complete data for this analysis. Results indicated significant effects of sex, maternal employment, and the interaction of the two in affecting young adults' attitudes.[2] Socioeconomic status (SES, computed by adding parental annual salaries for each participant) did not have an effect in the analysis.[3]

Effects of Sex.   Results indicated several significant differences between men and women in their job and family plans and expectations (see Table 12.1). First, men reported significantly greater importance of marriage before having children, and significantly greater importance of children being raised by married partners than women, results that are consistent with previous research indicating that young men express more traditional attitudes toward nonmarital childbearing than women (Trent & South, 1992). However, women in the present study expected to spend a significantly greater number of hours with their children per week than men, suggesting a more traditional view of parenting by both men and women in the current study. Men and women did not differ in their ratings of the importance of a happy family to fulfilling life goals.

---

[2]Multivariate results for sex: [$F(19, 329) = 10.23$, $p < .001$, $\eta^2 = .37$]; maternal employment [$F(19, 329) = 2.38$, $p < .001$, $\eta^2 = .12$]; and interaction [$F(19, 329) = 1.94$, $p < .02$, $\eta^2 = .10$].

[3]Results reported are those computed without SES as a covariate.

TABLE 12.1
Mean Work and Family Attitudes of Young Men and Women[a]

	Men (n = 73)		Women (n = 278)		
	Mean	SD	Mean	SD	F-value
Marriage/Family Plans					
Time per week w/ spouse[b]	87.5	28.2	84.9	26.7	<1
Time per week w/ children[b]	49.8	27.8	78.7	23.4	93.69***
Number of children planned	3.6	1.8	3.2	1.7	2.38
Age at first child	24.5	3.7	23.6	2.7	<1
Importance of marriage before childbearing	4.7	.74	4.3	1.1	4.51*
Importance of married parents	4.6	.91	4.0	1.3	9.68**
Importance of one parent at home for children	2.6	.89	2.8	.96	<1
Importance of family to life goals	4.8	.61	4.7	.64	<1
Job Plans					
Age at first job	24.5	3.9	23.6	3.0	8.62**
Hours of work per day	8.6	1.8	8.0	1.5	8.92**
Age at retirement	61.2	9.3	59.9	8.4	3.79*
Importance of a good job to life goals	4.2	.78	3.8	.99	12.51***
Job Features	45.8	6.3	46.7	5.6	<1
Job Flexibility	23.9	3.5	24.9	3.3	6.10*

Note. Degrees of freedom for all F-values are 1, 347. Total error rate for significant univariate tests = .11; without age at retirement and importance of marriage before children, α = .024.

***$p < .001$. **$p < .01$. *$p < .05$.

[a]All dependent variables analyzed in MANOVA are not included in this table.

[b]Table entry is hours per week.

Second, results indicated that some of the job plans of young men and women were significantly different. Women in the present study reported a significantly younger age at the time of first full-time job than men, while men expected to work significantly more hours per day and expected older age at retirement than women. Men also reported significantly greater importance of a good job to fulfilling life goals than women. Men and women did not differ in preferences for sick days or vacation days. Third, women reported significantly greater importance of job flexibility in the desirability of future jobs than men. Finally, frequency analyses indicated additional sex differences, with a greater number of men (9.2%) than women (1.6%) reporting that it was not okay if their spouse earned more money than they did, and a greater number of men (27.3%) than women (1.9%) reporting that if they themselves earned enough money, they would not want their spouse to work. With the exception age-at-first-job finding, these results suggest more traditional attitudes of young men toward work and family expectations compared to women.

Effects of Maternal Employment.   Results indicated several significant differences in the family and job plans of young adults whose mothers were employed and those whose mothers were not employed (see Table 12.2). First, young adults with employed mothers reported more liberal attitudes toward family plans than those with nonemployed mothers. Individuals with employed mothers reported significantly less importance of marriage before children, less importance of children being raised by married partners, and less importance of one parent always being at home with children than individuals with nonemployed mothers. Individuals with employed mothers also reported significantly older age at the birth of their first child, as well as plans for significantly fewer children of their own compared to individuals with nonemployed mothers.

Additional frequency analyses indicated that individuals with employed mothers were more likely to respond "I don't know" to the question, "Do you intend to have children?" (16%) than individuals with nonemployed mothers (6%); that a greater percentage of individuals with employed

TABLE 12.2
Mean Work and Family Attitudes of Young Adults
With Employed and Nonemployed Mothers[a]

	Employed Mother (n = 253)		Nonemployed Mother (n = 98)		
	Mean	SD	Mean	SD	F-value
Marriage/Family Plans					
Time per week w/ spouse[b]	83.0	26.7	91.7	26.8	1.03
Time per week w/ children[b]	71.6	25.5	75.4	30.6	<1
Number of children planned	3.0	1.4	4.1	2.0	21.88***
Age at first child	27.2	2.6	26.2	3.5	9.24**
Importance of marriage before childbearing	4.3	1.2	4.7	.68	5.71*
Importance of married parents	4.0	1.3	4.6	.87	9.43**
Importance of one parent at home for children	2.6	1.0	3.0	.72	12.57***
Importance of family to life goals	4.7	.70	4.9	.39	5.42*
Job Plans					
Age at first job	23.7	3.4	24.0	2.8	4.03*
Hours of work per day	8.1	1.6	8.0	1.7	<1
Age at retirement	61.1	8.0	57.8	9.6	2.96
Importance of a good job to life goals	4.0	.90	3.7	1.1	2.39
Job Features	46.5	5.8	46.5	5.7	<1
Job Flexibility	24.5	3.4	25.2	3.0	1.33

Note. Degrees of freedom for all *F*-values are 1, 347. Total error rate for significant univariate tests = .09; without age at first job, α = .043.
***p < .001. **p < .01. *p < .05.
[a]All dependent variables analyzed in MANOVA are not included in this table.
[b]Table entry is hours per week.

mothers reported that husbands and wives should share equal responsibility for childcare (78%) compared to individuals with nonemployed mothers (58%); and that a greater percentage of individuals with employed mothers reported that husbands and wives should be equally responsible for housework (87%) compared to individuals with nonemployed mothers (69%). These results complement previous studies indicating that maternal employment is associated with more liberal work and family attitudes of young women (Bridges & Etaugh, 1996; Willetts-Bloom & Nock, 1994), although they are somewhat unique in terms of relations between maternal employment and the work and family attitudes of young men (Helms-Erikson et al., 2000; Jackson & Tein, 1998; Keith, 1988; Thorn & Gilbert, 1998).

Second, individuals with employed mothers also reported somewhat different job expectations than individuals with unemployed mothers. Individuals with employed mothers reported significantly younger age at first full-time job than individuals with nonemployed mothers, and they also reported significantly higher expected age at retirement than individuals with nonemployed mothers. These results are consistent with previous research documenting more positive work orientations of young women with employed mothers (Betz & Fitzgerald, 1987; Tsuzuki & Matsui, 1997), but again they are relatively unique in that they are based on the responses of both young men and women.

Interaction of Sex and Maternal Employment.   Of particular interest are different effects of maternal employment in affecting work and family plans and expectations of young men and women. Analyses indicated several significant differences between the work and family attitudes of young men and women with employed and nonemployed mothers. First, young women with employed mothers reported the fewest number of planned hours per week spent with a spouse (M = 81.5), while young women with nonemployed mothers reported the greatest number of planned hours with a spouse per week (M = 94.1). The opposite pattern was apparent for young men: those with employed mothers planned to spend more time per week with their spouse (M = 89.0) compared to those with nonemployed mothers (M = 84.2). Similar results were found for the planned number of hours per week spent with children. Young women with employed mothers reported planning to spend fewer hours per week with children (M = 76.1) compared to young women with nonemployed mothers (M = 85.7), while young men with employed mothers reported planning to spend more hours per week with children (M = 53.5) compared to young men with nonemployed mothers (M = 41.8). These results are particularly interesting because they appear to reflect both young women's awareness that employed mothers are likely to spend less time at home with spouses and children, and young men's awareness that with an employed wife, husbands are likely to spend more time at home with spouses and children. This awareness of young men and women can be tied to their experience of having an employed mother.

Second, young men and women with employed and nonemployed mothers also differed somewhat on their job plans and expectations. Interestingly, both young men and women with employed mothers, and women with nonemployed mothers, reported similar expected age at the time of first full-time job (means = 23.4 to 23.8). However, young men with nonemployed mothers reported a significantly older expected age at the time of first full-time job (M = 26.0). Further, the sex by maternal employment interaction was also significant for expected age at retirement, with both men and women with employed mothers, and men with nonemployed mothers reporting similar expected age at retirement (means = 61.1 to 61.4). Women with nonemployed mothers, however, reported a significantly younger expected age at retirement (M = 56.7). These results suggest that individuals with working mothers are likely to expect to engage in full-time work at younger ages and to continue to work until older ages, while young men with nonemployed mothers expect a greater delay between education and full-time work, and young women with nonemployed mothers expect to quit working at an earlier age.

Additional frequency analyses were conducted to examine differences in the responses of men and women with employed and nonemployed mothers. First, frequency analyses indicated that a significantly greater number of men and women with employed mothers reported that husbands and wives were equally responsible for housework (86% and 87%, respectively) compared to men and women with nonemployed mothers (66% and 70%, respectively). Similarly, a significantly greater number of men and women with employed mothers reported that husbands and wives should share equal responsibility for child care (74% and 79%, respectively) compared to men and women with nonemployed mothers (53% and 60%, respectively). Finally, significantly greater numbers of men and women with nonemployed mothers reported that if there spouse earned enough money, they would not want their spouse to work (38% and 3%, respectively) compared to men and women with employed mothers (22% and 1%, respectively).

CONCLUSIONS AND FUTURE DIRECTIONS

Despite some inconsistency in the literature, particularly in research on adolescents, much previous research and results of the current study suggest that both sex and maternal employment have a meaningful influence on the work and family plans and expectations of young adults, with results of the current study indicating moderate to large effects. Consistent with previous findings indicating that young men are likely to express more traditional attitudes toward family and marriage than women (Helms-Erikson et al., 2000; Thornton, 1989), the current results indicated that young men rated marriage before childbearing and children being raised by married parents as significantly more important than did young women. Furthermore, young men expected to spend significantly fewer hours with their children each week and a greater preference for a nonworking spouse than women, consistent with more traditional views of family. Although they expect to work at a younger age than men and express less traditional attitudes toward marriage, young women in the current study expressed greater concern about work–family balance, rating job flexibility in terms of family issues as more important than did men, and expressing an interest in working fewer hours per day and spending more time with their children than men. These results are consistent with previous research indicating that young women's future plans include both a focus on career and motherhood (Murrell et al., 1991; Schroeder et al., 1992).

The current study also indicated several meaningful effects of maternal employment on the work and family plans of young adults. First, consistent with previous research indicating that offspring of working mothers tend to express egalitarian, liberal attitudes toward marriage and parenting (Castellino et al., 1998; Trent & South, 1992; Tuck et al., 1994), young men and women with working mothers expressed more liberal attitudes toward family life than those whose mothers did not engage in paid work. Specifically, children of working mothers expressed more positive attitudes toward having children outside of marriage, raising children with only one parent, and having someone other than a parent at home caring for children. Second, young adults with employed mothers planned to have fewer children and to have them at an older age than young adults with nonemployed mothers, suggesting that young adults who grew up with a working mother realize that parents in larger families are likely to experience greater work–family conflict, especially when parents have children at a younger age (Duxbury & Higgins, 2001).

Interestingly, the current results also indicated that although women with employed mothers planned to spend less time per week with their spouse and children compared to women with nonemployed mothers, men with employed mothers planned to spend *more* time per week with their spouse and children compared to men with nonemployed mothers, again suggesting that young men (as well as women) with working mothers develop more nontraditional, egalitarian attitudes toward parenting than offspring with nonemployed mothers. Men with employed mothers also expressed more nontraditional, role-sharing attitudes concerning housework and child care, as well as greater acceptance of wives' working and earning money, than men and women with nonemployed mothers. In contrast, men with nonemployed mothers, compared to all other groups, reported an older expected age at the time of first full-time job, perhaps suggesting that these young men are more comfortable relying on parents and less urgent in obtaining full-time work, as their mothers remain available to them for caretaking.

Research on maternal employment and its effects on young adult offspring will undoubtedly continue, given the growing number of mothers who are employed (particularly during children's infancy and preschool years) and the increasingly common finding that maternal employment is associated with more nontraditional, liberal sex role and work–family attitudes. Future research may pay particular attention to several issues. First, although societal attitudes toward working women have changed considerably (Dambrot, Papp, & Whitmore, 1984), research suggests that there are several negative stereotypes commonly held about women who work, especially women who work when their children are very young. Employed mothers are frequently viewed as less dedicated to families, less sensitive to the needs of others, more selfish, and less affectionate than mothers who stay at home with their children (Etaugh & Nekolny, 1990). The work performance of working mothers is also viewed more negatively, as children are often expected to adversely affect job performance (Etaugh & Poertner, 1989). Perhaps as general evaluations of working mothers become more positive, and as the sex-role ideologies of young men and women continue to converge (Moen, 1999; Oppenheimer, 1997), the family and work attitudes of young adult offspring of working mothers may also change.

Future research on the effects of maternal employment may also focus more intently on the experiences of young adult offspring who are members of ethnic minority groups. Although some research has focused on sex-role ideology and work–family attitudes of African American and Asian groups (Bridges & Etaugh, 1996; Matsui et al., 1999; Tsuzuki & Matsui, 1997), Latino groups have been largely overlooked. Given the more traditional cultural attitudes toward sex roles and the emphasis on familism among Latino groups (Rice, 1995), maternal employment is possibly less accepted and viewed more negatively in these populations. In addition, the attitudes of Latino fathers expressed toward maternal employment may be particularly relevant in the shaping of children's work–family attitudes. On the other hand, the necessity of maternal employment in American families may be especially pressing in Latino families, since Latino men have a higher rate of unemployment than White or Asian men, and their weekly wages for full-time work are lower than those of Black men and far lower than those of White men (Bureau of Labor Statistics, 2001). Future research may include comparisons of the effects of maternal employment on the work–family attitudes of offspring in White and Latino populations.

There are several limitations to the current study. First, several meaning-ful demographic and maternal employment variables were not assessed, in-cluding parental marital status, length and continuity of maternal employ-ment, and respondent's age when mother began working outside the home. Because maternal employment is clearly related to divorce, as moth-ers are more likely to work outside the home when their marriages end (Chase-Lansdale & Hetherington, 1990), distinguishing between single-parent and dual-earner families is important in examining consequences for adolescent and young adult offspring (Duckett & Richards, 1995). In addition, as the current study and previous research on children indicate differences in effects of maternal employment based on whether mothers worked full- or part-time (Richards & Duckett, 1994), it seems important for research to examine how length and continuity of maternal employ-ment are related to outcomes for offspring. Previous research also suggests that maternal employment beginning earlier in childhood may be particu-larly meaningful in affecting young adults' attitudes (Barnett et al., 2003). Young adults with mothers who worked consistently throughout their en-tire childhoods perhaps have different work–family attitudes compared to young adults with mothers who worked sporadically or for shorter periods of time.

As the population of young adults with employed mothers grows, and as dual-earner families increasingly represent the modal American family, the dominant sex-role attitudes and work and family concerns in our society are likely to change. As such, knowledge concerning sex-role attitudes and sex-role related educational, career, and family goals may become fairly out-dated rather quickly. In addition, research indicates that conflicts between work and family are related to a variety of negative outcomes for workers and families, including decreased self-esteem (Pearlin, 1983), higher nega-tive affect (Paden & Buehler, 1995), and marital withdrawal and withdrawal from the family (MacEwen & Barling, 1994). With the continuing focus of both popular and scientific observers on the negative work, family, and mental health outcomes associated with high work–family conflict (Frone, 2000), it is becoming increasingly important to understand how individual attitudes toward work and family are developed, and how they can be changed. Attitudes toward employed mothers in the workplace are often negative, as they are viewed as less professional and less committed to their jobs than men and women without children (Sobkowski, 1989). As young adults with employed mothers enter the workforce themselves, their atti-tudes are likely to be influential in changing organizational attitudes to-ward working mothers. As they begin their own families, their attitudes to-ward work and family issues will become increasingly important in changing societal sex-role expectations and beliefs. Societal concern for and focus on work–family conflict is already increasing (Peake & Harris,

2002); continuing research on the effects of maternal employment on off-spring work–family attitudes and on society as a whole is critical in increasing societal and organizational responsiveness to the work and family concerns of the modern family.

ACKNOWLEDGMENTS

We wish to thank Diane Halpern for envisioning the project on which this chapter is based. We also wish to thank Devang Vussonji (CMC) for developing a Web-based survey, and Joy Pixley (UC Irvine) who provided review and comments.

REFERENCES

Ahmad-Shirali, K., & Bhardwaj, K. (1994). Family communication and adjustment of female adolescents of working mothers in the hills. *Journal of Personality and Clinical Studies, 10*(1/2), 59–64.

Armistead, L., Wierson, M., & Forehand, R. (1992). Adolescents and maternal employment: Is it harmful for a young adolescent to have an employed mother? *Journal of Early Adolescence, 10*(3), 260–278.

Baber, K. M., & Monaghan, P. (1988). College women's career and motherhood expectations: New options, old dilemmas. *Sex Roles, 19*, 189–203.

Barber, B. L., & Eccles, J. S. (1992). Long-term influence of divorce and single parenting on adolescent family- and work-related values, behaviors, and aspirations. *Psychological Bulletin, 111*, 108–126.

Barnett, R. C., Gareis, K. C., James, J. B., & Steele, J. (2003). Planning ahead: College seniors' concerns about career–marriage conflict. *Journal of Vocational Behavior, 62*, 305–319.

Barnett, R. C., & Hyde, J. S. (2001). Women, men, work, and family: An expansionist perspective. *American Psychologist, 56*, 781–796.

Betz, N. E., & Fitzgerald, L. F. (1987). *The career psychology of women.* New York: Academic Press.

Bond, J. T., Galinsky, E., & Swanberg, J. E. (1998). *The 1997 National Study of the Changing Workforce.* New York: Families and Work Institute.

Bridges, J. S. (1989). Sex differences in occupational values. *Sex Roles, 20*, 205–211.

Bridges, J. S., & Etaugh, C. (1995). College students' perceptions of mothers: Effects of maternal employment-childrearing pattern and motive for employment. *Sex Roles, 32*, 735–751.

Bridges, J. S., & Etaugh, C. (1996). Black and white college women's maternal employment outcome expectations and their desired timing of maternal employment. *Sex Roles, 35*(9/10), 543–562.

Bureau of Labor Statistics. (2000). *Statistical tables: Employment and the labor force.* Retrieved September 22, 2003, from http://www.bls.gov/opub/rtaw/stattab2.htm

Bureau of Labor Statistics. (2001). *Counting minorities: A brief history and look at the future.* Retrieved September 25, 2003, from http://www.bls.gov/opup/rtaw/pdf/chapter1.pdf

Castellino, D. R., Lerner, J. V., Lerner, R. M., & von Eye, A. (1998). Maternal employment and education: Predictors of young adolescent career trajectories. *Applied Developmental Science, 2*(3), 114–126.

Chase-Lansdale, P. L., & Hetherington, E. M. (1990). The impact of divorce on life-span development: Short and long-term effects. In P. B. Baltes, D. L. Featherman, & R. M. Lerner (Eds.), *Life-span development and behavior: Vol. 10* (pp. 105–150). Hillsdale, NJ: Lawrence Erlbaum Associates.

Cunningham, M. (2001). The influence of parental attitudes and behaviors on children's attitudes toward gender and household labor in early adulthood. *Journal of Marriage and the Family, 63,* 111–122.

Dambrot, F., Papp, M., & Whitmore, C. (1984). The sex-role attitudes of three generations of women. *Personality and Social Psychology Bulletin, 10,* 469–473.

Davey, F. H., & Stoppard, J. M. (1993). Some factors affecting the occupational expectations of female adolescents. *Journal of Vocational Behavior, 43,* 235–250.

Duckett, E., & Richards, M. H. (1995). Maternal employment and the quality of daily experience for young adolescents of single mothers. *Journal of Family Psychology, 9,* 418–432.

Duxbury, L., & Higgins, C. (2001). *Work–life balance in the new millennium: Where are we? Where do we need to go?* (W/12). Ottawa: Canadian Policy Research Networks.

Duxbury, L., Higgins, C., & Lee, C. (1994). Work–family conflict: A comparison by gender, family type, and perceived control. *Journal of Family Issues, 15*(3), 449–466.

Eccles, J. S. (1987). Gender roles and women's achievement-related decisions. *Psychology of Women Quarterly, 11,* 135–172.

Eccles, J. S. (1993). Understanding women's educational and occupational choices. *Psychology of Women Quarterly, 18,* 585–609.

Etaugh, C., & Nekolny, K. (1990). Effects of employment status on employment of mothers. *Sex Roles, 23,* 273–280.

Etaugh, C., & Poertner, P. (1989, August). *Perceptions of women? Influence of performance, marital, and parental variables.* Paper presented at the meeting of the American Psychological Association, New Orleans, LA.

Falkowski, C. K., & Falk, W. W. (1983). Homemaking as an occupational plan: Evidence from a national longitudinal study. *Journal of Vocational Behavior, 22,* 227–242.

Fiorentine, R. (1988). Increasing similarity in the values and life plans of male and female college students? Evidence and implications. *Sex Roles, 18,* 143–158.

Frone, M. R. (2000). Work–family conflict and employee psychiatric disorders: The National Co-Morbidity Survey. *Journal of Applied Psychology, 85,* 888–895.

Gottfredson, L. S. (1981). Circumscription and compromise: A developmental theory of occupational aspirations. *Journal of Counseling Psychology, 28,* 545–579.

Hallett, M. B., & Gilbert, L. A. (1997). Variables differentiating university women considering role-sharing and conventional dual-career marriages. *Journal of Vocational Behavior, 50,* 308–322.

Harvey, E. (1999). Short-term and long-term effects of parental employment on children of the National Longitudinal Survey of Youth. *Developmental Psychology, 35,* 445–459.

Hayghe, H. V. (1990, March). Family members in the work force. *Monthly Labor Review,* 14–19.

Heilman, M., & Martell, R. (1986). Exposure to successful women: Antidote to sex discrimination in applicant screening decisions. *Organizational Behavior and Human Decision Processes, 37,* 376–390.

Helms-Erikson, H., Tanner, J. L., Crouter, A. C., & McHale, S. M. (2000). Do women's provider-role attitudes moderate the links between work and family? *Journal of Family Psychology, 14,* 658–670.

Herzog, A. R., & Bachman, J. G. (1982). *Sex role attitudes among high school seniors.* Ann Arbor, MI: Institute for Social Research.

Hochschild, A. (1989). *The second shift.* New York: Avon.

Hoffman, L. W. (1989). Effects of maternal employment in the two-parent family. *American Psychologist, 44,* 283–292.

Huston, A. C. (1983). Sex-typing. In P. H. Mussen & E. M. Hetherington (Eds.), *Handbook of child psychology: Vol. 4. Socialization, personality, and social development.* New York: Wiley.

Jackson, D. W., & Tein, J. (1998). Adolescents' conceptualization of adult roles: Relationships with age, gender, work goal, and maternal employment. *Sex Roles, 38,* 987–1008.

Jacobsen, J. P., & Levin, L. M. (1997). Marriage and migration: Comparing gains and losses for migration for couples and singles. *Social Science Quarterly, 78,* 688–709.

Keith, P. M. (1988). The relationship of self-esteem, maternal employment, and work–family plans to sex role orientations of late adolescents. *Adolescence, 23,* 959–966.

Kiecolt, K. J., & Acock, A. C. (1988). The long-term effects of family structure on gender-role attitudes. *Journal of Marriage and the Family, 50,* 709–717.

Koski, L. K., & Subich, L. M. (1985). Career and homemaking choices of college preparatory and vocational education students. *The Vocational Guidance Quarterly, 34,* 116–123.

Lamb, M. E. (Ed.). (1998). *Parenting and child development in "nontraditional" families.* Mahwah, NJ: Lawrence Erlbaum Associates.

MacEwen, K. E., & Barling, J. (1994). Daily consequences of work interference with family and family interference with work. *Work and Stress, 8*(3), 244–254.

Markus, H., & Wurf, E. (1987). The dynamic self-concept: A social psychological perspective. *Annual Review of Psychology, 38,* 299–331.

Matsui, T., Tsuzuki, Y., & Onglatco, M. (1999). Some motivational bases for work and home orientation among Japanese college women: A rewards/costs analysis. *Journal of Vocational Behavior, 54,* 114–126.

Menaghan, E. G. (1994). The daily grind: Work stressors, family patterns, and intergenerational outcomes. In W. R. Avison & I. H. Gotlib (Eds.), *Stress and mental health: Contemporary issues and prospects for the future.* New York: Plenum Press.

Milkie, M. A., & Peltola, P. (1999). Playing all the roles: Gender and the work–family balancing act. *Journal of Marriage and the Family, 61,* 476–490.

Moen, P. (1999). *The Cornell couples and careers study.* Ithaca, NY: Cornell Employment and Family Careers Institute, Cornell University.

Murrell, A. J., Frieze, I. H., & Frost, J. L. (1991). Aspiring to careers in male- and female-dominated professions: A study of Black and White college women. *Psychology of Women Quarterly, 15,* 103–126.

Novack, L. L., & Novack, D. R. (1996). Being female in the eighties and nineties: Conflicts between new opportunities and traditional expectations among White, middle class, heterosexual college women. *Sex Roles, 35,* 57–77.

O'Connell, L., Betz, M., & Kurth, S. (1989). Plans for balancing work and family life: Do women pursuing nontraditional and traditional occupations differ? *Sex Roles, 20,* 35–45.

O'Neal Weeks, M., Wise, G. W., & Duncan, C. (1984). The relationship between sex-role attitudes and career orientations of high school females and their mothers. *Adolescence, 75,* 595–607.

Oppenheimer, V. K. (1997). Women's employment and the gain to marriage: The specialization and trading model. *Annual Review of Sociology, 23,* 431–453.

Paden, S. L., & Buehler, C. (1995). Coping with the dual-income lifestyle. *Journal of Marriage and the Family, 57,* 101–110.

Parcel, T. L., & Menaghan, E. G. (1994). *Parents' jobs and children's lives.* New York: Aldine de Gruyter.

Paulson, S. E. (1996). Maternal employment and adolescent achievement revisited: An ecological perspective. *Family Relations, 45*(2), 201–208.

Peake, A., & Harris, K. L. (2002). Young adults' attitudes toward multiple role planning: The influence of gender, career traditionality and marriage plans. *Journal of Vocational Behavior, 60,* 405–421.

Pearlin, L. I. (1983). Role strains and personal stress. In H. H. Kaplan (Ed.), *Psychosocial stress: Trends in theory and research* (pp. 3–32). New York: Academic Press.

Perry-Jenkins, M. (1993). Family roles and responsibilities: What has changed and what has remained the same? In J. Frankel (Ed.), *The employed mother and the family context* (pp. 245–259). New York: Springer-Verlag.

Perry-Jenkins, M., Repetti, R. L., & Crouter, A. C. (2000). Work and family in the 1990s. *Journal of Marriage and the Family, 62*, 981–998.

Perry-Jenkins, M., Seery, B., & Crouter, A. C. (1992). Linkages between women's provider-role attitudes, psychological well-being, and family relationships. *Psychology of Women Quarterly, 16*, 311–329.

Pixley, J. E., & Moen, P. (2003). Prioritizing his and her careers. In P. Moen (Ed.), *It's about time: Couples' career strains, strategies, and successes* (pp. 183–200). Ithaca, NY: Cornell University Press.

Rice, F. P. (1995). *Intimate relationships, marriages, and families* (3rd ed.). Mountain View, CA: Mayfield.

Richards, M. H., & Duckett, E. (1994). Maternal employment and young adolescents' daily experience with and without parents. *Child Development, 65*, 225–236.

Rosenfield, S. (1989). The effects of women's employment: Personal control and sex difference in mental health. *Journal of Health and Social Behavior, 21*, 33–42.

Schroeder, K. A., Blood, L. L., & Maluso, D. (1992). An intergenerational analysis of expectations for women's career and family roles. *Sex Roles, 26*, 273–291.

Schulenberg, J. E., Vondracek, F. W., & Crouter, A. C. (1984). The influence of the family on vocational development. *Journal of Marriage and the Family, 46*, 129–143.

Shelton, B. A. (1990). The distribution of household tasks: Does wife's employment status make a difference? *Journal of Family Issues, 11*(2), 115–135.

Sobkowski, A. (1989, May/June). The mommy track controversy. *Executive Female*, pp. 40–42, 67–68.

Spade, J. Z., & Reese, C. A. (1991). We've come a long way maybe: College students' plans for work and family. *Sex Roles, 24*, 309–321.

Starrels, M. E. (1992). Attitude similarity between mothers and children regarding maternal employment. *Journal of Marriage and the Family, 54*, 91–103.

Stephan, C. W., & Corder, J. (1985). The effects of dual-career families on adolescents' sex role attitudes, work and family plans, and choices of important others. *Journal of Marriage and the Family, 47*, 921–929.

Thorn, B. L., & Gilbert, L. A. (1998). Antecedents of work and family role expectations of college men. *Journal of Family Psychology, 12*, 259–267.

Thornton, A. (1989). Changing attitudes toward family issues in the United States. *Journal of Marriage and the Family, 51*, 877–893.

Trent, K., & South, S. J. (1992). Sociodemographic status, parental background, childhood family structure, and attitudes toward family formation. *Journal of Marriage and the Family, 54*, 427–439.

Tsuzuki, Y., & Matsui, T. (1997). Factors influencing intention to continue work throughout the life span among Japanese college women: A path analysis. *College Student Journal, 31*, 216–223.

Tuck, B., Rolfe, J., & Adair, V. (1994). Adolescents' attitude toward gender roles within work and its relationship to gender type and parental occupation. *Sex Roles, 31*, 547–558.

U.S. Bureau of the Census. (1994). *Statistical abstract of the United States: 1994* (114th ed.). Washington, DC: U.S. Government Printing Office.

Willets-Bloom, M. C., & Nock, S. L. (1994). The influence of maternal employment on gender role attitudes of men and women. *Sex Roles, 30*, 371–389.

Zuckerman, D. M. (1981). Family background, sex-role attitudes, and life goals of technical college and university students. *Sex Roles, 7*, 1109–1126.

Chapter 13

Maternal and Dual-Earner Employment and Children's Development: Redefining the Research Agenda

Adele Eskeles Gottfried
California State University, Northridge

Over the course of the 20th century and into the 21st, the United States has seen a dramatic demographic trend that shows a large majority of mothers are employed (Bianchi, 2000; A. E. Gottfried, A. W. Gottfried, & Bathurst, 2002). Not only has this trend occurred for mothers of school age children, but also for mothers of infants and preschoolers. The present chapter will not provide an exhaustive review of literature concerning the impact of maternal employment on children's development. Such reviews have already been provided with the overall conclusion that maternal employment per se is not a detriment to children's development from infancy through adolescence (e.g., see Etaugh, 1974; A. E. Gottfried & A. W. Gottfried, 1988a, 1988b; A. E. Gottfried, A. W. Gottfried, & Bathurst, 1995, 2002; Hoffman, 1974, 1984, 1989; Hoffman & Youngblade, 1999; Lerner, 1994). Rather it is the context of parental employment, rather than maternal employment per se, that is the potent and explanatory factor related to children's development. This chapter presents issues that should redefine the future research agenda regarding maternal and dual-earner employment and children's development.

TRENDS IN THE RESEARCH ON MATERNAL EMPLOYMENT AND CHILDREN'S DEVELOPMENT

Phases of Research

Historically, the research on maternal employment and children's development can be divided into three general sequential phases, which also define the central issues in this field of study (A. E. Gottfried et al., 2002). Phase 1 can best be described as the period that investigators searched for the direct effects of maternal employment on children's development. It began with an empirical question guided by the expectation that maternal employment would be detrimental to children's development due to maternal absence during the time mother was working (A. E. Gottfried et al., 1995). In this early phase of research, researchers made direct comparisons of the children of employed and nonemployed mothers, usually without examining parenting directly, and the implication was that any difference between the groups was due to the direct impact that employment had on the maternal role (A. E. Gottfried, 1988). Early research on maternal employment was influenced by negative expectations of maternal employment on parenting and consequently on children's development. Many studies expected to detect detriment to children (e.g., Hand, 1957). Maternal absence through employment was believed to be deprivational, and research was designed to test the maternal deprivation perspective (Burchinal, 1963; Nye, Perry, & Ogles, 1963). Psychoanalytic theory provided a foundation for this perspective because the mother was considered to be of unparalleled importance to her child's psychological development (Bretherton, 1993).

Research has not substantiated the expected detriment to children presumably caused by maternal employment. One might draw the conclusion that maternal employment per se is neither facilitative nor detrimental to parenting and children's development. This conclusion is based on extensive empirical data across research studies and exhaustive reviews of research (Etaugh, 1974; A. E. Gottfried & A. W. Gottfried, 1988a; A. E. Gottfried et al., 1995, 2002; A. E. Gottfried, A. W. Gottfried, Bathurst, & Killian, 1999; Hoffman, 1989; Lerner, 1994; Spitze, 1995; Zaslow, Rabinovich, & Suwalsky, 1991). Not only did early Phase 1 research fail to consider the multifaceted role of parenting, the research did not account for heterogeneity within the employed and nonemployed mother groups, such as family socioeconomic status (SES), maternal occupational status and work hours, number of children in the home, mothers' and fathers' involvement, home environment, and maternal well-being. These factors could be responsible for differences between the groups that were obtained (A. E. Gottfried et al., 1995).

Researchers increasingly saw the need to move beyond the direct effects approach of Phase 1 research, and the research has entered Phase 2, which characterizes the current trend. The research within this phase is predicated by the view that maternal employment is embedded within the complex network of cultural, developmental, environmental, family, and socioeconomic factors. In order to fully understand the role of maternal employment in parenting and children's development, these factors need to be taken into account. Phase 2 concerns delineating the maternal employment variable into more refined issues and is characterized as adopting a mediational viewpoint. Hence, it has replaced the direct effects approach that guided the research issues of Phase 1. Phase 2 research is instead concerned with the processes that mediate between maternal employment and children's development, and therefore maternal employment is viewed as playing an indirect role in children's development. Variables such as family SES, mothers' work hours and occupational status, maternal attitudes toward employment and parenting, role division between employed mothers and fathers, paternal involvement, and the quality of home environment play a dominant role in researchers' formulation of hypotheses and models to test (e.g., Hoffman & Youngblade, 1999; Lerner, 1994).

Although Phase 2 research has contributed to our knowledge about the role played by parental employment in family functioning and children's development, it continues to perpetuate adverse views of the impact of maternal employment. For example, themes such as maternal stress and role strain have been two such variables studied (e.g., Barling, 1990; Repetti & Wood, 1997). Although this approach has contributed to an increased understanding of the indirect manner in which work roles and conditions may impact children through parenting, its focus on work stress and role strains also serves to limit new conceptualizations of the role of maternal employment in parenting and children's development. It is important for the definition of research issues to advance beyond this perspective because when research is framed to focus on stress, researchers are less likely to attend to the positive and adaptive functions of maternal and dual-earner employment with regard to parenting and children's development.

A. E. Gottfried et al. (2002) proposed that maternal employment research will make additional headway only when new research questions are formed in which maternal and dual-earner employment are conceptualized more positively, and in which families are viewed as adaptive. Families themselves are implicitly developing new definitions of parenting roles between mothers and fathers. Therefore, the role of these new definitions and adaptive features of the family should be used to understand the effects of maternal and dual-earner employment for parenting and children's development. Unfortunately, in the time since this proposal was originally advanced, not only has there been no movement in the field to redirect the research issues, but a trend to search for negativity about mothers' employment has continued.

Perspectives in the Research

Whereas there are no overarching theories that pervade this field, the literature is characterized by many themes and perspectives. These theoretical perspectives include the following: maternal deprivation, compensation, developmental impingement, and adaptation (A. E. Gottfried et al., 2002; A. E. Gottfried & A. W. Gottfried, 1994; A. E. Gottfried et al., 1994, 1995, 1999). These perspectives are particularly important because their basic underpinnings provide an interpretation of the data that serves to structure the research questions posed. For example, the *maternal deprivation* perspective posits that, when the mother is no longer the primary caregiver, deprivation occurs and children's development suffers as a consequence. This perspective was derived from the psychoanalytic view of family functioning in which the mother–child relationship is regarded as being of principal significance in the child's psychological development (Bretherton, 1993). Hence, according to this perspective, in early research, maternal employment was conceptualized as a form of maternal absence due to employment, and hence the child was considered to be deprived of being with the mother while she was at work (Burchinal, 1963; Nye, Perry, & Ogles, 1963). Today, few studies discuss maternal absence due to employment, albeit the legacy of this approach continues to exist in the form of an underlying skepticism that maternal employment, even if the norm, is still not optimal, and in the framing of questions that seek to determine negative outcomes.

The *compensation* perspective typically holds that fathers' increased involvement due to mothers' employment serves to compensate for the mothers' absence when she is at work. Certainly, the data strongly support a pattern of increased paternal involvement in dual-earner families (Bonney, Kelley, & Levant, 1999; Deutsch, Lussier, & Servis, 1993; Fagan, 1998; A. E. Gottfried et al., 1988, 1995, 1999, 2002; Grych & Clark, 1999; Hoffman & Youngblade, 1999; NICHD Early Child Care Research Network, 2000). However, the compensation perspective continues to operate under the presumption of deficit; that is, special family effort is required to overcome the presumed deficit resulting from mothers being at work instead of at home with their children (A. E. Gottfried & A. W. Gottfried, 1994). Rather than viewing families with employed mothers as different from the norm because they hold different societal and family roles, possess more egalitarian gender role definitions (Deutsch, 1999), or see the fathers' increase in shared child-care responsibilities as a choice of the couple, instead, fathers' involvement may be viewed as a response to the mothers' work rather than an input to the decision to work. Alternatives to this view need to be considered. Research on attitudinal and ideological selection factors that influence parents' choices regarding employment and family roles, and the resulting impact on children's development, has not yet been conducted. Such attitudes have been studied contemporaneously or subsequent to parental employment, but not as precursors to the decision for mothers to be employed or maintain a dual-earner home.

Another perspective pertaining to maternal and dual-earner employment is *developmental impingement*, which emerged from work on redefined

or nontraditional families that includes maternal and dual-earner employment (A. E. Gottfried & A. W. Gottfried, 1994). The developmental impingement perspective includes four basic principles:

1. There is no presumption of deficit, detriment, or benefit to children
   being reared in families with alternative structures;
2. The developmental level and other characteristics (e.g., gender, culture) of the child must be taken into account because the impact of
   certain variables may differ across such factors;
3. The impact of any alternative family form must be examined across a
   broad array of developmental outcomes to determine its general-
   izability and pervasiveness, rather than studying a single outcome
   measure of children's development at a single point in time. If the
   findings were negative or positive, explicit statements about maternal
   employment effects would be based on limited evidence. Hence,
   multivariate and longitudinal studies can best address the breadth
   and cross-time developmental aspects of effects;
4. A related concern is the need to generalize results across ecological
   levels and to examine, for example, extrafamilial societal influences
   that may have a spectrum of possible outcomes (e.g., positive, negative, none).

In the maternal and dual-earner employment research, the developmental
impingement perspective is beginning to accrue support. There is increasingly more maternal and dual-earner research on lower- and middle-SES
groups, varying cultural groups, and internationally (A. E. Gottfried et al.,
1994, 1999, 2002). The developmental impingement perspective was an impetus for our proposal to examine family adaptations regarding maternal
and dual-earner families (A. E. Gottfried et al., 1995; A. E. Gottfried et al.,
1999).

Another perspective concerns *family adaptations* regarding maternal employment and dual-earner families (A. E. Gottfried et al., 1994, 1995, 1999;
Spain & Bianchi, 1996). Family adaptation concerns practices and changes
that support effective family functioning. These would include, for example, increased father participation, greater participation of children in
housework, greater independence training of young children, nontraditional work schedules and alternating schedules of mothers and fathers,
work flexibility, and the like. Adaptation requires a change in perspective
from deficit and compensation to neutrality consistent with the developmental impingement perspective.

Other perspectives have been proposed as well, including the mediation
perspective (e.g., Hoffman & Youngblade, 1999), which views parenting be-

haviors as being the causal factors between maternal work on the one hand and children's development on the other; the life-span contextual view (Lerner, 1994), in which maternal employment is but one process in the context of a multiplicity of processes which interact with children's development throughout the life span; contributions from work and sociology literatures including work and family interaction such as: spillover of effects from work-to-family or family-to-work (e.g., satisfaction or stress in either work or family may impact the other realm; Edwards & Rothbard, 2000); egalitarian versus gender-based views of family roles which may influence mothers' and fathers' child involvement and division of household labor (Coltrane, 1996; Deutsch, 1999); ecological approaches which include time use (Richards & Duckett, 1994) and child monitoring (Crouter, Helms-Erikson, Updegraff, & McHale, 1999; VanderVen, Cullen, Carrozza, & Wright, 2001); and job conditions such as family friendly business policies and programs (Hughes & Galinsky, 1988; Levine & Pittinsky, 1997), work schedules (Presser, 1988, 1999), and job complexity (Greenberger, O'Neil, & Nagel, 1994; Parcel & Menaghan, 1994; Ryu & Mortimer, 1996). Each of these approaches has made a contribution to our understanding of the complex interweave of variables among work, parenting, and ultimately children's development. These factors may not be mutually exclusive inasmuch as aspects in one area may impact another. For example, changes in father involvement with children as related to mothers' employment may simultaneously indicate changes in role definitions, and also have implications for the developmental impingement model in which children's increased exposure to fathers may be beneficial. A multiplicity of theories and perspectives characterizes the field, which presents a future challenge to integrating these approaches.

RESULTS OF THE FULLERTON
LONGITUDINAL STUDY

From our research on the role of maternal employment in children's development, we realized that a new perspective was needed to develop new theories and research issues, as well as to provide a structure for interpretation (A. E. Gottfried et al., 1988, 1994, 1995, 1999, 2002). The results of other major longitudinal studies, and literature in the field, pointed to the same need (Galambos, Petersen, & Lenerz, 1988; Goldberg & Easterbrooks, 1988; Hock, DeMeis, & McBride, 1988; Hoffman & Youngblade, 1999; Lerner & Galambos, 1988; Owen & Cox, 1988).

In a longitudinal study of development from ages 1 through 24 years, known as the Fullerton Longitudinal Study (FLS), mothers' and fathers' employment were prospectively examined regarding their relationship to children's development across a wide breadth of developmental domains (intellectual, cognitive, affective, social, academic, motivational, and behavioral adjustment); detailed measures of proximal home environment; parental involvement with their children; and maternal attitudes toward employment. In addition to these developmental and proximal environmental measures, distal and family demographic measures were studied including SES, parental occupation, parental work hours, parental education level, and the like, permitting analyses of the dual-earner employment context in the family, not only mother's employment.

The FLS was initiated with 130 healthy 1-year-old infants and their families with not less than 80% of the participants returning for any assessment. The sample represents a wide range of the middle-class as measured by the Hollingshead Four Factor Index of Social Status (A. W. Gottfried, 1985; A. W. Gottfried, A. E. Gottfried, Bathurst, Guerin, & Parramore, 2003; Hollingshead, 1975) ranging from semiskilled workers through professionals. Developmental assessments were conducted every 6 months from ages 1 through 3.5 years, and yearly from age 5 through adolescence. At age 24, participants were surveyed as to their current educational progress. A longitudinal study of children from ages 1 through 24 years affords us the opportunity to determine whether there were any short- or long-term patterns of relationships between maternal employment and children's development both contemporaneously and prospectively. We were also able to investigate hypothesized "sleeper" effects, the consistency of relationships between maternal employment and children's development on measures repeatedly administered across the ages, as well as the continuity of mothers' employment. At the initiation of the study 36% of mothers were employed, and by the time the children reached age 17 years, 83% of the mothers were employed. The overwhelming majority of mothers were employed by the end of adolescence, and therefore in data analyses over the course of the study, the comparison of employed and nonemployed mothers is based on an increasingly larger employed group and an increasingly smaller nonemployed group. This itself represents an aspect of the developmental impingement perspective with regard to the changing of maternal roles to which the children were exposed during their childhood.

Extensive, multivariate analyses, controlling for factors such as family SES, marital status, and number of children, were conducted. The most prominent findings of this research are the absence of statistically significant effects of maternal employment status examined across a broad array of developmental measures from infancy, preschool years, school age, and early adolescence. Examination of part-time versus full-time employment through age 8 showed no significant difference between part- and full-time employment status in relation to the outcome measures. This finding was consistent with those of Goldberg and Easterbrooks (1988), and Lerner and Galambos (1988). Hence, part- and full-time employment status was merged in subsequent analyses.

Our findings did show that in order to more fully understand the role of maternal employment in children's development across infancy, childhood, and adolescence, it is necessary to investigate a network of family and contextual factors which impinge upon the child. The most salient contextual family factors that emerged from our research included fathers' involvement, maternal attitudes toward parenting and employment, and parental occupational status. When mothers were employed, fathers were significantly more involved with their children particularly during the weekdays when mothers tended to be at work. Increased fathers' involvement proved to be a longitudinal trend from ages 3.5 through 17. Fathers were significantly more involved in caretaking, playing, nurturing, stimulating, and spending time with their children through age 17 beginning when mothers were employed when children were 3.5 years. These early years proved to be quite important in providing a continuous and future pattern of increased father involvement which persisted throughout the children's development. Furthermore, as mothers' employment hours increased, fathers' involvement with their children also significantly increased.

Regarding maternal attitudes toward the dual roles of parenting and employment, across the ages, more positive attitudes toward this balance were related to children's higher academic achievement, more positive attitudes toward and interest in school, greater academic intrinsic motivation for school learning, fewer behavior problems, greater maternal involvement with the child, higher educational stimulation, greater family cohesion and less conflict (A. E. Gottfried et al., 1988, 2002). Aspects of employment and parenting that were related to more favorable attitudes included greater job flexibility, fewer work hours, mothers experiencing greater emotional and practical support in the parenting role, greater satisfaction with parenting, greater involvement with their child, and more effective limit setting with their child. Maternal attitudes were not related to fathers' work conditions.

Other analyses were conducted to examine the balance of mothers' and fathers' work roles in relation to children's development. These dual-earner analyses included mothers' and fathers' occupational statuses, work hours, and work flexibility, which were studied in relation to children's development. Results showed that both mothers' and fathers' occupational statuses were significantly, pervasively, and positively related to children's academic achievement, the stimulation of the home environment, and parents' educational aspirations for their children. Whereas many of the significant findings indicated that mothers' and fathers' occupational statuses were both related to these outcomes, there were findings showing individual significant, positive contributions of mothers' occupational status to children's academic intrinsic motivation, aspects of the physical environment, and educational aspirations, whereas fathers' occupation alone positively predicted children's age 12 intelligence and achievement scores, child's independence, and mothers' time involvement. Mothers' occupational status was inversely related to amount of TV viewing (less viewing with higher occupation). Furthermore, employed mothers had more favorable educational attitudes regarding their children at ages 5 and 7. Analyses of parental work hours and job flexibility indicated that they themselves bore no reliable significant relationships to children's outcomes. As both mothers and fathers worked longer hours, their amount of time involvement with their children decreased, and as mothers worked longer hours, father time with children increased.

Overwhelmingly, across the span of the FLS, children's development was related to their home environment (A. E. Gottfried et al., 1988, 1994, 1995, 1999, 2002; A. E. Gottfried, Fleming, & A. W. Gottfried, 1998; A. W. Gottfried & A. E. Gottfried, 1984). Maternal employment status per se was not significantly related to children's development. Whereas there were many more individual findings than can be reported herein, the full complement of findings from the FLS illustrate the point that a balance of factors and family adaptations must be accounted for in order to understand the role of maternal employment in its relationship to children's development. For example, parental occupational status, maternal satisfaction with the dual roles of parenting and employment, and father involvement with children, emerged as important factors in this study with which to understand the family context, balance of factors, and adaptations made by families to support their children's development. Furthermore, children's outcomes were observed over a long-term period and based on many variables, not just a single outcome. It may be concluded that when work related variables are significantly related to children's outcomes, their interpretation requires an appreciation of the interplay of family factors that impinge on the child. To the extent that parental employment is related to environment, both in favorable and unfavorable ways, children's development is likely to be affected.

These conclusions are consistent with the extensive literature that has emerged across the field (Etaugh, 1974; A. E. Gottfried & A. W Gottfried, 1988a; A. E. Gottfried et al., 1995, 2002; A. E. Gottfried et al., 1999; Hoffman, 1989; Lerner, 1994; Spitze, 1995; Zaslow et al., 1991). In fact, Hoffman (1988) concluded that maternal employment is "not so robust a variable that it can be linked directly to a child characteristic. Maternal employment operates through its effects on the family environment and on the child care arrangements" (p. xi). Inasmuch as there is simply no credible evidence that maternal employment is itself detrimental to children's development, it is time to abandon this issue and study the context of specific family processes that will advance effective family functioning and optimize children's outcomes in employed parent families.

INTERPRETING THE LITERATURE IN THE CONTEXT
OF FAMILY PROCESSES AND FAMILY ADAPTATION

Whereas there continues to be a plethora of maternal employment research conducted, there needs to be a more consistent effort to interpret research results in a family process and family adaptation context. The goal of this section is to provide such an interpretation to some recent studies. In this regard, the interpretations made will have implications for directing a new research agenda.

Research documenting the role of context and culture indicates the importance of accounting for these factors. One developmental factor, gender, has received a great deal of attention, but its effect varies across studies. Some studies show no significant differences in the role of maternal employment for girls and boys, as found across studies reported in A. E. Gottfried and A. W. Gottfried (1988b) and those reviewed by Lerner (1994); and others finding positive or negative effects for one gender or another. For example, some studies have found that daughters have higher aspirations and more egalitarian sex-role attitudes when mothers are employed (reviewed in A. E. Gottfried et al., 2002; Lerner, 1994), and some have found that boys have lower achievement (Brooks-Gunn, Han, & Waldfogel, 2002), particularly if they are middle class (Lerner, 1994). (See also Riggio & Desrochers, chapter 12, this volume.)

A recent study of children's social behavior and maternal employment regarding single mothers in welfare programs with preschool-age children indicated that girls were significantly less aggressive when mothers were employed; whereas, there was no significant difference for boys' aggression (Fuller et al., 2002). Regardless of gender, maternal employment bore no relation to adverse outcomes. These authors concluded that proximal home environment was more robust in relation to children's social development than mothers' employment.

In another study the expectation that infant sons of employed mothers would have more insecure attachments was not supported across a broad range of mothers ranging from professionals (e.g., medical doctors) to working class (child care aide; Harrison & Ungerer, 2002). This lack of consistency across studies itself indicates that factors other than maternal employment must be examined as related to the specific gender findings of particular studies. When one study finds what appears to be an adverse or favorable finding for one gender or another, the researcher needs to delve beyond maternal employment and gender themselves and examine such factors as home environment, attitudes toward the employment roles of mothers and fathers in relationship to child gender, and parental involvement with their children to determine the source of such differences. For example, it may be speculated that employed parents of daughters may develop more egalitarian gender-role attitudes, which may impact the attitudes of their children. Perhaps some of the adverse findings for boys has to do with the adequacy of parental monitoring of child behavior, a variable suggested to be important in the maternal employment literature (Crouter et al., 1999; Vander Ven et al., 2001). There is no inherent reason as to why maternal employment would be more or less favorable or detrimental for either girls or boys, and the inconsistent findings across studies attests to this.

Regarding socioeconomic context, research evidence continues to accrue indicating that maternal employment is associated with a host of favorable outcomes for children of lower SES, regardless of whether employment is freely chosen or not as is the case with welfare reform. Findings indicate that cognitive and academic achievements as well as social development are more positive when poorer mothers are employed. This is evidence that has not just occurred in the past few years, but has been accumulating for decades (Cherry & Eaton, 1977; A. E. Gottfried et al., 1995; Heyns, 1982; Hoffman & Youngblade, 1999; Rieber & Womack, 1969; Zaslow & Emig, 1997). The extra resources afforded by the increase in family income has often been one such explanatory process accounting for this variable.

Of particular relevance to this issue is the recent evidence regarding the impact of welfare reform, or involuntary employment, on children's outcomes. At the inception of this social program, a number of publications suggested that when mothers must work involuntarily, there could be new stressors added to the family life (Wilson, Ellwood, & Brooks-Gunn, 1995; Zaslow & Emig, 1997). By this time, a number of studies have been published regarding the impact of welfare to work on children's outcomes, documenting positive findings for both the mothers' parenting and children's outcomes (Dunifon, Kalil, & Danziger, 2003; Fuller et al., 2002; Gennetian & Miller, 2002; Gennetian & Morris, 2003). Rather than the potential adverse outcomes which were expected, the findings are, on the contrary, positive. Conclusions as to reasons for these outcomes range from increased resources to higher maternal self-esteem. Again, the role of SES is of exceptional importance in interpreting these results. It is not maternal employment per se, but rather the nature of the environment, attitudes, and family processes that must be taken into account. These findings provide further support for studying family adaptations.

As a corollary to these findings, McLoyd and her colleagues have found that unemployment is itself stressful and detrimental in low-SES families (McLoyd, Jayaratne, Ceballo, & Borquez, 1994). In fact, unemployment is associated with a host of adverse outcomes, as is poverty itself (Brooks-Gunn & Duncan, 1997). These two lines of evidence, that of positive aspects of maternal employment in lower SES families, and the adverse impact of unemployment and poverty, speak to the need to facilitate maternal employment in such families.

The expectation of a negative impact of maternal employment seems to persist for middle-class families, despite the broad absence of such evidence. Perhaps because maternal employment violates the traditional societal norm of the single-male-earner family with mother not employed, an expectation of negativity is perpetuated (A. E. Gottfried et al., 1999). The single-male-earner family may continue to be considered the standard against which all others families are compared. If so, this is an anachronism inasmuch as the two-parent, single-male-earner family with mother being the primary caretaker of the children is the minority family (A. E. Gottfried & A. W. Gottfried, 1994). Maternal employment for personal development and satisfaction may be viewed as selfish and harmful if such employment is not absolutely necessary for family income (A. E. Gottfried et al., 1999). Perhaps in poorer families mothers' employment is justified as a necessity, whereas in homes with more economic resources mothers' employment is viewed as a luxury, and perhaps negatively prejudged.

If negative beliefs about maternal employment are held by certain middle-SES parents who themselves ascribe to more traditional family values, then it would be understandable that these specific mothers would feel guilty about their employment, and such negative attitudes could affect the climate of the home, the sensitivity of child care they provide, or stimulation level of the environment. These aspects of family environment may then, in turn, affect children's development. This explanation would indicate that maternal employment per se is not detrimental, but rather one must look beyond to the values and attitudes of families. Indeed, research has shown that it is the congruence between maternal employment status and maternal employment preference that is important, not maternal employment per se (A. E. Gottfried et al., 1995; Lerner & Galambos, 1988). Hence, the values and attitudes of mothers and fathers regarding their employment and parenting roles are needed in order to elucidate these processes.

Using the family process and family adaptation perspectives, other research may likewise be interpreted. For example, findings by Brooks-Gunn et al. (2002), using the NICHD Child Care Consortium sample, do not show a consistent impact of maternal employment in the first year of life. Indeed, for European-American families, maternal employment within the first year had a negative relation to one of three cognitive measures when mothers were employed sometime within the first 9 months after their child's birth, but not earlier or later. Furthermore, this finding held true only for married mothers who were employed more than 30 hours per week. No significant effect was found for mothers who worked less than 30 hours per week, for single mothers who worked either more or less than 30 hours per week, or for minority mothers. These findings themselves, if reliable, indicate that it is not maternal employment nor the intensity of employment per se, that plays a role in children's outcome, but rather the context of particular familial circumstances within which these conditions occur. Although these researchers found some contextual factors reduced the relationship between maternal employment and the measure of cognitive outcome, such as maternal sensitivity, quality of child care, home environment, and marital status, the authors nevertheless concluded that their findings "suggest that there may be something particularly problematic about having a mother who went to work between 6 and 9 months and/or something unusual about the children whose mothers began employment at this time" (p. 1066). This conclusion seems to be an overgeneralization and unwarranted due the inconsistency of results across measures and family types. Additionally, other factors may have played a role but were not examined in this study including maternal occupational status, consistency of mothers' employment over time, maternal separation anxiety (e.g., see Hock et al., 1988), and maternal attitudes toward the dual roles of employment and parenting, all variables shown to be important in the maternal employment literature. Because the negative findings occurred for married mothers, this pattern of findings suggests that these mothers held more traditional values and attitudes that were compromised by employment of more than 30 hours a week.

In another study using a sample from the National Longitudinal Study of Youth, Han, Waldfogel, and Brooks-Gunn (2001) found that early maternal employment during the first year and later bore no relationship to the cognitive and behavioral outcomes of African-American children. For European-American children, only those whose mothers had an unstable employment pattern (employed in the first year, but not later) had lower achievement scores at ages 5 through 7. For children whose mothers were consistently employed, no adverse findings occurred. Child gender differences were not obtained. Hence, the context of employment is essential in understanding maternal employment. Again, maternal employment per se was not related to child outcomes. It may be that maternal employment was interpreted more negatively by European American compared to African-American families. Additionally, since instability of employment was related to a negative outcome, not employment itself, exiting the work force after a period of employment may indicate the existence of other maternal or family problems, and these may be related to child outcome. Results for behavior problems were inconsistent as well, showing no relationships to internalizing behavior problems, but rather to externalizing problems at ages 4 and 7–8 (not ages 5–6) only if the mother was employed in the first 3 quarters after birth and not thereafter. The contextual factors involved in these associations need further investigation as the explanatory factors.

A study reported by Harrison and Ungerer (2002) provided contrary evidence showing that early return to employment was associated with more secure attachment in Australian 12-month olds. Mothers of secure infants had a higher commitment to work and less anxiety about using non-parental child care than mothers of insecure infants. These job-related contextual factors played a role in these outcomes.

A recent study indicated that parenting quality of mothers in two-parent families was more negative with their 9-month olds when they reported more negative interpersonal interactions at work (Costigan, Cox, & Cauce, 2003). This is another example of context as influencing parent–child interactions, in this instance, the work context. However, the study does not address the adaptations that families can make in order to overcome such spillover other than to say that "The results also suggest that employment policies that facilitate a positive and rewarding work environment will have beneficial effects that extend beyond enhanced employee well-being" (p. 407).

In a study of Finnish parents in dual-earner families, Leinonen, Solantaus, and Punamäki (2003) found mothers' and fathers' punitive parenting was related to economic pressures. However, under such circumstances, social support of mothers tended to reduce punitive mothering. The authors also described Finnish society as a welfare state in which both mothers and fathers are expected to be employed.

FAMILY ADAPTATIONS AND PUBLIC POLICY

Research issues need to be framed to identify factors associated with successful family adaptations. Such issues have the potential to develop public policy and business practices. For example, results of such research are continually published not only in professional journals, but also in media for the general public. Hence, it is essential that information be presented to the public in a fair and balanced manner, with the intricacies of the issues of context and adaptation described in understandable terms. To illustrate the potential significance of the research, evidence in A. E. Gottfried, A. W. Gottfried, & Bathurst (1985) was cited and provided a foundation for a California State Supreme Court ruling (Burchard v. Garay, 1986) regarding child custody. The State Supreme Court ruled that a mother's or father's employment status could not be used to discriminate against her/him in deciding a child's custody arrangement. The results regarding a lack of significant direct effect of maternal employment status on children's development provided a basis for this decision.

Bianchi (2000) stated that, "it would appear that the dramatic movement into the labor force by women of childbearing age in the United States has been accomplished with relatively little consequence for children" (p. 401), a conclusion consistent with the current author's interpretation of the literature. In her presentation of factors that might account for this, Bianchi (2000) relies heavily on concepts consistent with the family adaptation view. One prime factor has been that mothers' time with children has remained fairly stable regardless of their increase in employment hours. Bianchi suggests that this is made possible by reallocating priorities such as reducing personal time, housework, volunteer work, and free-time pursuits. As a corollary, fathers' time spent with their children has increased over the years. Bianchi concluded that "In two-parent families, children's time with mothers and fathers increased sufficiently to counteract any decrease of time in the home associated with increased maternal employment" (p. 411). Increased father involvement has been shown to be a family adaptation related to maternal employment.

Flexibility of Employment

Hill, Ferris, and Märtinson (2003) surveyed IBM employees, both males and females, who worked in either a traditional office setting, virtual office setting, or home office setting using telecommuting. The latter work environment was related to the most positive perceptions of work/life balance, including families with children, and greater perceptions of personal and family success. Work quality was not compromised by home telecommuting. The authors included an extensive review of literature on telecommuting documenting its relationship to positive motivation and job morale. Considering the literature on mother's attitudes toward the dual roles of employment and parenting, working at home may be an alternative that promotes both career and family life. In an earlier survey of IBM employees (Hill, Hawkins, Ferris, & Weitzman, 2001), of those who worked 40 to 50 hours per week, only 28% of those with either flextime or flexplace reported difficulty with work–family balance as compared to 46% of workers with no flexibility of schedule or location. This indicates that work conditions play a role in family context surrounding parental employment.

Family adaptation may also be noted in the context of work restructuring and family responsive work policies. (See Murphy & Zagorski, chapter 3, this volume for more on the role of organizational management.) Work restructuring may take various forms, including flextime, shift work, job sharing, part-time employment, a compressed work week, work at home, personal days for family responsibilities, time bank, relocation assistance, and benefits. In studies of dual-earner families with children, Brett and Yogev (1988) and Karambayya and Reilly (1992) found that women engaged in more restructuring on a regular basis than did men. Men's restructuring was more likely to be in response to a special need and was more temporary (Karambayya & Reilly, 1992).

Nontraditional Work Schedules

Nontraditional work schedules have emerged as family adaptations (A. E. Gottfried et al., 1999). For example, Presser (1994) found that the degree of nonoverlap in work hours in married, dual-earner families was related to increases in housework completed by husbands and wives. When husbands were home alone particularly during the day, their housework increased. Brayfield (1995) found that fathers in dual-earner families with preschool children were more likely to engage in child care when their work hours differed from those of the mothers. When fathers worked nonday hours, they were more likely to be the primary caretakers for preschool-age children, but were more likely to be the caretakers for school-age children when they worked day hours. This probably relates to the correspondence between fathers' work schedules and children's child-care needs at different ages.

REDEFINING THE RESEARCH AGENDA

Maternal employment is here to stay. Given this reality, and given the by now familiar finding that maternal employment per se is not detrimental to children's development, it is now time to change the focus of research. We must identify and delineate the adaptations of such families, and become more vocal about the balance of factors that interplay in every family, across SES, ethnicity, marital status, single-earner or dual-earner employment. Whereas this agenda was called for in earlier publications (A. E. Gottfried et al., 1999; 2002), there continues to be little research focusing on detecting competencies of maternal and dual-earner families, nor their differences compared to families in which mothers are not employed. For example, positive spillover from work to family or vice versa, has been associated with numerous positive outcomes such as better physical and mental health and well-being, but there has been little research conducted on the antecedents (Hammer, Colton, Caubet, & Brockwood, 2002). Furthermore, multiple role occupancy has been theorized to be beneficial by accruing benefits from achievements in some areas balancing disappointments in others (Hammer et al., 2002).

Research continues to convey a negative bias by searching for and detecting adverse consequences of maternal employment. This is reflected in the research issues chosen for study, and in the frameworks used to generate interpretations. It is fruitless to attempt to explain relationships between parental employment and child outcomes without interpreting the context of maternal employment in terms of work-related variables, parental occupational status, maternal attitudes, fathers' availability, home environment, attitudes toward different forms of child care, economic resources, gender-role attitudes of families, and the like. Indeed, child-care quality has also entered the list of contextual factors related to this issue (e.g., Belsky, 2001; Brooks-Gunn et al., 2002).

It is time to change the research agenda in the maternal employment field from the search for negativity to the systematic investigation of conditions which facilitate the work–family balance, and child outcomes, in working families. Furthermore, the developmental impingement perspective is an important conceptual framework to adopt to frame research issues and interpret findings (A. E. Gottfried & A. W. Gottfried, 1994). This perspective includes and advocates for the broad consideration of factors including multivariate domains of development, ecological contexts, and consideration of the reliability and consistency of findings both contemporaneously and across time, using a value neutral framework that does not prejudge outcomes as either negative or positive. Until this perspective is adopted, the field will continue to provide premature and partial, hence biased, interpretations of data.

Moreover, research needs to be instituted on the potential competencies that employed parents may possess and how these may be communicated to their children. For example, when mothers are employed they are exposed to the larger world environment beyond the home. How such exposure may impact parenting and children's development has been completely unexplored. Another needed area for study is the role of egalitarian gender roles and their relationships to parental employment and children's development.

It is hoped that the issues presented herein provide an impetus toward redefining the research agenda on maternal employment toward conceptualizing new issues, which will have an impact on children, families, work, and public policy. With concerted efforts, forthcoming research will be directed toward elucidating these significant issues regarding the impact of parental employment on children's development for creating and implementing policies and recommendations based on a balanced view of research findings for working families which do not arouse unnecessary fear and guilt.

REFERENCES

Barling, J. (1990). *Employment, stress, and family functioning.* New York: Wiley.

Belsky, J. (2001). Emanuel Miller Lecture: Developmental risks (still) associated with early child care. *Journal of Child Psychology and Psychiatry, 42,* 845–859.

Bianchi, S. (2000). Maternal employment and time with children: Dramatic change or surprising continuity? *Demography, 37,* 401–414.

Bonney, J. F., Kelley, M. L., & Levant, R. F. (1999). A model of fathers' behavioral involvement in child care in dual-earner families. *Journal of Family Issues, 13,* 401–415.

Brayfield, A. (1995). Juggling jobs and kids: The impact of employment schedules on fathers' caring for children. *Journal of Marriage and the Family, 57,* 321–332.

Bretherton, I. (1993). Theoretical contributions from developmental psychology. In P. G. Boss, W. J. Doherty, R. LaRossa, W. R. Schumm, & S. K. Steinmetz (Eds.), *Sourcebook of family theories and methods: A contextual approach* (pp. 275–297). New York: Plenum.

Brett, J. M., & Yogev, S. (1988). Restructuring work for family: How dual-earner couples with children manage. *Journal of Social Behavior and Personality, 3,* 159–174.

Brooks-Gunn, J., & Duncan, G. J. (1997). The effects of poverty on children. *The Future of Children,* Summer/Fall, 55–71.

Brooks-Gunn, J., Han, W.-J., & Waldfogel, J. (2002). Maternal employment and child cognitive outcomes in the first three years of life: The NICHD study of early child care. *Child Development, 73,* 1052–1072.

Burchard V. Garay 42 Cal. 3d; *Cal.Rptr.,* P.2d, (Sept. 1986).

Burchinal, L. G. (1963). Personality characteristics of children. In F. I. Nye & L. W. Hoffman (Eds.), *The employed mother in America* (pp. 106–124). Chicago: Rand McNally.

Cherry, F. F., & Eaton, E. L. (1977). Physical and cognitive development in children of low-income mothers working in the child's early years. *Child Development, 48,* 158–166.

Coltrane, S. (1996). *Family man.* New York: Oxford University Press.

Costigan, C. L., Cox, M. J., & Cauce, A. M. (2003). Work-parenting linkages among dual-earner couples at the transition to parenthood. *Journal of Family Psychology, 17,* 397–408.

Crouter, A. C., Helms-Erikson, H., Updegraff, K., & McHale, S. (1999). Conditions underlying parents' knowledge about children's daily lives in middle childhood: Between- and within-family comparisons. *Child Development, 70,* 246–259.

Deutsch, F. M. (1999). *Halving it all: How equally shared parenting works.* Cambridge, MA: Harvard University Press.

Deutsch, F. M., Lussier, J. B., & Servis, L. J. (1993). Husbands at home: Predictors of paternal participation in childcare and housework. *Journal of Personality and Social Psychology, 65,* 1154–1166.

Dunifon, R., Kalil, A., & Danziger, S. K. (2003). Maternal work behavior under welfare reform: How does the transition from welfare to work affect child development? *Children and Youth Services Review, 25,* 55–82.

Edwards, J. R., & Rothbard, N. P. (2000). Mechanisms linking work and family: Clarifying the relationship between work and family constructs. *Academy of Management Review, 25,* 178–200.

Etaugh, C. (1974). Effects of maternal employment on children: A review of recent research. *Merrill-Palmer Quarterly, 20,* 71–98.

Fagan, J. (1998). Correlates of low-income African-American and Puerto Rican fathers' involvement with their children. *Journal of Black Psychology, 24,* 351–367.

Fuller, B., Caspary, G., Kagan, S. L., Gauthier, C., Huang, D. S., Carroll, J., & McCarthy, J. (2002). Does maternal employment influence poor children's social development. *Early Childhood Research Quarterly, 17,* 470–497.

Galambos, N. L., Petersen, A. C., & Lenerz, K. (1988). Maternal employment and sex typing in early adolescence: Contemporaneous and longitudinal relations. In A. E. Gottfried & A. W. Gottfried (Eds.), *Maternal employment and children's development: Longitudinal research* (pp. 155–189). New York: Plenum.

Gennetian, L. A., & Miller, C. (2002). Children and welfare reform: A view from an experimental welfare program in Minnesota. *Child Development, 73,* 601–620.

Gennetian, L. A., & Morris, P. A. (2003). The effects of time limits and make-work-pay strategies on the well-being of children: Experimental evidence from two welfare reform programs. *Children and Youth Services, 25,* 17–54.

Goldberg, W. A., & Easterbrooks, M. A. (1988). Maternal employment When children are toddlers and kindergartners. In A. E. Gottfried & A. W. Gottfried (Eds.), *Maternal employment and children's development: Longitudinal research* (pp. 121–154). New York: Plenum.

Gottfried, A. E. (1988). Maternal employment and children's development: An introduction to the issues. In A. E. Gottfried & A. W. Gottfried (Eds.), *Maternal employment and children's development: Longitudinal research* (pp. 3–8). New York: Plenum.

Gottfried, A. E., Bathurst, K., & Gottfried, A. W. (1994). Role of maternal and dual-earner employment status in children's development: A longitudinal study from infancy through early adolescence. In A. E. Gottfried & A. W. Gottfried (Eds.), *Redefining families: Implications for children's development* (pp. 55–97). New York: Plenum.

Gottfried, A. E., Fleming, J. S., & Gottfried, A. W. (1998). Role of cognitively stimulating home environment in children's academic intrinsic motivation: A longitudinal study. *Child Development, 69,* 1448–1460.

Gottfried, A. E., & Gottfried, A. W. (1988a). *Maternal employment and children's development: Longitudinal research.* New York: Plenum.

Gottfried, A. E., & Gottfried, A. W. (1988b). Maternal employment and children's development: An integration of longitudinal findings with implications for social policy. In A. E. Gottfried & A. W. Gottfried (Eds.), *Maternal employment and children's development: Longitudinal research* (pp. 269–287). New York: Plenum.

Gottfried, A. E., & Gottfried, A. W. (1994). Impact of redefined families on children's development: Conclusions, conceptual perspectives, and social implications. In A. E. Gottfried & A. W. Gottfried (Eds.), *Redefining families: Implications for children's development* (pp. 221–229). New York: Plenum.

Gottfried, A. E., Gottfried, A. W., & Bathurst, K. (1985, August). *Maternal employment and young children's development: A longitudinal study.* Paper presented at the annual meeting of the American Psychological Association, Los Angeles.

Gottfried, A. E., Gottfried, A. W., & Bathurst, K. (1988). Maternal employment, family environment, and children's development: Infancy through the school years. In A. E. Gottfried & A. W. Gottfried (Eds.), *Maternal employment and children's development: Longitudinal research* (pp. 11–58). New York: Plenum.

Gottfried, A. E., Gottfried, A. W., & Bathurst, K. (1995). Maternal and dual-earner employment status and parenting. In M. H. Bornstein (Ed.), *Handbook of parenting* (Vol. 2, pp. 139–160). Mahwah, NJ: Lawrence Erlbaum Associates.

Gottfried, A. E., Gottfried, A. W., & Bathurst, K. (2002). Maternal and dual-earner employment status and parenting. In M. H. Bornstein (Ed.), *Handbook of parenting, 2nd edition* (Vol. 2, pp. 207–229). Mahwah, NJ: Lawrence Erlbaum Associates.

Gottfried, A. E., Gottfried, A. W., Bathurst, K., & Killian, C. (1999). Maternal and dual-earner employment: Family environment, adaptations, and the developmental impingement perspective. In M. Lamb (Ed.), *Parenting and child development in "nontraditional" families* (pp. 15–37). Mahwah, NJ: Lawrence Erlbaum Associates.

Gottfried, A. W. (1985). Measures of socioeconomic status in child development research: Data and recommendations. *Merrill-Palmer Quarterly, 32,* 85–92.

Gottfried, A. W., & Gottfried, A. E. (1984). Home environment and cognitive development in young children of middle-socioeconomic-status families. In A. W. Gottfried (Ed.), *Home environment and early cognitive development: Longitudinal research* (pp. 57–115). New York: Academic Press.

Gottfried, A. W., Gottfried, A. E., Bathurst, K., Guerin, D. W., & Parramore, M. (2003). Socioeconomic status in children's development and family environment: Infancy through adolescence. In M. Bornstein (Ed.), *Socioeconomic status and parenting* (pp. 189–207). Mahwah, NJ: Lawrence Erlbaum Associates.

Greenberger, E., O'Neil, R., & Nagel, S. K. (1994). Linking workplace and homeplace: Relations between the nature of adults' work and their parenting behaviors. *Developmental Psychology, 30,* 990–1002.

Grych, J. H., & Clark, R. (1999). Maternal employment and development of the father-infant relationship in the first year. *Developmental Psychology, 35,* 893–903.

Hammer, L. G., Colton, C. L., Caubet, S. L., & Brockwood, K. J. (2002). The unbalanced life: Work and family conflict. In J. C. Thomas & M. Hersen (Eds.), *Handbook of mental health in the workplace* (pp. 83–101). Thousand Oaks, CA: Sage.

Han, W., Waldfogel, J., & Brooks-Gunn, J. (2001). The effects of early maternal employment on later cognitive and behavioral outcomes. *Journal of Marriage and Family, 63,* 336–354.

Hand, H. (1957). Working mothers and maladjusted children. *The Journal of Educational Sociology, 30,* 245–246.

Harrison, L. J., & Ungerer, J. A. (2002). Maternal employment and infant-mother attachment security at 12 months postpartum. *Developmental Psychology, 38,* 758–773.

Heyns, B. (1982). The influence of parents' work on children's school achievement. In S. B. Kamerman & C. D. Hayes (Eds.), *Families that work: Children in a changing world* (pp. 229–267). Washington, DC: National Academy Press.

Hill, E. J., Ferris, J., & Märtinson, V. (2003). Does it matter where you work? A comparison of how three work venues (traditional office, virtual office, and home office) influence aspects of work and personal/family life. *Journal of Vocational Behavior, 63,* 220–241.

Hill, E. J., Hawkins, A. J., Ferris, M., & Weitzman, M. (2001). Finding an extra day a week: The positive influence of perceived job flexibility on work and family balance. *Family Relations, 50,* 49–58.

Hock, E., DeMeis, D., & McBride, S. (1988). Maternal separation anxiety: Its role in the balance of employment and motherhood in mothers of infants. In A. E. Gottfried & A. W. Gottfried (Eds.), *Maternal employment and children's development: Longitudinal research* (pp. 191–229). New York: Plenum.

Hoffman, L. W. (1974). Effects of maternal employment on the child: A review of the research. *Developmental Psychology, 10,* 204–228.

Hoffman, L. W. (1984). Maternal employment and the young child. In M. Perlmutter (Ed.), *Parent-child interactions and parent-child relations in child development: The Minnesota Symposia on Child Psychology, Vol. 17* (pp. 101–127). Hillsdale, NJ: Lawrence Erlbaum Associates.

Hoffman, L. W. (1988). Foreword. In A. E. Gottfried & A. W. Gottfried (Eds.), *Maternal employment and children's development: Longitudinal research* (pp. ix–xiii). New York: Plenum.

Hoffman, L. W. (1989). Effects of maternal employment in the two-parent family. *American Psychologist, 44,* 283–292.

Hoffman, L. W., & Youngblade, L. M. (1999). *Mothers at work: Effects on children's well-being.* New York: Cambridge University Press.

Hollingshead, A. B. (1975). *Four factor index of social status.* Unpublished manuscript, Department of Sociology, Yale University.

Hughes, D., & Galinsky, E. (1988). Balancing work and family lives: Research and corporate applications. In A. E. Gottfried & A. W. Gottfried (Eds.), *Maternal employment and children's development: Longitudinal research* (pp. 233–268). New York: Plenum.

Karambayya, R., & Reilly, A. H. (1992). Dual earner couples: Attitudes and actions in restructuring work for family. *Journal of Organizational Behavior, 13,* 585–601.

Leinonen, J. A., Solantaus, T. S., & Punamäki, R. (2003). Social support and the quality of parenting under economic pressure and workload in Finland: The role of family structure and parental gender. *Journal of Family Psychology, 17,* 409–418.

Lerner, J. V. (1994). *Working women and their families.* Thousand Oaks, CA: Sage.

Lerner, J. V., & Galambos, N. L. (1988). The influences of maternal employment across life: The New York Longitudinal Study. In A. E. Gottfried & A. W. Gottfried (Eds.), *Maternal employment and children's development: Longitudinal research* (pp. 59–83). New York: Plenum.

Levine, J. A., & Pittinsky, T. L. (1997). *Working fathers: New strategies for balancing work and family.* New York: Harcourt, Brace.

McLoyd, V. C., Jayaratne, T. E., Ceballo, R., & Borquez, J. (1994). Unemployment and work interruption among African American single mothers: Effects on parenting and adolescent socioemotional functioning. *Child Development, 65,* 562–589.

NICHD Early Child Care Research Network. (2000). Factors associated with fathers' caregiving activities and sensitivity with young children. *Journal of Family Psychology, 14,* 200–219.

Nye, F. I., Perry, J. B., & Ogles, R. H. (1963). Anxiety and anti-social behavior in preschool children. In F. I. Nye & L. W. Hoffman (Eds.), *The employed mother in America* (pp. 3–17). Chicago: Rand McNally.

Owen, M. T., & Cox, M. J. (1988). Maternal employment and the transition to parenthood. In A. E. Gottfried & A. W. Gottfried (Eds.), *Maternal employment and children's development: Longitudinal research* (pp. 85–119). New York: Plenum.

Parcel, T. L., & Menaghan, E. G. (1994). *Parents' jobs and children's lives.* New York: Aldine de Gruyter.

Presser, H. B. (1988). Shift work and child care among young dual-earner American parents. *Journal of Marriage and the Family, 50,* 133–148.

Presser, H. B. (1994). Employment schedules among dual-earner spouses and the division of household labor by gender. *American Sociological Review, 59,* 348–364.

Presser, H. B. (1999). Toward a 24-hour economy. *Science, 284,* 1778–1779.

Repetti, R. L., & Wood, J. (1997). Families accommodating to chronic stress: Unintended and unnoticed processes. In B. H. Gottlieb (Ed.), *Coping with chronic stress* (pp. 191–220). New York: Plenum.

Richards, M. H., & Duckett, E. (1994). The relationship of maternal employment to early adolescent daily experience with and without parents. *Child Development, 65,* 225–236.

Rieber, M., & Womack, M. (1969). The intelligence of preschool children as related to ethnic and demographic variables. *Exceptional Children, 34,* 609–614.

Ryu, S., & Mortimer, J. (1996). The "occupational linkage hypothesis" applied to occupational value formation in adolescence. In J. T. Mortimer & M. D. Finch (Eds.), *Adolescents, work, and family* (pp. 167–190). Thousand Oaks, CA: Sage.

Spain, D., & Bianchi, S. M. (1996). *Balancing act: Motherhood, marriage, and employment among American women.* New York: Russell Sage Foundation.

Spitze, G. (1995). Women's employment and family relations. In G. L. Bowen & J. F. Pittman (Eds.), *The work and family interface: Toward a contextual effects perspective* (pp. 230–250). Minneapolis: National Council on Family Relations.

Vander Ven, T. M., Cullen, F. T., Carrozza, M. A., & Wright, J. P. (2001). Home alone: The impact of maternal employment on delinquency. *Social Problems, 48,* 236–257.

Wilson, J. B., Ellwood, D. T., & Brooks-Gunn, J. (1995). Welfare-to-work through the eyes of children. In P. L. Chase-Lansdale & J. Brooks-Gunn (Eds.), *Escape from poverty: What makes a difference for children* (pp. 63–86). New York: Cambridge University Press.

Zaslow, M. J., & Emig, C. A. (1997). When low-income mothers go to work: Implications for children. *The future of children: Welfare to work, 7,* 110–114.

Zaslow, B. A., Rabinovich, B. A., & Suwalsky, J. T. D. (1991). From maternal employment to child outcomes: Preexisting group differences and moderating variables. In J. V. Lerner & N. L. Galambos (Eds.), *Employed mothers and their children* (pp. 237–282). New York: Garland Press.

Chapter 14

Children's Perspectives of Employed Mothers and Fathers: Closing the Gap Between Public Debates and Research Findings

Ellen Galinsky
Families and Work Institute

Many of us who study the work and family lives of children and families hope that our work makes a difference. We care about doing the most rigorous research, about adding to theory and knowledge, but we also care about the children and families who are the subjects and objects of our studies. We hope that—in some measure—their lives are improved by the hours we spend developing the hypotheses that form the basis of our inquiries; constructing the models that then inform our research; translating these models into valid constructs and measures; administering questionnaires or observational procedures; and then poring over the findings to find the story behind the numbers.

Yet, in the field of work and family life, in which I have spent close to 30 years, there is a gap between what studies show and the content of the debates that continue to occur in the media, in offices, on factory floors, and around kitchen tables. In this chapter, I compare and contrast what employed parents think about the issues of work and family with the empirical research on the topics. It is my hope that by calling attention to these differences, the gap between the public debates and research findings will narrow.

BACKGROUND: THE ASK THE CHILDREN STUDY

For this chapter, I draw most heavily on the findings of a study of employed parents and children that I conducted, the Ask the Children study (Galinsky, 2000). It includes a nationally representative sample of 1,023 children

219

ages 8 to 18 years. These children were surveyed in their classrooms in May and June of 1998 and represent the diversity that encompasses children in the United States today. They come from high-, middle-, or low-income families; from a wide range of ethnic groups; from two-parent and single-parent homes; and from families with employed and nonemployed fathers and mothers. This study also includes a nationally representative sample of 605 employed mothers and fathers with children birth through 18 who were interviewed by telephone in June of 1998. These parents and children were not from the same families, however, prior to the quantitative surveys and telephone interviews, my colleagues and I conducted qualitative interviews with 171 children ages 4 to 18 years and parents from within the same families.

FOUR DEBATES THAT REVEAL A GAP BETWEEN PUBLIC OPINION AND RESEARCH FINDINGS

Debate 1: Is Having an Employed Mother Good or Bad for Children?

There is no question that this debate continues to resonate with the public. From the 1960s when the losses of parental connections for children in orphanages were compared to the losses suffered by the children of employed mothers to the present time, the public continues to question whether maternal employment causes harm.

In the Ask the Children study, a representative group of employed parents were asked how strongly they agree or disagree with the following statement: "A mother who works outside the home can have just as good a relationship with her children as a mother who does not work." Overall, 76% of employed parents agree somewhat or strongly with this statement (see Fig. 14.1). One would expect employed parents to endorse their own lifestyle, but it is noteworthy that one in four parents disagree.

Who are these parents who disagree? Fathers are much more likely to disagree (30%) than mothers (18%). There are no differences between fathers and mothers in dual-earner couples on this issue, whereas—as one might expect—there are large differences between fathers with employed spouses and those with spouse at home.

Economics play a role in parents' views. For example, this study asked parents how they feel about maternal employment when mothers really need the money and found that almost all employed parents (97%) somewhat or strongly agree that "It is OK for mothers to work if they really do need the money" (see Fig. 14.2). But a closer look indicates that there is some ambivalence, particularly among fathers, who are less likely than

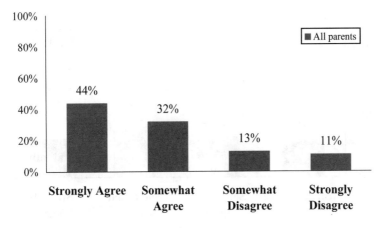

FIG. 14.1.   A mother who works outside the home can have just as good a relationship with her children as a mother who does not work.

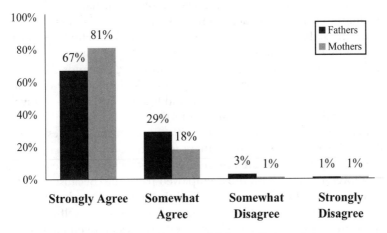

FIG. 14.2.   It is OK for mothers to work if they really do need the money.

mothers to believe that mothers should work—even if they need money: 67% of fathers strongly agree compared with 81% of mothers.

How do employed parents feel about mothers who hold jobs but can afford to stay home? This study reveals even more ambivalence. Overall, 47.5% agree with the statement, "Mothers who really don't need to earn money shouldn't work," compared with 97% who agree that "it is OK for mothers to work if they really need the money" (see Fig. 14.3).

Not unexpectedly, fathers with nonemployed wives endorse their own lifestyle by being more likely to agree (60%) than fathers with employed wives (48%) that "mothers who really don't need to earn money shouldn't work."

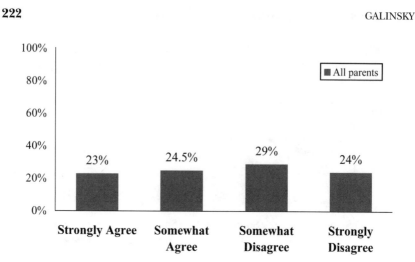

FIG. 14.3.   Mothers who really don't need the money shouldn't work.

To probe whether and how mothers' employment harms children, we asked children to assess (in fact, to grade) how they were being parented on 12 parenting skills that research indicates are linked to children's healthy development and school success. These include "raising me with good values"; "being someone I can go to when I am upset"; "spends time talking with me"; "appreciates me for who I am"; "provides family traditions and rituals"; "encourages me to want to learn and to enjoy learning"; "is involved with my school or child care"; and so forth.

Perhaps surprisingly, there are no differences in the "grades" given by children who have employed mothers with those who have mothers at home full time. Nor are there differences between children whose mothers are employed full time with those employed part time. Because not all the items were asked of children in the third through sixth grades, Table 14.1 presents the results for children in the seventh through twelfth grades. If this study were the only one to show no differences between children with employed mothers and those with mothers at home, this finding could be dismissed. However, this finding echoes several decades of research that indicates that you cannot predict a child's outcomes *simply* based on whether or not his or her mother works. As Lois Hoffman and her colleagues at the University of Michigan pointed out, the positive and negative effects of mothers' employment on children's social and academic competence are not direct ones, "they are carried by the effects on the family environment" (Hoffman & Youngblade, 1999, p. 26). Similarly, the National Institute of Child Health and Human Development (NICHD, 1997) study of approximately 1,200 children from 10 communities across the country from birth through their seventh year found that mothers' employment and whether a child is in child care do not necessarily affect the bond between mother and

TABLE 14.1
What Grade Would You Give Your Mother on . . .

Children Grades 7–12	A	B	C	D	F
Being there for me when I am sick?	81	11	5	2	1
Raising me with good values?	75	15	6	3	2
Making me feel important and loved?	64	20	10	5	1
Being able to attend important events in my life?	64	20	10	3	3.5
Appreciating me for who I am?	64	18	8	6	5
Encouraging me to want to learn and to enjoy learning?	59	23	11.5	3	3
Being involved in what is happening to me at school?	46	25	14	10	6
Being someone I can go to when I am upset?	46	22	14	8	9
Spending time talking with me?	43	33	14	6	4
Establishing family routines and traditions with me?	38	29	17	10	6
Knowing what is really going on in my life?	35	31	15	10	9
Controlling her temper when something I do makes her angry?	29	27.5	20.5	12	11

Note. The values represent the percentage of children that selected each grade.

child. Infants are more likely to be securely attached to their mothers when their mothers are warm and responsive, no matter the employment status of the mother. Maternal employment is linked to problems in attachment primarily when the mother is less warm and responsive and when the child experiences one or more of the following conditions: poor quality child care, more than minimal amounts of time in child care, or more frequent changes in the child-care arrangement.

In other words, what matters most is how children are mothered, particularly whether mothers are warm and responsive, firm yet caring, and whether the children are priorities in their mothers' lives. It is also important how maternal employment affects the larger environment in which the children live. In sum, having an employed mother is not necessarily good or bad for children. It depends. Is there a problem? In my view, yes. But the problem is not simply that mothers are employed. The problem, according to the Ask the Children study, resides in the finding that between 9% and 43% of children do not see their mothers as parenting them very well (they give their mothers a C or lower)—regardless of whether the mother is at home full time or employed.

Debate 2: Is It Mothering or Fathering?

The debates about the impact of work on children have primarily focused on mothers (Levine & Pittinsky, 1997). Although mothers' employment is seen as potentially harmful to children because it takes them away from their children, fathers' employment is typically not questioned. In fact, it is fathers' *un*employment that is depicted as potentially harmful to children

(Bronfenbrenner & Crouter, 1982). Accordingly, the father's role is seen primarily as that of an economic provider. In the Ask the Children study, employed parents were asked to respond to the statement: "It is much better for everyone involved if the man earns the money and the woman takes care of the home and the children" (see Fig. 14.4). Fifty-one percent of employed parents agree.

Employed fathers are more likely to support this statement than employed mothers (58% of employed fathers agree compared with 44% of employed mothers). The difference is not between fathers and mothers where both parents are employed, but between fathers with wives at home and fathers whose wives work. In fact, 75% of fathers with wives at home agree with this statement compared with 52% of those with wives who are employed. On the other hand, almost three-fourths (74%) agree that: "Children do just as well if the mother has primary responsibility for earning the money and the father has primary responsibility for caring for the children." In sum, although many employed parents accept the traditional view that fathers' main role is that of economic provider, they also accept the notion that children would do well if fathers were in charge of caring for them (see Fig. 14.5).

If one turns to children, the importance of fathers—whatever their role—is very evident. For example, children were asked if they had too little, enough, or too much time with their mothers and fathers. This study found that children are more likely to say that they have too little time with their fathers (35%) than their mothers (28%). In the qualitative interviews conducted for this study, many of the children who did not have fathers involved in their lives spoke of yearning for them.

Studies support what children are asking for. For example, research finds that children whose fathers are more involved during infancy score

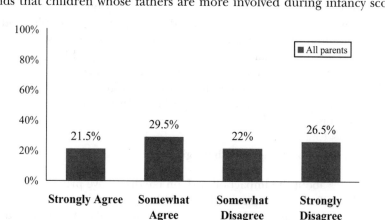

FIG. 14.4. It is much better for everyone involved if the man earns the money and the woman takes care of the home and children.

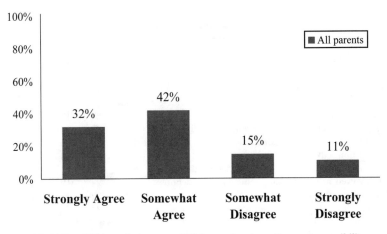

FIG. 14.5.   Children do just as well if the mother has primary responsibility for earning the money and the father has primary responsibility for caring for the children.

better on tests assessing their mental and motor development (Pedersen, Zaslow, Suwalsky, & Caine, 1980) and manage stress better in the school-age years (Parke, 1996). These payoffs continue when fathers are more involved with their children in the preschool and school-age years; for example, children demonstrate a greater ability to take initiative (Radin, 1981). In adolescence, father involvement seems to reduce the risk of drug use, juvenile delinquency, and teen pregnancy (Harris, Furstenburg, & Marmer, 1996). Hoffman and Youngblade (1999) found that when fathers have a larger share of child-care responsibilities, children's achievement test scores are higher. As with mothers, the point is not simply to have fathers involved. Children fare better when their fathers are warm and responsive (Lamb, 1986).

Is there a problem here? Yes, but it is not whether mothers or fathers play significant caregiving roles in children's lives. Both do. The problem, as with mothers, is that between 14% and 42% of children do not feel that their fathers are parenting them very well (see Table 14.2).

Debate 3: Is Child Care Good or Bad for Children?

Whenever I testify in Congress about the child-care research we conduct at the Families and Work Institute, the debate typically veers into the assumption that child care is bad for children because it supplants parental care. In these debates, child care is referred to as "stranger care" and children in child care are described as "day-care reared." A recent study by Public Agenda (2000) found that parents likewise see child care as potentially

TABLE 14.2
What Grade Would You Give Your Father on . . .

Children Grades 7–12	A	B	C	D	F
Raising me with good values?	69	18	8	4	2
Appreciating me for who I am?	58	21	11	8	2
Encouraging me to want to learn and to enjoy learning?	57.5	24	12	4	2
Making me feel important and loved?	57	22	13	6	2
Being able to attend important events in my life?	55	22	13	5	5.5
Being there for me when I am sick?	51.5	20	16	8	4
Spending time talking with me?	43	24	19	10	4
Establishing family routines and traditions with me?	41	26	15	11	7
Being involved in what is happening to me at school?	38	24	19	12	7
Being someone I can go to when I am upset?	38	22	15	12	13
Controlling his temper when something I do makes him angry?	31	27	20	10	12
Knowing what is really going on in my life?	31	30	17	12.5	10

Note. The values represent the percentage of children that selected each grade.

competitive with their care. As their report stated, "one of the most striking findings in this survey is the palpable fear parents have of turning their children over to strangers, even day care professionals" (p. 1). For example, more than 6 in 10 parents (63%) in a nationally representative sample of parents with a child age 5 or under say that they are very concerned about abuse and neglect in child care.

Literature reviews of research reveal that child care does not supplant parent care. Parents are first and foremost in children's lives and their importance is not diminished or replaced by child-care providers (Gamble & Zigler, 1986; NICHD, 1997). In fact, the opposite can be true. For example, the conceptual model used in the Ask the Children study (designed to investigate how work and parenting fit together) reveals, in contrast to the public debates, that child care can be a support for parents. Families who have family and friends to turn to when they have a problem with their child, who feel comfortable accessing that support, and who see the nonparental child care they have used as "very positive" for their child's development, manage their work and family responsibilities more positively than those parents who do not have child rearing support. These factors are like bedrock, providing the essential support parents need for navigating work and family life.

Furthermore, when child care is working, it can feel like an extended family to the parents and children. In selecting child care, parents typically look for someone who is known, or who is known to someone they know (Galinsky, Howes, Kontos, & Shinn, 1994; Howes, Galinsky, Shinn, Sibley, Abbott-Shim, & McCarthy, 1998; Kontos, Howes, Smith, & Galinsky, 1995).

But regardless of whether the child-care provider begins as a stranger or a friend, a relative or a professional provider, the qualitative interviews conducted for the Ask the Children study revealed whether the child care felt right to the parents by the words they used to describe it. Parents would say, "She is like a sister to me," or "She brings wonderful new things to my children's lives" (Galinsky, 2000; Galinsky & Hooks, 1977; Zinsser, 1991). Similarly, when children felt very comfortable with and close to their child-care provider, they described her (or sometimes him) as feeling like kith and kin.

So is child care good or bad for children? It is not bad for children because it supplants parent care. But it can be bad for children if the care is of low quality. The bad news, from the Ask the Children study, is that only 20% of parents report that their child care has been very positive for their child's development. This percentage is similar to the percentages of good-to-excellent quality child care found in three observational studies conducted between 1988 and 1995 (Child Outcomes Study Team, 1995; Galinsky, Howes, Kontos, & Shinn, 1994; Whitebook, Howes, & Phillips, 1990). However, the good news is that change is possible. The research we have conducted of efforts in several states or communities to improve the quality of child care reveal that it is very possible to do so in ways that positively affect children's development (see, e.g., Galinsky, Howes, & Kontos, 1995; Howes et al., 1998; Sibley, Abbott-Shim, & Galinsky, 1994).

Debate 4: Is It Quality Time or Quantity Time?

There is no question that time is a burning issue for employed parents. The majority of mothers and fathers in the Ask the Children study (53%) feel that they have too little time with their child. Furthermore, they are critical of many employed parents for putting their material desires and strivings for success ahead of their obligations to care for their children. More than two in five (42%) feel that employed mothers care more about being successful at work than meeting the needs of their children (see Fig. 14.6). Interestingly, there is no difference between mothers and fathers on their response to this statement, although there is a difference between those who work part-time and full-time. Sixty percent of parents who work less than 35 hours a week agree with this statement compared with 40% of those who work more than 35 hours a week. Obviously, parents who work fewer hours are both living in a way that supports their priorities and are judgmental about mothers who do not appear to put their children first.

What about parents' views of fathers? Because the debates tend to center on mothers, it is perhaps surprising that employed parents are more likely to see *fathers*—not mothers—as putting their desires for success ahead of their concerns for their children (see Fig. 14.7). Overall, 62% of employed

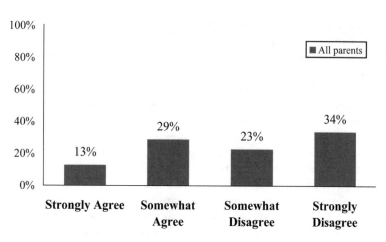

FIG. 14.6.   Many working mothers seem to care more about being successful at work than meeting the needs of their children.

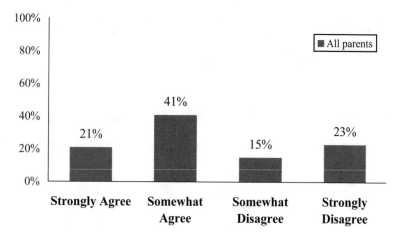

FIG. 14.7.   Many working fathers seem to care more about being successful at work than meeting the needs of their children.

parents feel this way. Again, there is no difference between mothers and fathers in holding this point of view.

So why has time become such an issue for parents? The Families and Work Institute's National Study of the Changing Workforce finds—to the surprise of many—that children in dual-earner families are spending more time with their parents today than they did 20 years ago. This increase is due to three factors: The amount of time that mothers spend with their children has held constant; fathers have increased the amount of time they spend with children (on workdays, this increase amounts to

30 minutes); and dual earners are having fewer children (Bond, Swanberg, & Galinsky, 1998).

In assessing time diary entries, Suzanne Bianchi from the University of Maryland has come to a similar conclusion (Bianchi, 2000). If employed parents are spending approximately as much or more time with their children than in earlier decades, why are parents today feeling so stretched, so pressed for time? Perhaps it is because the time spent with their children has become more fragmented. Or as the boundaries between work and family life have become increasingly blurred, perhaps families are multitasking more, turning from their children to their email, voice mail, or other work and then back to their children again. The National Study of the Changing Workforce reveals that parents are more likely to bring work home today than they did 20 years ago. It also reveals that the pace of work has quickened and become more demanding and this pressure spills over into home life (Bond et al., 1998).

Whatever the causes, the result has been an intensified debate about quality time versus quantity time. The Ask the Children study provides an opportunity to explore this debate from the vantage point of children. To do so, I looked at how much time children report spending with their parents as well as what happens in that time—the activities that parents and children do together, whether the time is rushed or calm, and whether children feel that their parents can really focus on them when they are together. I found that all of these factors are predictive of how children assess their parents' parenting skills and how successful they feel their parents are in managing work and family life. The amount of time children spend with their parents and what happens in that time both are important.

Once again, the debates we have been having mask what I consider a very real problem: the level of stress and exhaustion that parents bring home from work. When asked if they could make one wish to change the way their mother's and/or their father's work affects their lives, the largest proportion of children wish that their mothers and fathers would be less stressed and less tired. Thirty-four percent make this wish for their mothers. And 27.5% make this wish for their fathers (see Figs. 14.8 and 14.9).

WHY THE DEBATES PERSIST

Changing these debates requires changing the way parents think about and see the world. At the core of each of these controversies is an assumption of the centrality of the mother to her children's development and well-being. The debates are questioning whether she should spend any time away from her children, including the time she may be spending as an economic provider, except if the family "really needs the money." And, if she is employed,

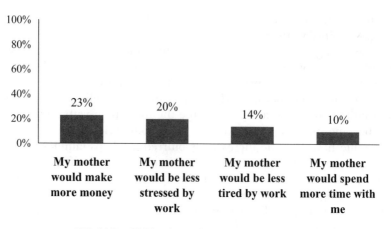

FIG. 14.8.   Children's top four wishes for mothers.

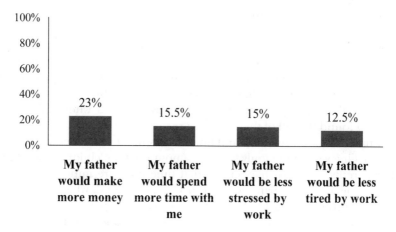

FIG. 14.9.   Children's top four wishes for fathers.

how much time is "enough" to be with her children? Furthermore, can anyone else really provide good care for the children—the father as well as
child-care providers, or will children's ties to these other people weaken the
bonds between the mother and her children? In sum, if the child has a
good relationship with his or her mother, the relationship will not necessarily be affected (read damaged) by short separations or by the child's connections to others. It is interesting to speculate why this notion has been
hard to accept.

As I found in the research I conducted for my book, *The Six Stages of Parenthood* (Galinsky, 1987), sharing the care of a child can be emotionally
wrenching. Especially during the early years, the parent who is in charge—
usually the mother—feels drawn to the child, worries for the child's safety

when separated, and feels competitive with others who break into this parent–child circle. One mother of a 6-week-old describes her desire to be with her child as so strong that everything else is an "annoyance, an interruption." What she would really like to do is to "get into a little burrow with this baby." And when she is separated from her child for a while, "my image of myself is of an elephant mother charging through the jungle because she hears her babies squeal" (Galinsky, 1987, p. 75).

Changing also requires parents to be open to the fact their past views and actions might not have been written in stone. According to one mother in interviews I have conducted, "this is very threatening." These feelings help explain why the tension between employed and at-home mothers is difficult to abate. According to another mother, the thinking goes: "If another mother does things differently and that's okay, it may mean that the way I have been doing things is not absolutely necessary." It can be hard to accept that two very different, seemingly contradictory, parenting choices could each have merit.

Finally, changing requires an alternative way of thinking. In our culture, we are steeped in black–white either–or thinking. Perhaps this dichotomous way of thinking has its roots in our western culture; perhaps it has been fanned by the media that sells its wares by pitting competing arguments against each other. So to change, one would have to embrace a style of thinking that encompasses the nuances of an argument rather than simply its polar extremes.

RESISTANCE TO CHANGE AND ITS IMPACT
ON "ASKING THE CHILDREN"

I believe that this resistance to change has stood in the way of "asking the children." It is surprising that this study is one of the few that includes a comprehensive investigation of how children feel about their employed parents. After all, we are more than 30 years into the societal change that the Hudson Institute calls "the most significant change in the history of the American workplace—the rapid increase of women in the work force" (Judy & D'Amico, 1997). The Bureau of Labor Statistics has recently charted the employment of mothers at an all time high in 1998, 59% of mothers returned to work in the first year after giving birth, compared with 31% in 1976 (Bachu & O'Connell, 2000). Most studies examining the impact of maternal and dual-earner employment have collected data on children's development and family adaptation, without including children's perspectives.

There are several plausible reasons why children have typically not been included as informants in the work–family literature. Many of the studies focus on very young children who are less able to speak on their own behalf. Additionally, because so much of the literature has examined the potential harm to children of having employed mothers, perhaps there has been a fear of hearing directly about these experiences from children. Or perhaps children are seen as imperfect reporters, because they are only able to defend the lives they have led. Or including children's voices in this ongoing debate may be seen as abdicating adult responsibility to children. Although the resistance to listen to children remains strong, as Thorne (1998) noted, times are changing—we are moving from viewing children as "becoming" adults-in-the-making to seeing them as actors in the present. I believe that the Ask the Children study is part of this emerging trend.

What Is Missed by Not Asking the Children

Because a number of people are stuck in debates that do not fit the data, this study finds they may have missed very important insights about how children feel and what they know about their parents' work and family life. Here are several examples:

Children Are Concerned About Their Parents' Stress.   Recall that when children were granted one wish to change the way their mother's/father's work affects their lives, the largest proportion wished that their parents would be less stressed, less tired. Parents were asked to make a wish for themselves: "If *you* were granted one wish to change the way that your work affects your child's life, what would that wish be?" It was an open-ended question so parents could say anything they wanted. The largest majority of parents— 22%—say "have more time with their child." An additional 16% wish they could "work less time." Parents were also asked: "If *your child* were granted one wish to change the way that your work affects his/her life, what would that wish be?" The largest group of parents, 21%, thinks their child would want "more time with me." An additional 19% think their child would want them to work less time, and 16% say their children would want them "not to have to go to work." In total, 56% focus on increasing their time with their child. Interestingly, only 2% of parents guess what so many children wish for—less stressed and tired parents.

Children Are Worried About Their Parents.   Another thing that parents may miss is that their children worry about them. Parents report that they are used to the notion that they, the parents, worry about their children, but their children worrying about them? Perhaps a surprising thought. The Ask the Children study reveals that one third of children 8 through 18 (32%) worry about their parents often or very often. If one includes the children who say they "sometimes" worry about their parents, the percentage rises to almost two thirds of children (65%) who worry. The largest proportion of children (37%) report that they worry because "we are a family and families worry about each other." Another 25.5% worry because their parents are very stressed and 11% worry because their parents are very tired.

Children Do Not Think That Their Parents Like Their Jobs as Much as Parents Do.   The Ask the Children study found that while three in five parents like their jobs "a lot," only two in five children think that their parents like their jobs "a lot." Possibly parents see work as competitive with their children, so they do not share very much about their jobs. In addition, parents often come home and complain about work, without realizing that their actions are a living laboratory in which children learn about the world of work.

A Number of Children Do Not Know Too Much About Their Parents'—Especially Their Fathers'—Jobs.   Work has traditionally been seen as the province of fathers who have served as the primary breadwinners, however, it is interesting that children know more about the kind of work their mothers do than what their fathers do. Two thirds of children 8 to 18 years old (66%) know "a lot" about their mothers' work compared with 54% who know "a lot" about their fathers' work. One of the few other studies that tapped children's knowledge of their parents' work and working condition found the same thing: Children claim significantly more knowledge about their mothers' than their fathers' jobs (Piotrkowski, 1987).

HOPES FOR THE FUTURE

It is my hope that the gap between what research finds and the nature of what the public debates begins to narrow and this and the other studies reported today are part of closing that gap. Moving beyond the either–or arguments will help parents better navigate the sometimes turbulent waters of working and having a family. For example, when many people think about how parents' work affect children, they talk about how old the child was when the mother went back to work and how much time parents spend working each day. Yet research finds that it is not simply that parents work, it is "how" they work that makes a difference.

In the Ask the Children study, I developed a model to identify those aspects of jobs that matter. I found four factors make a difference: having a reasonably demanding job; having a job that permits parents to focus on their work; having a job that is meaningful, challenging, provides opportunities to learn, and job autonomy; and having a workplace environment with good interpersonal and supportive relationships where parents do not feel they have to choose between having a job and parenting, and where they are treated with respect. Parents who work in these environments are in better moods and have more energy for parenting, which, in turn, can affect their interactions with their children, and children's development. The chain of effects, however, does not stop with home life. Parents with good situations at work, who come home in better moods and with more energy for their children, and who have children who are developing well, reinvest this energy back at work.

As implied in the title of this book, we no longer think about work and family as a balancing act because it implies an either–or scale, where if you give to one part of your life, you take away from the other part. As you can see, our studies find that work and family can enrich each other. By knowing that "how" they work can affect their home life, parents can begin to change their frame of reference; can make even small changes at work that will enable them to come home in a better mood and with greater energy for their children.

My ultimate hope, however, is that we continue "asking the children." I know all too well what happens when there are no conversations. Time and time again in the qualitative interviews I did for this study, I heard misunderstanding and misinformation from children when there was no talking. I heard about fears and grievances. I heard "secrets." One child thought that her mother had stopped working at home because she was too noisy, when in fact her mother's plan to move from her home office had been in the works for a long time and had nothing to do with the child's making noise. Several children hated their child care (and for very good reason) but had never said so.

When parents and children talk together about these issues, reasonable changes can be made. One teenager had wished for years that her parents had gone on school field trips when she was young. As a result of a conversation, this family took a field trip. It is a lark, but it is not a lark either. It was unfinished business that was eating away at the child. Also as a result of a conversation, a mother who worked at home and whose business calls had interrupted her time with her child no longer puts her child off with "just a minute." She has become more realistic about the time the calls will take and tries not to schedule calls just at the moment her children arrive home from school.

Why does the bank in my neighborhood have the slogan "it is the right relationship?" Because even with the bank, it is all about relationships. Parents set the rules and the traditions, and navigate the course that their work and family lives take. Within that context, however, it is important to create a climate where parents can listen to and talk to their children about whatever is important in their lives. Recall that children did not give their parents very high marks for knowing what is really going on in their lives. According to a 12-year-old child:

Listen. Listen to what your kids say, because you know, sometimes it's very important. And sometimes a kid can have a great idea and it could even affect you. Because, you know, kids are people.

REFERENCES

Bachu, A., & O'Connell, M. (2000). Fertility of American women: June 1998. In *Current Population Reports* (U.S. Census Bureau Publication P20-526). Washington, DC: U.S. Census Bureau.

Bianchi, S. (2000). Maternal employment and time with children: Dramatic change or surprising continuity? *Demography, 37*, 401–414.

Bond, J. T., Swanberg, J., & Galinsky, E. (1998). *The national study of the changing workforce.* New York: Families and Work Institute.

Bronfenbrenner, U., & Crouter, A. C. (1982). Work and family in time and space. In S. B. Kamerman & C. D. Hayes (Eds.), *Families and work: Children in a changing world* (pp. 39–83). Washington, DC: National Academy Press.

Child Outcomes and Study Team. (1995). *Cost, quality and child outcomes in child care centers.* Denver, CO: Economics Department, University of Colorado.

Galinsky, E. (1987). *The six stages of parenthood.* Reading, MA: Addison-Wesley.

Galinsky, E. (2000). *Ask the children: The breakthrough study that reveals how to succeed at work and parenting.* New York: Quill.

Galinsky, E., & Hooks, W. H. (1977). *The new extended family: Day care that works.* Boston: Houghton Mifflin.

Galinsky, E., Howes, C., & Kontos, S. (1995). *The family child care training study: Highlights of findings.* New York: Families and Work Institute.

Galinsky, E., Howes, C., Kontos, S., & Shinn, S. (1994). *The study of children in family child care and relative care: Highlights and findings.* New York: Families and Work Institute.

Gamble, T. J., & Zigler, E. (1986). Effects of infant day care: Another look at the evidence. *American Journal of Orthopsychiatry, 56*, 26–42.

Harris, K. M., Furstenburg, F. F., Jr., & Marmer, J. K. (1996, August). *Parental involvement with adolescents in intact families: The influence of fathers over the life course.* Paper presented at the annual meetings of the American Sociological Association, New York.

Hoffman, L. W., & Youngblade, L. M. (1999). *Mothers at work: Effects on children's well-being.* New York: Cambridge University Press.

Howes, C., Galinsky, E., Shinn, M., Sibley, A., Abbott-Shim, M., & McCarthy, J. (1998). *The Florida child care quality improvement study: 1996 report.* New York: Families and Work Institute.

Howes, C., Smith, E., & Galinsky, E. (1995). *Florida child care quality improvement study: Interim report.* New York: Families and Work Institute.

Judy, R. W., & D'Amico, C. (1997). *Workforce 2020: Work and workers in the 21st century.* Indianapolis, IN: Hudson Institute.

Kontos, S., Howes, C., Shinn, M., & Galinsky, E. (1995). *Quality in family child care and relative care.* New York: Teachers College Press.

Lamb, M. E. (1986). *The father's role: Applied perspectives.* New York: Wiley.

Levine, J., & Pittinsky, T. L. (1997). *Working fathers: New strategies for balancing work and family.* New York: Addison-Wesley.

NICHD Early Child Care Research Network. (1997). The effects of infant child care and attachment security: Results of the NICHD study of early child care. *Child Development, 68,* 860–879.

Parke, R. D. (1996). *Fathers.* Cambridge, MA: Harvard University Press.

Pedersen, F. A., Zaslow, N., Suwalsky, J., & Caine, R. (1980). Parent–infant and husband–wife interactions observed at five months. In F. Pedersen (Ed.), *The father–infant relationship* (pp. 82–92). New York: Praeger.

Piotrkowski, C. S. (1987). Children and adolescents look at their parent's jobs. In J. H. Lweko (Ed.), *How children and adolescents view the world of work.* San Francisco, CA: Jossey-Bass.

Public Agenda. (2000). *Necessary compromises: How parents, employers and children's advocates view child care today.* New York: Public Agenda.

Radin, N. (1981). The role of the father in cognitive, academic, and intellectual development. In M. E. Lamb (Ed.), *The role of the father in child development.* New York: Wiley.

Sibley, A., Abbott-Shim, M., & Galinsky, E. (1994). *Child care licensing: Georgia impact study.* New York: Families and Work Institute.

Thorne, B. (1998). *Selected bibliography on the sociology of childhood.* Berkeley, CA: University of California, Berkeley.

Whitebook, M., Howes, C., & Phillips, D. A. (1990). *Who cares? Child care teachers and the quality of care in America, Final report of the National Child Care Staffing Study.* Oakland, CA: Child Care Employee Project.

Zinsser, C. (1991). *Raised in East Urban: Child care changes in a working class community.* New York: Teachers College Press.

Chapter 15

Imagining the Future: A Dialogue on the Societal Value of Care

Faith A. Wohl
President
Child Care Action Campaign

Changing the metaphor, as the title of this book urges, is one way to think differently about an important issue. Another is to change the context in which that thinking is done. That was, in fact, the impetus behind Child Care Action Campaign's decision to position its strategic thinking about advocacy for child care in a new time frame—the year 2020—in the hope that doing so would permit accelerated progress on present-day solutions.

Late in the summer of 2001, as the organization worked on its strategic plan, one fact seemed both clear and unarguable. The national dialogue on child care was truly stuck. The public conversation was using the same vocabulary, advancing the same arguments, facing the same barriers as it had in the 1980s. Evidence was, to some degree, empirical: Those who had worked in the field for many years could see that legislative issues and coverage in the media had not changed in 25 years.

However, more rigorous evidence could be found in a report from the National Council of Jewish Women, "Opening a New Window on Child Care." This report marked the 25th anniversary of NCJW's landmark study, "Windows on Day Care," often acknowledged as the first nationwide survey of child-care facilities and services. The report compared the needs facing the field and the solutions that had been recommended in the late 1970s with those in the new report, and found them literally the same, thus reflecting a sense of the lack of progress over more than a two-decade time frame.

Child Care Action Campaign (CCAC) also compared the findings and recommendations of its own study, "Child Care and the Bottom Line," published in 1988, with the current situation. Again, it found that more than two thirds of the recommendations made in that report had not been accomplished by 2001. Although there had been considerable progress in academic research on child care, as well as significant increases in federal and state funding, the national conversation had truly not advanced. Part of this was due to the fact that with the passage of welfare reform legislation in 1996, child care had become a state-based issue. It was now the captive of the unique political, economic, cultural, and financial climate of each of the 50 states.

FINDING A NEW DIRECTION

As an advocacy organization that had helped shape and drive the national dialogue since its founding in 1983, and that had served as the field's voice for much of that time, CCAC was determined to find the path on which to move the national discussion forward in a new direction. It wanted to jump-start thinking and lift the field's discussions away from its preoccupation with legislative tactics for the next appropriations round in Congress. Instead, it wanted to make real progress toward CCAC's organizational vision, "quality, affordable child care for every American family that needs it."

CCAC came to the conclusion that it would look to the year 2020—a generation ahead—to help guide and shape current thinking. Its interest was to understand why the United States seems unable to achieve quality care for every child, as have many countries in the developed world. It wanted to move the public dialogue forward in a new direction that would place the topic squarely on the nation's agenda.

The challenges to achieving such a goal seemed insurmountable, especially as the project was in its early stages of development when the attack on the World Trade Center devastated the nation in September 2001. Suddenly, the world was so frighteningly uncertain that planning for the future on a long-term basis seemed, if not foolhardy, then risky at best. In the face of this, CCAC decided to use a scenario planning methodology. This offered a process that is not only designed to take uncertainty into account but also to yield alternate possibilities for the future, not actual predictions. It engaged Susan G. Stickley, President of Stratus and senior practitioner, with the Global Business Network and an expert in scenario planning, to facilitate and partner with it in the process.

Many studies in the past had focused on child care, but few if any had looked at child care in the broader context of care, including health, elderly, and special needs care; none had looked a generation ahead into the future. CCAC chose to expand the exploration to this broader and different context in the hope of discovering synergies among the various fields, as well as underlying assumptions that were not apparent through a present-day child-care perspective alone. It also recognized that placing the intractable issue in a very different time frame could yield new solutions, as well as strategies to reach them.

THE IMPACT OF OUTSIDE FORCES

The success of a scenario planning process is the selection of the right question to use as a foundation for inquiry. This focal question would be at the heart of all discussions and considerable time was spent defining it. As Susan Stickley advised CCAC, the question would probably not originate in the "transactional space" of the field—around typical questions of affordability, quality, and access to care that had formed the trilemma of thinking in the field for many years. Nor was it likely to be about issues of compensation, turnover, or curriculum, all the customary subjects of discussions about early care and education. Rather, the focal question would probably emerge from the effect of outside forces, such as politics, culture, and world events, where most uncertainty and change is created.

The selected focal question was: "How do we best influence societal priorities in American life in a way that values both care and equality, to achieve a better, more caring future for children, families and society for the next generation?" As CCAC engaged in the process over the succeeding months, that question evolved into three parts:

1. "What are the most critical uncertainties affecting American life over the next generation that impact care?" The answer to this would lead to the development of alternate scenarios for the future.
2. "How do we achieve a better, more caring future for children and families and society?" This would yield the outline of a new strategy for Child Care Action Campaign.
3. "Do we need to influence societal priorities to achieve that better future?" The answer to this final question would be critical. It had long been assumed in the field that "if only we could change societal priorities, we could achieve the child care system we wanted and children needed." Would CCAC find this true or necessary?

The project was originally designed as a 3-month process to create a set of four relevant scenarios. However, after the initial think tank session held in New York City in January of 2002, CCAC could see both the power and effectiveness of the process, as well as the potential to change and influence thinking in a powerful way. The program was recast as a set of six consecutive think tanks to be conducted in cities around the United States, over a 14-month period, to capture regional perspectives.

This decision afforded the opportunity to engage a diverse audience in the process of re-conceiving the future of care. Participants in the six workshops reflected wide diversity, not only in region but also age, gender, ethnicity, and field of expertise. All told, about 120 leaders participated from fields as varied as ethics and literature, sociology and nursing, as well as key members of the child-care community. Together, they developed a scenario framework, defined a strategic agenda to achieve effective care and finally, explored whether societal priorities would need to be influenced to achieve a better, more caring future.

This very diverse group of experts agreed that the field was, indeed, stuck. The reasons they advanced included society's ambivalence toward mothers, which had become obvious during the welfare reform debate, when it was argued that poor mothers should go to work but that middle-class mothers should stay home. A literature review of public opinion polls showed that the public was apathetic and uninformed about the subject of care, but also made it clear that there was more support than the field had believed and that it could be strengthened. Consumer polls also revealed that parents, by and large, do not see government solutions as answers to their work and family dilemmas; they see the solutions as personal. Apathy was also an issue. Beyond those in the advocacy field, no real champion was demanding change, not even parents. All of these factors, and others, had mired the field and diminished its prospects for progress.

THE IMPETUS OF INTERNAL VALUES AND PRIORITIES

In beginning to consider the focal question, think tank participants had to first envision what could happen if societal priorities changed. One participant said, memorably, "care would be valued with reverence, like liberty." Another envisioned a "society reawakened to its spiritual underpinnings." In such a climate, "raising children would be seen as one of the most valuable endeavors." Aspirational statements like these lifted subsequent discussions to a very different plane than usually experienced at child-care meetings. Most important of all, the groups agreed that there would be different results if the solutions for the future were built around children and their needs, compared to supporting the needs of working parents as in current practice.

Scenario development is a process designed to reach down under the surface, forcing people to face their own inherent assumptions. Early validation of Child Care Action Campaign's belief that the issue is truly stuck came from the broad agreement of think tank participants with this position. Not only did they agree that the issue no longer has traction, but argued that it would take an earth-shattering event to lift and change public values. One small work group actually had to invent an invasion of aliens to allow themselves to believe in the magnitude of change necessary to complete an assigned exercise. Since all of the think tanks occurred after the events of September 11, which many believed had already changed the world forever, it is easy to see how and why the group had to reach that far. Although their approach was certainly not typical of the more pragmatic conversations that took place, it gave credence to how stuck participants believed the child-care issue was at that point.

Participants believed that child care was at a standstill because of societal priorities and values. Despite all the progress that had been made in the last 25 years to reshape workplaces to better accommodate the different needs of modern families, the changing work environment seemed to be outstripping that progress. Its long hours, demands for ever-increasing productivity and intense, short-term emphasis on the bottom line were putting more and greater stress on the interaction between work and family life. Leadership, the participants agreed, could not bring about the necessary change; in fact, some leaders were actually holding it back. Progress on child care had, indeed, come to a halt.

Discussions of driving forces in society that could bring about change included the sense that time is moving faster and distances are shorter, thanks to the ease and frequency of travel and the availability of electronic devices to maintain connections in the all-the-time-everywhere workplace. The dominance of global capitalism, the increasing influence of religion on national policy, and even the 24-hour global news cycle were also cited. Participants explored the contradiction inherent in the fact that unresolved cultural attitudes persist on the role of women, especially mothers of young children, in an economy that is dependent on women to work. They even noted the growing confusion over what it means to be an American, as large immigrant communities moved from past patterns of assimilation to determined preservation of culture, language, and family and child-rearing practices.

With the goal of building a four-quadrant matrix that could help define alternate futures, participants grouped these driving forces of change into continuums of critical uncertainties. The matrix itself would be formed by the intersection of two such continuums, both of which would need to be plausible, novel, challenging, and relevant to the topic. Ultimately, over several think tank sessions, two were chosen from a wide-ranging set of possibilities. One reflected the relationship between abundance and scarcity; the other, the source of responsibility, solutions, and values in the society, ranging from individualized at one end to systemic at the other. Simply stated, the matrix pictured the intersection of resources and values, and it was around the dynamics of those that the scenarios were developed. The impact of technology was also recognized, linking a high-tech emphasis with abundance and a high-touch/low-tech environment with scarcity.

IMAGINING FOUR DIFFERENT FUTURES

The scenarios were not intended to predict a specific future but rather to illuminate plausible alternatives, as current events and trends were extrapolated into the chosen time frame—the year 2020. The actual future might be one of these possibilities, or none of them. Likely, it would be some combination of all, close to the matrix center, where some aspects of all four scenarios would be in play. However, in their discussions, participants were encouraged to drive their thinking deliberately toward the outer edges of the matrix, to achieve maximum differentiation, and to see both unique and similar possibilities for care.

To test the plausibility of the scenarios, participants were asked to search for early indicators of ideas and events in the media—stories in today's newspapers, television reports, and magazine articles—that reported a trend, an innovation, or a new idea whose result could be projected into one of the futures. Participants brought rich and varied examples to every session, validating the possibility that our society could be headed in any one of the four scenario directions.

Two of the four possible futures existed in the top half of the matrix where resources were abundant. The participants named these "A New Destiny," and "Innovation Rules." The other two described futures in a scarcity environment; these were titled "Empty Pockets, Empty Promises" and "Tribes and Tribulations." After years of consistent economic growth and increasing wealth in the United States, it was difficult at first for many participants to imagine the degree of scarcity that might exist in the two scenarios in that half of the matrix. But as national and world economic events around the think tank discussions changed during 2002 and early 2003, the mood switched. For some, it became difficult to see how the United States could continue to prosper at the level many had expected, and as the two abundance scenarios projected.

Over the course of three of the think tanks, pictures of life in each of the four futures were developed through intense and far-ranging discussions. From these, CCAC prepared written narratives of each scenario. To make them relevant and readable, CCAC chose to tell the stories through the lens of a single family. Each scenario shows how that family, especially the father and first person spokesman, Jim Rivers, would experience life in the unique circumstances of each quadrant of the matrix. Also, each started with a "what if" question, designed to very briefly define the circumstances in which the United States would find itself because of the history of the years between the present and 2020. The purpose of the narratives is to bring a real-life focus to the large historical, political, and economic developments inherent in each window to the future. What follows uses some excerpts from the narratives to briefly tell the story of each quadrant.

The Year Is 2020: Innovation Rules

This scenario poses the question, *"What if the United States were to find itself in the grip of an explosion of technological advancement unparalleled in its history, spawning the knowledge economy and the age of knowledge workers."* Against that backdrop, the narrator introduces himself as Jim Rivers, president of a 3-year-old company called HistoGame. He describes himself and his work: "We design and develop video games that provide advanced concept curricula in a wide array of social studies disciplines for the secondary school market. I'm not quite used to calling myself, 'President.' For many years, I was just an ordinary social studies teacher at a large suburban high school near Chicago. But back in 2003, I read a brief newspaper article about how children were learning to succeed in the alternative universes of video games, while failing to pass high-stakes tests and meet new standards in class."

He went on to explain, "It suddenly occurred to me that the folks at Nintendo and Sony had figured out what some of us teachers never really learned in our methods classes back in college—how to captivate young minds in the 21st-century. As they used to say, back when I was a kid, a light bulb came on. Of course, we don't use light bulbs any more, but you get the idea. It took me 15 years to figure it out after that inspiration, but with a Microsoft Certificate in gaming technology and software design, along with start-up capital that was ridiculously easy to come by, HistoGame was born. And, I say proudly, not only is it booming but test scores are rising."

What happened to transform Jim Rivers, social studies teacher, into a high-tech entrepreneur? It was a potent combination: the triumph of innovation and a period of incredible abundance. The new technology resulted from the traumatic failure of the American intelligence community to detect and prevent September 11 as well as other attacks in the next few years (as predicated in this scenario). The President challenged a special collaboration of major defense contractors to develop new intelligence gathering and communications linkages to protect the United States. They accomplished the task on an urgent schedule, driven by fear, pride, and patriotism.

The results not only provided the nation with a new intelligence apparatus but also presaged a time when individuals with an idea to make things better could easily find the right technological break-through to make their dreams come true. The remarkable technical work flowing from the intelligence project, rooted in nanotechnology and quantum physics, generated a continuing explosion of new products. With the continued unraveling of government regulation, the provision of universal access to technology for all and an economy growing at the unparalleled annual rate of more than 8%, by 2020 unemployment had become a thing of the past. Funds once set aside for unemployment compensation were reinvested in new benefits, to intensify workforce training to keep up with technological progress, and to improve family life.

The only shadow falling over these incredibly good times was finding enough people to work. Many instant multimillionaires retired, to do charitable work or just live a life of leisure. With the population getting older and the birthrate down, the primary challenge became workforce development. So many workers, with lucrative employment contracts, chose to work part time, alternate day schedules and/or from home, that pressure on care systems was greatly relieved. Between different kinds of paid leave, 3-days-a-week work schedules, and better training in child development for all, families could take care of their own.

At the same time, the immediate need for older workers to work later in their life span and the need for more babies to build a future workforce, exemplified the heated competition for resources even in a time of extraordinary abundance. And as Jim Rivers said, "There is still the need for professional caregivers—for single-parent families, for example—but they are now well-trained and highly valued as knowledge workers. After all, they're caring for the generation that will invent our next new world."

Susan Stickley, CCAC's consultant, explained that this is actually what many in business today see as the so-called official future, that is, what they think will actually happen or at least hope it will. This picture of 2020 represents life as it's been lived in the past several years, where access to the Internet, to wireless technology and complex electronic appliances, has transformed daily reality. However, the other three scenarios suggest that life in the future may actually be very different.

The Year Is 2020: A New Destiny

This scenario posed the question, *"What if the United States acquired irrefutable data demanding a global vision of environmental and economic sustainability to avoid calamity, bringing forth an era of optimum growth and cooperation, a time of incredible abundance and a true economic and social renaissance."* We again meet Jim Rivers who, in this scenario, is a social studies teacher in a large suburban high school near Chicago. He says, "I feel incredibly fortunate to be a teacher today compared to what my mother experienced when she taught third grade as I grew up. Teachers today are not only very well-paid, but considered important to our society and our economy. I wish my mother could have lived long enough to see that, but unfortunately, the therapeutic that could have prevented her stroke wasn't discovered until two years ago."

Again, this scenario provides a compelling example of how good can sometimes arise from difficult circumstances. In this case, it was a series of really frightening epidemics around the world from new and mutated viruses. It all started with AIDS, but in the early years of this century, SARS, avian flu, mad cow disease, and many others swamped the poorly funded and antiquated Centers for Disease Control, putting untenable pressure on the nation's health system and millions of uninsured Americans. The government had to step in. In doing so, it demonstrated for the first time in a long time, proactive concern for the health of its citizens, if only to save the economy from total ruin.

The need for a seamless flow of centralized information from around the world led to the creation of a global DataCore on health, environmental, and economic issues. Quickly dubbed "WorldWise," the new system was capable of mapping with precision the extent of global health and environmental problems and their connection to American patterns of disease, environmental degradation, and economic issues. With these data in hand, the government had both a mandate and a method to ensure the survival of humanity, based on irrefutable data.

Drawing on what it learned, the United States poured public dollars into research, particularly for sustainable green technologies, including remarkable fuel cell technology for the automotive industry. This spurred renewed attention to solar power and wind turbine energy innovations, all of which accelerated the forward propulsion of economic prosperity. Marketing and installation of these cost-effective and environmentally sound green technologies created worldwide opportunities for work and wealth creation.

The passage of the UniCare Act in 2018 established permanent funding for intergenerational care programs and facilities. It provided a solid foundation of publicly funded and high-quality elder care, child care, elementary and secondary education, and other health resources in the community. This created real jobs for caregivers and teachers, as well as humane solutions based on measurable data, positive human impact, and sustainable benefits.

The contrast between this scenario and "Innovation Rules" is clear. In both cases, resources are abundant, but in one case, the driving spirit and values are entrepreneurial and individual; in the other, "A New Destiny," it is public initiative that draws bold solutions from a terrifying health problem. These ultimately catalyze environmental enhancement on a global scale.

The Year Is 2020: Empty Pockets, Empty Promises

As discussions moved to the bottom half of the matrix where resources are scarce, two very different futures emerged. This one posed the question: *"What if the unique democracy of the United States was near collapse, with scarce resources in the hands of a small but powerful elite, with government promising but unable to deliver change, with the nation's physical infrastructure crumbling as the result of a prolonged and expensive battle against terrorism."* Now Jim Rivers' initial introduction of himself is as an irritated citizen. As he says, "People are just fed up with the government spending billions on wars and nation building in other countries while, at the same time, letting real problems here at home go unfixed!" Now he's an unemployed history teacher, having lost his job in the last round of downsizing the schools to save money, so that the resources can be used to build new schools in Iraq or Palestine.

He comments that "ever since the World Trade Center disaster back in 2001, we've lived in a time of incredible tension and ongoing terrorism. It became a mandate for government deficit spending on defense to support that war as well as the hunt for Al Qaeda." By 2020, people like Jim are paying the price for years of war in the Mid-East, against terrorist networks, individuals, and nations. All of this has exhausted the patience of American citizens and emptied its government's pockets. The U.S. economy has also been in the midst of a prolonged recession, one that has created a seemingly permanent underclass. National borders were finally closed so that American workers would have the best chance to compete for the few new jobs being created by public works projects or small businesses. The desperation of its own people is fueling a destructive cycle of American isolationism on the world stage, with violence not only abroad but at home.

The private sector was caught between the proverbial rock and hard place, as continued threats of violence made markets at home volatile, while the cost of capital and the danger of travel from terrorism limited growth opportunities in developing nations. By 2020, with the Dow at 500 and the price of oil at $60/barrel, many major businesses have simply closed their doors.

In this world of isolation, terror, and poverty, children are again a source of labor, both in the home and on neighborhood farms. With so many family members out of work or working reduced schedules due to cost-cutting measures, with travel difficult because of fear, the neighborhood has become the nation. Within the neighborhood, families meet a lot of their needs by bartering their services and their crops and by sharing the work. In fact, one of the good things to come out of this long period of tension and terrorism is the growing importance of extended family, friends, and neighbors.

The Year Is 2020: Tribes and Tribulations

The fourth and final scenario also exists in the scarcity quadrant of the matrix but the focus is on individual, rather than systemic, solutions. It starts with this question: *"What if the United States' status as an economic superpower crumbled as the last shred of credible corporate ethics and practices melted away, while attempts to rebuild the economy were hobbled by the scarcest resources since the Depression?"* Jim Rivers is no longer a social studies teacher. He says, "The commute was increasingly expensive and dangerous; also it seemed important to stay closer to home, here in our small town where you feel like you know everyone." He supplements the modest pension from his teaching years by delivering daily newspapers on a local route and tutoring some of the neighborhood children.

The United States remains in the grip of the longest economic and technological recession in history, which began after the September 11, 2001 terrorist attacks. In fact, the nation is nearing a profound depression that could have catastrophic impact on already waning homeland security and health and human service initiatives. While terrorism has been a potent factor, the real culprit is the revelation of corporate accounting scandals and improprieties. They drove the stock market into a permanent downward trend. With a lack of investment capital to support innovation, the economy is stuck in a technological time warp.

Many asked themselves, how could the strongest and best economy go sour so quickly? How did we miss seeing the cracks in the facade until great American institutions came falling down, as quickly and as horrifyingly as the North and South Towers? Too much was happening at once; Americans were literally holding their collective breath. Consumers began to close their wallets in the face of possible war on three fronts, the continual reports of ongoing corporate scandals, and the growing gap between the haves and have-nots.

For some 10 years after the initial attack on the World Trade Center, the economic downturn fed on itself in a vicious cycle: Faltering financial markets led to an increasing number of business closings, unemployment figures rose to levels not seen in a hundred years. With an ever-growing number of citizens in need of the safety net of publicly funded services, and the GDP shrinking, public resources were stretched to a breaking point.

Not surprisingly, the country's biggest problem in 2020 is lack of trust. First, the lack of trust in corporations that led to financial ruin for many; then, lack of trust in the government for not anticipating the problem. With so many people in financial difficulty, there is now mistrust of anyone you don't know personally. America has turned into a collection of tribes, organized for protection as well as access to such basic resources as safe shelter, adequate food, and clean water. Americans at every level are circling the wagons at the neighborhood and village level.

With reductions in Social Security and stringent limits on Medicare and Medicaid, the worst impact of these difficult times is on the elderly. The lucky ones are active and can play a valued role in intergenerational communities. Others have become a burden and drain on society. They are the forgotten ones, suffering through quiet and lonely twilight years, in most cases dependent on their families to provide basic food and shelter. But Jim Rivers argues that it is the young who suffer the most. The financial downturn has changed the American mindset, from one of optimism and hope to one of fear and struggle. No one thinks and plans for the future; too much energy goes into daily living.

In a very real sense, that's what has already happened within the childcare field. With resources diminished, little strategic thought has been given to long-term needs. With struggles over millions of dollars in Federal appropriations instead of the billions really needed, energy has been dissipated and competition for waning resources has been fierce. The care fields may already be in the Tribes and Tribulations part of the matrix. While participants in the think tank discussions agreed that "Empty Pockets" represented the most clear and believable extension of today (2002–2004), "Tribes" could well be the right metaphor for the care fields with the resource difficulties and mistrust they already encounter.

BACK TO THE PRESENT

CCAC's facilitator, Susan Stickley, explained that in the business world, strategy is based on value propositions and the exchange of value. She said, "If you build a business strategy around true value, money will come. The non-profit world is no different." CCAC decided to use its final think tank to build its own "field of dreams," by learning from the younger generation. Undergraduate and graduate students from Boston area universities and colleges were asked to role play within each of the four scenarios, the key stakeholder groups: working parents, elderly, children, employers, care providers, and public policymakers. Thanks to the passion and insight of the students, the results were hopeful and uplifting.

It was at this meeting that the answer to the third part of the original focal question became clear—"if only we could change societal priorities, could we achieve the child care system we wanted and children needed?" As students enacted their parts in each of the scenarios, societal priorities were found to change spontaneously, according to the circumstances. However, the values underlying those priorities did not change. Through this think tank, CCAC could see the enormous influence of capitalism on our values as a society. With the energetic and imaginative participation of the students, it became clear how much decision making is based on economic success. The only stakeholders who benefited in each of the scenarios were employers and working parents, while those in need of care trailed badly on the priority list in *all* cases. Until child care and other forms of care can be viewed and measured as contributors to economic success, it will be difficult for care to achieve a higher priority and focus within public institutions, unless and until underlying societal values change.

The Boston meeting clarified how world events outside the advocacy field largely determined changes in priorities within each of the four possible futures. This is also true in today's real world. The effects of war and terrorism, of declines in the strength of the dollar on world markets, the cynicism resulting from corporate scandal and many other factors have all played a role in determining the value for care today and at different points in our nation's history. During World War II, for example, the compelling need for women to go to work in defense factories, while their husbands went to war in foreign countries, led to the creation of thousands of publicly funded high-quality child-care centers and extended-day school programs to support these working women. Yet the deeply held, underlying value—that mothers belong at home with their young children—stayed strong. At the end of the war, when the need changed, the vast majority of these centers were shuttered, the women sent home, and child care fell from the public agenda.

IMAGINING THE FUTURE

Child Care Action Campaign also found in all its scenarios for the future a surprising and diminished role for out-of-home care solutions, largely based on the changing interactions of values and resources, the twin arms of the matrix. In the two scenarios built around scarcity, families or communities found new ways to care for children or needed far less care because of pervasive unemployment. In the two scenarios in times of abundance, there was less reliance on caregivers because of the reduced need for a two-paycheck family. These findings are somewhat at odds with current views of the need for care and raise difficult and challenging questions for the child-care advocacy field and its strategies and tactics in the coming years. For example, how will families, neighborhoods, and local cooperatives receive the training and materials they need to be good caregivers, to enhance and support the development of children in their care? What will be the role of center-based care? How will the changing mix of children as American demographics continue to diversify affect values, priorities, and strategies?

There may well be a shift in values in the future, if the students who participated in the CCAC think tank are any bellwether. As the students discussed their personal values, not those of a stakeholder whose role they were playing, they exposed a set of values that was quite different. In many important ways, their values were far more supportive of a better, more caring future. Where they perceived in all the scenarios a set of values that included parental responsibility, economic drivers, and an emphasis on the individual, their dreams for the future were based on shared community responsibility, social rather than economic drivers, and concern for needs beyond the individual. In contrast to the perceived lack of value for care today and in the four scenarios for 2020, the students hoped for a world where care is deeply valued.

(Shortly after completing the think tanks, Child Care Action Campaign's Board of Directors decided to close the organization, which happened in May of 2003. Since CCAC was not able to execute the strategic agenda it developed through its scenario planning, hopefully this brief review of its work will inspire other organizations to think more fully and longer term about the future, because it may be very different than what we hope and expect.)

Chapter 16

Vision for the Future of Work and Family Interaction

Susan Elaine Murphy
Diane F. Halpern
Claremont McKenna College

American families are facing many challenges and as noted in several chapters, many are finding it difficult to meet the escalating costs of education and health care. Working families often struggle to find affordable, quality day care, and they rely on the income from two jobs to provide a living wage. Although families take responsibility to meet these challenges in whatever manner possible, often they cannot do it alone and increasingly, the government's role in family life is central to how we define ourselves as a country. Basic societal questions revolve around the need to determine how far we are willing and able to go to support families and what it means to be profamily in a political climate where the term *family* excludes some functioning family units and being profamily can have opposite meanings for different groups.

When the United States is compared to many European countries and Canada, U.S. policies appear to be almost antifamily. Sweden, for example, is one of the most accommodating countries for working families. Sweden implemented a generous parental leave policy and subsidized child care in the early 1970s. Today, both parents are entitled to 450 days of paid leave from work which they can share to care for a newborn or adopted child, 30 days of which they must each take alone, and parents can take this leave part time. The requirement of 30 days leave for each parent alone was enacted as a way of ensuring that fathers would provide sole care for their infants and thus develop early bonds with their children. The long-term effect of this policy is unknown, but one can imagine a generation of children and fathers who benefit from closer relationships. Also, parents can work reduced hours until their child is eight or formally begins school.

Moreover, Swedish employers also help with work–family interaction. Section five of the Swedish Equal Opportunity Act reads, "An employer shall facilitate the combination of gainful employment and parenthood with respect to both female and male employees" (Shahmehri, 2001). Sweden is not alone in its efforts to help citizens succeed at work and home. The Canadian Government supports work–life balance through a number of resources for employees and employers. Recently, the Canadian Department of Labour sponsored a nationwide survey of work–family policies. By providing information to companies, they show the way in which work–family policies make good business sense and provide national guidelines for introducing family-friendly strategies. The United Kingdom appears to have a similar level of effort as evidenced by government supported resources. Even Japan is now looking for ways to accommodate the increasing number of women and working mothers who are entering the workforce.

In the United States, Congress passed the Family Medical Leave Act (FMLA) of 1993 in response to the changing demographics of the workforce. Although many consider the FMLA a success, some employees still are hesitant to take the leave for fear of losing their jobs or eligibility for upcoming promotions despite the fact that their jobs and future promotions are protected by FMLA. They know the culture of their workplace and it is often difficult to overcome a negative culture, even with a strong law. The state of California, as well as other states, including Connecticut, Hawaii, Maine, Minnesota, New Jersey, Oregon, Rhode Island, Vermont, Washington, Wisconsin, and the District of Columbia has extended some of the provisions of the federal act. For example, the California Family Rights Act (CFRA Under SB 1661, effective July 1, 2004) will allow workers to receive up to 6 weeks of partially paid leave per year to care for a seriously ill child, spouse, parent, or domestic partner or to bond with a new child, making California first in the United States to offer paid family leave.

Many U.S. companies also offer various benefits such as flextime or telecommuting, and a few offer on-site day care or other accommodations for working mothers and fathers. Research studies have shown these programs to be effective in decreasing absenteeism, increasing productivity, and increasing worker satisfaction (e.g., Weber, 2003). Although these efforts have brought about change in the way many of us work, other research indicates that organizations still have a way to go if they want to see the full effectiveness of these programs. There is still resistance to any change from the status quo, and despite evidence of the effectiveness of flexible policies, many employers remain wary of employee abuse. For example, organizations must continue to take steps to improve the implementation of work–family policies and find ways to extend these policies to lower wage earners.

WORK AND FAMILY CONCERNS
ARE EVERYONE'S CONCERNS

When employees' multiple roles become incompatible and work and family interfere (e.g., manager meetings are scheduled before nursery school starts), everyone at the managers' meeting and nursery school is affected. Employers have a stake, and we as a nation have a stake as to whether individuals have the ability to successfully integrate their home and work lives. The children feel the stress which can lead to life-long health problems, work suffers, good employees may leave, and children may be endangered by being left alone when they are too young. This is everyone's problem.

We chose to focus on work and family for this book rather than the seemingly broader category of work life because what happens to families is important to everyone. Whether an individual has a spouse, or a couple has a child, every individual has some family tie. It may not be that child care is a pressing need for everyone, but elder care may soon be. In the opening chapter of this volume (Halpern & Murphy, chap. 1), we presented a number of reasons that work and family interaction is a concern to everyone. To reiterate, we all have some interest in providing all children with the support they need to become contributing members of society. After all, they will pay our Social Security. Overburdened working parents experience increased levels of stress and burnout, which can lead to serious consequences for families. For example, stressed families may be more likely to exhibit unresolved marital conflict and may engage in more verbal or physical abuse of spouses or children. Children who grow up in families with high levels of stress, however manifested, can experience deleterious effects of all sorts. The stress affecting working families can also increase stress related health illnesses, which in turn increases everyone's insurance premiums. It is clear that we all have a stake in keeping America's families strong, regardless of who you include in your own categorical boundaries for the term *family*.

WHAT DO WE KNOW ABOUT INCREASING
THE POSITIVE INTERACTION
BETWEEN WORK AND FAMILY?

Working families are here to stay. And the desire to have it all (i.e., a satisfying job and a satisfying home life), is still a very attractive goal to many working families. In this volume, we outlined a number of topics that play an important role in the effective interaction of work and family, including the contribution of research, what organizations can and are doing, the implications of the changing family forms, and the overall positive effects of working families on children. Of course, family members should have the choice to work for pay outside the home, but it is important to recognize that this is not a real choice for most families who need two salaries to make ends meet.

Work–family research significantly influences both corporate and government policies designed to benefit working families. In addition, the research in the last 30 years on this topic has provided a number of findings that have answered important questions for families. Such questions as, do organizational policies for work and family benefit both the organization and the family? The answer is, yes. Or, do different family forms harm children? The answer is, probably not. There is no research that shows there is a single family form that is necessary for good child development. Most people value fathers and mothers, but healthy children grow in loving families of all sorts. However, without asking the right questions, or recognizing the right answers, research can quickly become irrelevant for those policymakers trying to improve life for working families. A method for ensuring that research is useful is to examine the issue of work–family interaction across disciplines. We began this volume with research perspectives on work and family from a psychologist, economist, and political scientist. In chapter 2, it became clear that to study the interaction of work and family we need to consider different research perspectives to understand the full implications of work–family policies.

We know it is important for organizations, both at the top management levels and at the supervisory level, to assist employees in achieving effective work–family interaction. Organizations must ensure that the policies they offer are implemented fairly and supported throughout the organization and check to ensure that the policies they offer are the ones their employees want and need (chap. 3). Moreover, organizations need to recognize that management at all levels must increase awareness and understanding of the demands faced by working families, as well as serving as role models of appropriate work–family interaction, if possible. There are many positive outcomes associated with appropriately implemented work–family policies including reduced absenteeism, reductions in work stress and burnout (chap. 8), and improved productivity.

Perhaps the strongest case for family-friendly policies can be found in chapter 4. Chapter 4 shows that organizations offering work and family policies experience additional positive outcomes. Specifically, these family-friendly corporations provide greater shareholder returns than the average market return. Sharing research findings such as these will induce more organizations to implement effective work–family policies. Organizations have employed different methods for addressing work–family issues, and have learned a great deal about what is or is not effective in terms of both the process and the policies. Representatives from five companies, and a branch of the military, the Army, shared their ongoing experiences with various policies to accommodate working families (chaps. 5, 6, & 7). We learned from these examples that many businesses and the Army are attempting to attract more working mothers and fathers because they realize that it makes good business sense and that without these policies they would lose these valuable employees to competitors and, in the case of the Army, the number of families who choose to re-enlist.

We also know how families are faring with increased family and work demands in today's fast-paced work environment. As shown in chapter 11, dual-career families are the norm, and although they do face a number of stressors, they are effectively coping in many different ways. Fathers have begun to take on an increased proportion of household and child-care duties even though their increased share is still less than that of their working spouse. It is important to note that helping working families manage the transitions from home to work to school is an important part of educating a workforce for higher skilled jobs. These are especially important for African-American families whose children have not had equal access to education, and thus have not been able to reap the benefits that are usually associated with higher education and other work opportunities (chap. 9). The African-American–Caucasian education and wage gap is still very wide and much more work needs to be done to bridge this gap so that adolescent African Americans can achieve the same linkages between education and wages for paid work that are available to other racial groups.

The paradoxical relationship families have with technology will become increasingly important in encouraging positive work–family interactions. Chapter 10 explores how technology takes away from family life by allowing one's job to impinge on home life, and how at the same time, technology such as cellular phones, pagers, videophones, and text messaging allow mothers and fathers to stay in touch with their families when away from home. It is a love–hate relationship with technology that improves how we work and makes work inescapable.

To understand the implications of work–family interaction, it is important to consider the effects of working families on the children. Researchers are considering new research paradigms that take into account the full context of the issue of working families rather than limiting the question to whether or not working mothers harm children (chap. 13). Asking children directly about the effects of working families on their lives (chap. 14), and to demonstrate long-term effects such as those shown in young people's attitudes toward their ideas about combining work and family in the future (chap. 12) are two additional methods for producing effective research in this area. A final consideration comes from the fact that children's outcomes are strongly affected by the type of child care available to working families. Continuing efforts to determine what political, cultural, and other factors will produce effective child care in this country are very important for the future of working families (chap. 15).

WHAT DON'T WE KNOW?

When it comes to solutions for working families, there is no one-size-fits-all because families come in many sizes and different configurations—step families, foster families, single parents, same-sex couples, dual-earners, multiple generations, in addition to the now minority prototype of a male wage-earner and stay-at-home wife. Despite the fact that families face many common challenges, family form (e.g., single mother, divorced parents, homosexual couples with children, etc.) and family income are important considerations when devising policies and making individual recommendations.

For a family of four in the United States, the poverty level is $14,348 and 11.3 % fall below that line (which is 31.1 million individuals or 6.2 million American families). The median household income in the United States was $42,409 in 2002. Low-income jobs offer much less in the way of flexibility because even a few hours of missed work can mean the difference between being able to pay the rent or having enough money to buy groceries. A recent U.S. Census report shows that single mothers now make up 26% of those living in poverty. Much of the research on work–family interaction does not take into account what specific needs exist for specific types of families. We need much more research that considers the full range of working family forms and incomes and offers public policy recommendations that make sense across socioeconomic levels.

OUR VISION OF THE FUTURE

Imagine a place where work and family interacted such that the benefits from one not only spilled over into the other domain, but at the nexus of the two life domains, we find people living richer and more fulfilled lives because of the interaction of work and family. This vision could include life-long learning where adults and children engage in educational experiences that add value to their lives and provide valuable job skills, such as learning to use computer programs that help them to express themselves more clearly and communicate in foreign languages. Job advancement leads to better living conditions and children learn about work motivation from the adults in their lives. A common vision is an important tool for a number of reasons. First, a vision is useful because it provides a tangible future goal. The specificity of the goal, as well as how it might vary for different working family forms, helps define where we need to go and also what the world will look like once the vision is realized. A common vision also may allow different groups to understand their specific responsibility in achieving the vision. Second, for the vision to be effective, everyone must understand the importance of the vision for others and themselves. How do we ensure understanding and buy in? We need to make sure the vision is articulated carefully and the reason for the vision is clear. We provide clear messages that work and family life can facilitate each other and that the old metaphor of balance where a gain in one necessarily means a loss in the other is a wrong metaphor. Once the vision is out there, each person needs to take ownership. Third, we also must consider what it will take in time and resources to sustain and support the vision.

WHO IS GOING TO HELP ACCOMPLISH THE VISION?

It is not possible to point the finger at one group and say that it their responsibility to see that the vision is attained. It will instead take a number of groups working on their own and working together to achieve the vision. Understandably, it is the responsibility of organizations (profit and not-for profit) to provide policies that work for families that interact with the organization. It is also the responsibility of government whether through policy, legislature, or incentives to help U.S. families. It is part of our value system. We value families and as part of our value, we support families in ways that are fiscally sound. Equally important, however, is that families take responsibility to demand effective and fair policies. For the most part, families have not demanded family-friendly policies because they feared negative retaliation in the workplace or they would be labeled as uncaring parents by the "super parents" who did not make such demands. By changing the metaphor and vision to one that clearly sees dual gains for work and family, families can demand policies that will achieve this goal. Finally, it is the responsibility of researchers to find answers to the right questions that businesses can use to facilitate work–family interaction. In this section, we explore the actions each of these groups can take.

What Can Employers Do?

Attention to work–family interaction is not a form of social responsibility for organizations, it is a business imperative. But even as a business imperative, it requires that an organization truly understands what it means to accommodate working families. James Goodnight, SAS co-founder and CEO, understands this and has been recognized for his efforts. SAS was voted one of *Working Mother's* "100 Best Companies for Working Mothers," as well as being included in *Fortune's* "100 Best Companies to Work for in America" and *Business Week's* "Best Companies for Work and Family." According to Goodnight, SAS' worker-friendly program is based on the philosophy: if you treat all employees as adults, then they'll behave like adults.

Unfortunately, most employers still run their organizations as if they are full of "unencumbered" workers. According to Williams (2000),

> An unencumbered worker is an employee who behaves in the workplace as if he or she has a wife at home full time, performing all of the unpaid care work that families require. This "gold standard" worker is an employee who works full time, year round; is available to work overtime as required by the employer; and takes no time off for child bearing or child rearing. The expectation is that personal problems will not be brought into the workplace, and that conflicting demands will be resolved in favor of the requirements of the job. Indeed, workers in the U.S. can be—and frequently are—marginalized and even fired if their care responsibilities interfere with their jobs. (Appelbaum, Bailey, Berg, & Kalleberg, 2002, p. 8)

It is important that employers move organizations from the above mindset to a more informed realization that work–family policies can in fact benefit the organization. Recent statistics, however, have shown that employers have been cutting back on the number of employees who can use flextime. It is the responsibility of human resource managers to evaluate how this can cost the organization in increased absences or lowered work performance.

What Can Government Do?

Part of our vision for working families includes the ability for families to make a decent living based on one income if they choose to. The economic growth of the last 20 years, some argue, has been at the expense of the middle class and lower wage earners. According to Krugman, *New York Times* columnist, a Congressional Budget Office report showed that over the last 20 years, the rich really have gotten richer and the poor, poorer—the top 1% saw their income rise by 157%, with middle-income Americans increasing their income by 10%, and the poor just getting what they usually do—poorer (Lind, 2004). The wages for single mothers have been growing the slowest.

Some explain the increasing difference between the very wealthy and the lower income ranges as resulting from the loss of higher paying manufacturing jobs as U.S. companies attempt to keep domestic wages low to compete internationally, or as companies export many of those jobs to countries where $2.00 a day is an acceptable wage. All of this differential in income is justified in the name of shareholder profits.

What can the Federal government do to help working families if it cannot or is not willing to affect the disparity in the distribution of wealth in the United States? First, the Federal government serves as a role model in offering much in the way of good work–family benefits for its own workers. These include alternative work schedules, telecommuting, part-time employment, and job sharing. Also, child care and elder care referral services are provided by many Federal agencies.

Government policies might address the disparity between benefits for different types of workers. Some researchers have argued that lower hourly wage earners should be given more flexibility to accommodate family needs, because they typically are in jobs where they have the least flexibility. If both parents must work, or desire to work, there are other accommodations that might be introduced by federal and state government. A recent book published by the Economic Policy Institute (a nonprofit, nonpartisan think tank) examines what they call shared work. A few of the policies they propose include U.S. policies needed to facilitate a system of shared work and valued care:

- *Hours-of-work legislation* to allow for a shorter standard work week for all, flexibility for workers, longer part-time hours, and limits on mandatory overtime.
- *Adjustment-of-hours legislation* to allow workers to request up to a 20% reduction in hours and pro-rated reductions in pay and benefits.
- *Equal opportunity and non-discrimination provisions* to protect workers on part-time schedules from discrimination in pay or benefits.
- *Sharing of the cost of care* by investing in day care and elder care infrastructure, and by providing subsidies for child care and elder care, short-term careers' leave, subsidized wages or tax credits for caregivers, universal preschool, and after- and before-school programs for children.
- *Untying of benefits from individual employers* by making access to health insurance available to everyone without regard to employment status, and by establishing funds similar to unemployment insurance for maternity leave, parental leave, and long-term family medical leave.
- *Updating of income security protections* such as unemployment insurance and old age pensions to reflect the changes and great variety in family structure and in work arrangements. (Appelbaum et al., 2002, p. viii)

Other recommendations have included money for universal preschool, which would give students early exposure to letters and numbers, to help poor children start school ready to learn and provide some relief care for children of working parents.

Earlier in this chapter we mentioned some of the steps Sweden has taken to accommodate working families. U.S. companies can also take lessons from the United Kingdom. For example, beginning last year parents with children under 6-years old, or with disabled children under 18, were given the right to request a flexible working pattern. The government also requests that employers must consider these requests seriously. Over the past 3 years, the government has sponsored a campaign to increase work–life balance, based on the increasing number of dual-career families in the United Kingdom. The government is also quite aware that when employees are required to respond to customer demands 24 hours a day this severely affects the quality of family life.

In Canada, the Labour Department provides evidence for the business case for the effectiveness of work and family initiatives. The government also provides a useful framework for organizations to assess their workplace. For example, employers can answer 20 questions that help identify opportunities for meaningful change by reviewing current practices and results in their workplaces. The sponsored Website has other resources for organizations. The Website summarizes studies that give organizations research evidence statistics about reductions in absenteeism and stress levels, increases in recruitment, retention, and productivity, as well as methods for making the organization accountable for enforcing the work–family policies adopted by the organization. Through policies, support, and example, we can look to our Federal and state governments to prioritize increasing work–family interaction to better the lives of America's working families. There are many possible ways public policies can facilitate better work and family integration.

What Can Families Do to Achieve the Vision?

Researchers and public policy analysts sometimes avoid discussing what families can do to achieve work–family interaction, because asking what the families can do to make their work and family lives better feels a little like blaming the victim. Many families face intense economic pressures that require both husband and wife to work to achieve a middle-class existence, but some families do have control in determining how they choose to integrate work and family. Some families attempt to find jobs with shorter commutes, fewer travel requirements, and less work that needs to be brought home. Mothers and fathers need to make sure they are asking their organizations for whatever arrangements might be possible to help them take care of their families and their work. For example, Charlene Begley is a mother of three and president and CEO of GE's Transportation Systems. Three years ago, she admitted to a women's networking group that she never worked weekends, even as she was moving up the ranks of GE, and she still does not work weekends. She worked diligently during the week to get all of her work done so that the weekends were dedicated to family (Brady, 2003). We acknowledge that many families may not have this level of flexibility, but all families should be encouraged to do what they can. Earlier in this volume, we mentioned how some employees use the invisible mommy and daddy fast track (Hall, 1990). Although we do not advocate being dishonest with one's employer, many workers are not yet in a position where they can work counter to the company norms, and have to do what they can to accommodate family. Coontz (1998) mentioned that many women, rather than working toward better jobs, tend to take more traditionally feminine, low-paying jobs, which are the ones that have much less flexibility. Educating children about job choices are important so that they one day will have the opportunities to work in occupations that allow them to attend to their family life.

On the home front, there are other steps families have taken to turn the home into a sanctuary in order to avoid the hassles of work. These families have also looked at their lives in an attempt to cut out unnecessary activities and expenditures. A movement started a few years ago that is dedicated to life simplification. These groups believe in cutting back on the materially abundant and overscheduled lives that many people lead. Many families are just cramming more into their daily schedules than is comfortably possible. There is something to be said for those groups that promote the simple life, although for some working families they are working at the edges to make ends meet and do not have the luxury of choice in these matters. Double shifts at a plant, or late evening child care are a necessity. But some families can and should examine what is needed to accomplish a more comforting home environment. The "simplicity" movement encourages finding a simpler life, and in fact, there is a magazine called *Simple Living* that gives advice on how to live more simply. There are other methods that look at ways to reduce the effects of work on nonwork life. For example, books such as *Downshifting: How to Work Less and Enjoy Life More* (Drake, 2001) or *Taking Back Our Lives in the Age of Corporate Dominance* (Schwartz & Stoddard, 2000) try to convince people that there is another way to live.

Another way to reduce some of the stress that families feel is for all families to be more accepting of each other's choices. Family structures have changed, but that does not mean that one family structure is necessarily better than another. A recent episode of the talk show, *Dr. Phil*, showed an ugly exchange between a group of stay-at-home mothers and mothers who worked outside of the home. This is the traditional "Mommy Wars," between those mothers who have made different choices and feel that they must defend their choices because each has sacrificed and feels that her own sacrifice must be justified and declared correct (Johnston & Swanson, 2003).

All working mothers need support and understanding, regardless of why they work, and all mothers that make the choice to care for their children full time deserve similar support and understanding. There does not have to be a victor in the Mommy Wars. People make choices that are right for themselves and their very often complicated circumstances. Fathers need more support as well. Some studies find that in today's society, men still are not acknowledged for taking on an increased parenting role—not from their employers, their friends, nor the children's grandparents, and their wives (Coontz, 1998). Some writers have even coined the term "invisible dilemma" for men's level of work–family conflict, something men do not talk about and the media has not picked up on (Levine & Pittinsky, 1998).

For many other families, there may be no choice in how they spend their work and family time. The only guidance for them is to vote with their feet. That is, find employers who are more accommodating of working families. Of course, this is easier said than done, but if employers feel more pressure, change will eventually come.

What Can Social Scientists Do?

Social scientists such as psychologists, economists, sociologists, political scientists, anthropologists, as well as historians and human resource and organizational behavior researchers have all investigated issues surrounding work and family, albeit from different perspectives. This comprehensive coverage of the area is very encouraging, but the field has yet to take advantage of all the potential benefits of cross-disciplinary research. We need more researchers who work to build connections among topic areas as well as utilize different research approaches in the field. A first step to bring researchers together might be to determine the "big" questions in the area. For example, if we take the topic of "family friendly" work policies, the question might be, "are they effective?" A psychologist may measure effectiveness by looking at outcomes such as organizational continuance attitudes, others such as economists or human resource researchers may want to know the relationships between dollars spent on a program and dollars saved in absenteeism or made in increased productivity.

Unifying theories may also help identify important questions. For example, the field of work–family conflict has been criticized for lacking a theoretical basis. However, a number of recent research studies have attempted to apply theoretical lenses to understand how conflict occurs and its consequences. These studies may provide more answers that organizations can use in planning and implementing work–families policies by focusing on the methods that reduce work and family conflict effectively.

Also, future research should encompass many forms and situations families may face, it appears fairly homogeneous with respect to research populations, with few exceptions. The field is also fairly homogeneous with respect to research paradigms. Much of the published research in the organizational literature relies exclusively on quantitative research methods such as surveys, as does some of the sociological research. However, reviews of historical context of work and family and more qualitative studies are needed to more fully understand the underlying issues for working mothers and fathers.

Most importantly, regardless of the discipline investigating work and family issues, it is important that this research gives business and government results that are useful and that these results are disseminated widely. Organizations should be provided with methods for measuring the impact of programs, an understanding of effective implementation plans, as well as ways to meet employee needs by including them in the process of devising policies.

CONCLUSION

The goal of work family interaction is lofty. To achieve this vision it will take the work of all.

REFERENCES

Appelbaum, E., Bailey, T., Berg, P., & Kalleberg, A. R. (2002). *Shared work-valued care: New norms for organizing market work and unpaid care work.* Washington, DC: Economic Policy Institute.

Brady, D. (2003). People: Crashing GE's glass ceiling. *Business Week,* July 28. Retrieved January 7, 2004 from http://www.businessweek.com:/print/magazine/content/03_30/b3843105. htm?mz

Coontz, S. (1998). *The way we really are: Coming to terms with America's changing families.* New York: Basic Books.

Drake, J. D. (2001). *Downshifting: How to work less and enjoy life more.* San Francisco: Berrett-Koehler.

Hall, D. T. (1990). Promoting work/family balance: An organization change approach. *Organizational Dynamics, 18,* 5–18.

Johnston, D. D., & Swanson, D. H. (2003). Invisible mothers: A content analysis of motherhood ideologies and myths in magazines. *Sex Roles, 49*(1–2), 21–33.

Levine, J., & Pittinsky, T. (1998). *Working fathers: New strategies for balancing work and family.* San Diego: Harvest Books.

Lind, M. (2004). Are we still a middle-class nation? *The Atlantic Monthly, 293*(1). Retrieved on January 22, 2004 from http://www.theatlantic.com/issues/2004/01/lind.htm

Schwartz, E., & Stoddard, S. (2000). *Taking back our lives in the age of corporate dominance.* San Francisco: Berrett-Koehler.

Shahmehri, B. (2001). More than welcome: families come first in Sweden. *Mothering*, Nov-Dec. Retrieved January 4, 2004 from http://www.findarticles.com/cf_dls/m0838/2001_Nov-Dec/100807143/p1/article.jhtml

Weber, G. (2003). Flexible jobs mean fewer absences. *Workforce Management*, *82*(12), p. 26.

Williams, J. (2000). *Unbending gender: Why family and work conflict and what to do about it.* New York: Oxford University Press.

Author Index

Subject Index